BEYOND
literal
BELIEF

BEYOND literal BELIEF
RELIGION AS METAPHOR

DAVID TACEY

garratt
PUBLISHING

Published in Australia by
Garratt Publishing
32 Glenvale Crescent
Mulgrave VIC 3170

Australian edition copyright © 2015 David Tacey.
First published in 2015 by Transaction Publishers, 10 Corporate Place South, Suite 102, Piscataway, New Jersey 08854. This Australian edition is published by arrangement with Transaction Publishers.

All rights reserved. Except as provided by Australian copyright law, no part of this publication may be reproduced in any manner without prior permission in writing from the publisher.

Cover design by Red Bilby Media
Printed in Australia by McPhersons Printing Group

National Library of Australia Cataloguing-in-Publication entry
Creator: Tacey, David J. (David John), 1953- author.

Title: Beyond Literal Belief : Religion as Metaphor / David Tacey.

ISBN: 9781925009798 (paperback)

Subjects: Christianity--21st century.
Mysteries, Religious.
Philosophy and religion.
Theology, Doctrinal.
Dogma.

Dewey Number: 230

C. G. Jung. The Collected Works of C. G. Jung. © 1977–2015 Princeton University Press. Reprinted by permission of Princeton University Press.

C. G. Jung. The Collected Works of C. G. Jung. © 1977–2015 Routledge. Reprinted by permission of Taylor & Francis Books UK.

The author and publisher gratefully acknowledge the permission granted to reproduce the copyright material in this book. Every effort has been made to trace copyright holders and to obtain their permission for the use of copyright material.

The publisher apologises for any errors or omissions in the above list and would be grateful if notified of any corrections that should be incorporated in future reprints or editions of this book.

Dedicated to future generations:
may you make more sense of religion than the
generations before you.

Faith is unwilling to give up the primitive, childlike relationship to mind-created figures; it collides with science and gets its deserts, for it refuses to share in the spiritual adventure of our age.
— C. G. Jung

Every religion is true when understood metaphorically. But when it gets stuck to its own metaphors, interpreting them as facts, then you are in trouble.
— Joseph Campbell

My point is not that those ancient people told literal stories and we are now smart enough to take them symbolically, but that they told them symbolically and we are now dumb enough to take them literally. They knew what they were doing; we don't.
— John Dominic Crossan

Contents

Preface · xi

Acknowledgments · xv

Personal Introduction · xvii

1 Miracles as Imagination · 1
   Mythos and History; The Miracles of Jesus;
   Metaphor and Its Hazards; Preserving the
   Spiritual Meaning

2 Religion as Metaphor · 15
   The Literary Mode of Scripture; Myth,
   Metaphor and Jesus; Literal Thinking as Idolatry;
   Religion as Unconscious Poetry; Pious Fraud;
   The Greatest Story Ever Sold?

3 The Soul's Symbolic Code · 37
   Why Myth Matters; Myth as Ancient
   Psychology; When Mythos became Logos;
   The Ancestral Mind; Mythos, Soul, Eternity;
   Mythos in Art and Entertainment; Mythos as a
   Structure of Thought; Mythos Downgraded;
   Myths, Dreams, Religions; Something Continues
   to Speak

4 Jesus the Metaphor · 59
   Imagination and Reality; Fear of Myth;
   The Secret Life of Us; Personifying; Spirit
   Personified in Jesus; Ongoing Incarnation;
   The Messenger as the Message; An Eastern Moment
   in the West; Gnosticism and Other Heresies;

Absolutism, Violence, and Conflict; When Jesus became God; Onward Christian Soldiers; Jesus the Mirror of Our Projections

5 The Myth of the Virgin Birth   87
The Dead Hand of Patriarchy; Can We Be "Moved" By Myths?; Sexual Politics and the Uses of Myth; The Myth and Its Background; Divine Insemination; Spiritual Rebirth; Institutional Literalism; The Less We Believe the Better

6 Waking Up   107
The Kingdom; Putting on the New Self; Waking Up to a Higher Authority; Reversal of the Ego's Values; Losing and Finding Life; The Mustard Seed; Many are Called, Few Choose; Completion, Not Perfection; Transformation, Not Repentance; Jesus, Socrates, and Waking Up

7 Apocalypse   131
Apocalypse as Psychology; Coming of the New Self; Destruction and Renewal; Spiritual Event and Pathological Obsession; Violation of the Ego's Boundaries; New Self as Original Self; Judgment; Destruction and Punishment; God as Interruption; Rapture; Founding a New Order

8 Satan and Literalism   151
Nicodemus and the Rebirth Story; Incest Fantasies and Sexual Abuse; Satan as the Personification of Literalism; The Sublimation of Base Instincts

9 Resurrection: Ascending to Where?   167
The Resurrection Conundrum; Joseph Campbell's Straight Talking; Jung: Cutting through Spiritual Materialism; Paul's Mysticism; The Parable of Emmaus; Emmaus Never Happened, Emmaus Always Happens; The Unacknowledged God in Our Midst

10 Psyche and Symbol	187

      Dreaming the Myth Onward; Reworking
      the Past; The Therapeutic Function of Myth;
      Myth as Psychic Truth; Mystery Without Literalism;
      Respect to a God Unknown; The Assumption
      of Mary; Elevation of the Symbolic

11 After Belief	209

      After Literalism; Faith Without Belief;
      Vision and Uncommon Sense; Bultmann's
      Progressive Thinking; Saving the Myths;
      Throwing Out the Baby; Progressives in the
      Rationalistic Mode; The Sea of Faith at Ebb Tide;
      From Passive Belief to Active Faith;
      Stages of Faith; Recreating the Fables

Conclusion: Unveiling the Soul	233

      Rebirth of the Sacred; From the God-Shaped Hole;
      Depth Psychology as Midwife; Psyche as an Opening
      to Infinity

Index	249

Preface

Many of us in Western societies have given up religious practices and taken on secular attitudes. Of those who maintain a spiritual attitude, some have turned to Eastern pathways and New Age interests. A few have clung to their natal Jewish or Christian traditions, often for cultural or community reasons. Some have turned fundamentalist, in a bid to strengthen religion in unpropitious times. Like many of my generation who grew up in the Christian tradition, I lost interest in religion in early adulthood, not seeing its relevance. The miracles and wonders seemed bizarrely out of step with the world around me. But today I realize that there is an error in Christianity that has brought on this disconnect between religion and society. The religious story has been misinterpreted as history and fact. This worked while believers remained uneducated; in fact the claim that everything was historical added to its appeal. But as the West became more sophisticated, people abandoned religion in droves. They treated it with contempt, as an insult to their intelligence. The problem is not with the scriptures as such, but with how they are interpreted.

The original sin of religion is literalism, the habit of reading texts literally. This is not only an intellectual problem, which has given many a distorted view of the world, but it is also the cause of sectarian conflict and religious violence. Literalism engenders idolatry and aggression, and is the bane of civilization. It is the reason why the new atheists of the post–9/11 era are trying to get rid of religion. Getting rid of religion is an absurdity, but getting rid of literalism is something we need to seriously consider. This book will argue that scriptures were written primarily as myth and have been misunderstood as history. We have to reconfigure religion in light of the knowledge that has emerged from various quarters over the last 150 years. In this book I will attempt to interweave personal reflections with the insights of several disciplines, including contemporary scripture scholarship and depth psychology, in a bid to present a new view of religion and its metaphorical approach to the spirit. It is important that this new approach be conveyed to a wide audience in accessible language.

Scholars around the world have been saying for some time that the stories of the Bible are not to be read literally. Not only this, but more startling is the news that the stories were not intended to be taken literally. This is known only to a few specialists; it is not known, as yet, to the general public. Nor is it known to a great many clergy. Clergy often turn a blind eye to scholarship and treat the scriptural narratives as historical. They think this is treating them with respect, but they are destroying their true meaning by constructing them as eyewitness accounts of real events. One cannot blame individual priests or ministers for this confusion; it is a crisis of Western culture not to be able to discern the deeper dimension of religion. We are technologically advanced, but spiritually impoverished.

History is present in these ancient works, but it is overwhelmed by myth and wrapped in metaphor. All the "big" moments of scripture, the miracles and wonders, are acts of imagination, not acts of history. Unfortunately, myth and metaphor have such poor reputations, often synonymous with lies or deceit, that many assume I am adopting a negative approach to religion. Some imagine I am trying to reduce it to incoherence, but the opposite is the case. I have great respect for religion, and value faith as a guiding light in culture and life. But a distinction needs to be made between belief and faith. If religion is seen as "belief in impossible events," it hardly has much of a future in an age of science. Faith, however, is a different matter. My hope is that faith will be reignited by the realization that we need to read scripture nonliterally, as stories of soul and spirit.

This book follows a pattern found in my life and in other lives. The pattern begins with literal religious belief in childhood, shifts to reason and doubt in early adulthood, and moves to a deeper yet questioning faith as a mature adult. Mature faith leads to the realization that scriptures point to spiritual realities that do not exist in a literal sense, but may be considered true in nonliteral terms. If our imaginations are poor, we need miracles or signs to buoy us up. Once we become educated, naïve belief is crushed and we are unable to find a spiritual orientation. When our imaginations are reignited, we realize that scriptures can be "true" again, but in different ways from previously imagined. They can be true as metaphors, and if we regain respect for metaphors and myths, we are able to rediscover a spiritual life for ourselves and civilization.

Preface

I am hoping that adults of all ages, and of all beliefs and non-beliefs, will read this book and be energized by it. I am hoping that students will find their way to this book, as young adults need something more than the cynical, debunking mindset that is offered by the media and society. Due to the influence of Richard Dawkins and the new atheists, it has become commonplace to see religion as delusional.[1] In the early twentieth century Freud wrote *The Future of an Illusion*, in which he claimed religion was a universal obsessional neurosis.[2] He covered the same territory as Dawkins, and the only difference is that Freud's illusion became Dawkins' delusion. Both arrive at atheism as the best response to the crisis of religion, but Freud is slightly kinder, arguing that despite its illusory nature, religion provides social cohesion. As time goes by, attacks on religion become more sweeping and desperate. Atheists are right to reject religious statements if they are claimed to be historical. But atheists do not seem to realize they are attacking a misunderstanding. Freud and Dawkins are laboring under illusions of their own.

The argument of this book is that religion is not delusional but metaphorical. It is only delusional if we take the metaphors literally. Once we understand this, a lot of puzzling things make sense. The atheists throw out too much, and there is precious cargo in religion that "enlightened" people are losing. I am not in favor of nihilism, nor am I keen on fundamentalism. I think the challenge today is to overcome these -isms and aspire to a mystical vision that beckons us at this time. It is what religion has pointed to all along, but it has taken the West some time to get there. Some will find this book challenging and perhaps offensive. But it only offends a certain attitude that is based on misconceptions. Truth can be uncomfortable, and if we have to go through a period of discomfort before we realize that metaphor is the primary carrier of truth, then so be it. Our times are leaning toward atheism, but I want to arrest this development and tilt the balance the other way, toward a renewed interest in faith. The problem is, will this faith be recognized as faith, or seen as make-believe? It is a risk I have to take, because that is what faith is, a risky business, a leap into the unknown.

David Tacey
Professor of Literature
La Trobe University, Melbourne
August 15, 2014

Notes

1. Richard Dawkins, *The God Delusion* (London: Bantam Press, 2006).
2. Sigmund Freud, *The Future of an Illusion* (1927), in *The Standard Edition of the Complete Psychological Works*, Vol. 21 (London: The Hogarth Press, 1953).

Jung epigraph, C. G. Jung, "Psychological Commentary on 'The Tibetan Book of the Great Liberation'" (1939/1954), *Psychology and Religion: West and East, The Collected Works of C.G. Jung*, Vol. 11 (London: Routledge, 1969) § 763.
Campbell epigraph, Joseph Campbell, *The Power of Myth* (New York: Doubleday, 1991), p. 67.
Crossan epigraph, John Dominic Crossan, *Who is Jesus?* (Louisville, KY: Westminster John Knox Press, 1996), p. 79.

Acknowledgments

I would like to thank a number of people who have contributed directly or indirectly to this book. Conversations with philosophers Richard Kearney and Kevin Hart have been helpful, and correspondence with John Caputo was clarifying. Talks with scripture scholar Kevin Treston and media presenter Brian Coyne were seminal, and discussions with psychologist Peter Todd and psychoanalysts Murray Stein, Mark Saban, and John Dourley have been important. Years ago, conversations with Thomas Moore and Joseph Campbell in America, and John O'Donohue in England, planted seeds that have born fruit.

Anne Boyd, Janet Galos, Helen Littleton, Peter Vardy, Bernie Neville, John Carroll, Wayne Hudson, and Matthew Del Nevo asked challenging questions and offered useful suggestions. Conversations with radical clerics John Spong, Don Cupitt, and Lloyd Geering were illuminating, even if I disagreed with them. I recall a defining conversation with Alan Jones, former dean of Grace Cathedral (San Francisco), at the Merton Institute in Kentucky. Jones said he found himself saying, "It's a metaphor, stupid" to those who enquired about supernatural aspects of scripture. People were keen to know how he, an educated man, managed to believe them. He replied that some religious statements are not meant to be "believed," but reflected on for their significance.

I thank my partner and distinguished poet, Lisa Jacobson, for her interest in this project and her encouragement when the way was tough.

I would like to acknowledge the writings of C. G. Jung, Alvin Kuhn, Tom Harpur, Eugen Drewermann, Dominic Crossan, Karen Armstrong, Northrop Frye, and Richard Holloway. Without their distinguished works, I would not have been able to complete this book.

Personal Introduction

Take care not to interpret physically what is intended spiritually.
— *The Cloud of Unknowing*[1]

As a child I used to believe that the miracles and wonders of my natal faith were literally true. My parents inculcated this view, and I tried my best not to disappoint them. Some of the children in my neighborhood questioned what was taught in the churches, but I plugged my ears and tried not to listen. I knew that faith was important to my family and did not want to lose it. I was required to believe in the Word of God and if this meant literal adherence to the "words of God" then so be it. If the Bible said Jesus had a virgin birth or a physical resurrection, or walked on water, or fed the five thousand, this must be true, because it came from the holy book. It was the "greatest story ever told." I was to accept this without questioning and not doubt God's ability to perform miracles. These wonders were to become the cornerstones of my faith. But as childhood came to an end I was forced to concede with St Paul: "When I was a child I thought like a child and reasoned like a child—but now that I am an adult I have put away childish things."[2]

I clung to my early faith until I was about thirteen, when it began to dissolve in the course of my education. Indeed, thirteen is about the outer limit of the developmental phase that can accept religion as it is presented. As I began to find out more about the world and how it works, and to think about God in a deeper way, my belief in these miracles dissolved. I realized that religion was basically mythological, but regarded as history and fact. I noted that my schoolteachers, and later, university professors, regarded it with contempt, and although I did not share their contempt, I felt that this kind of religion might be fatally flawed. It can speak to children but not to grown-ups. It is little wonder that what is called "faith" is in short supply, if it is based on such a misunderstanding of scripture. Believing in impossible events is not faith but credulity, and leads not to an understanding of God but to mere superstition.

When I was fifteen, my sister, a few years older than me, announced that religion was a fraud. She said it was mythological and to her mind that meant it was false. This is a real problem in society today: as soon as the mythic dimension of religion is glimpsed, it is regarded as lies. As I will go on to say, we need to recover respect for myth and metaphor, and appreciate their capacity to reveal truth. Spiritual truth is different from literal truth. At the time, I did not have the language to convey this to my sister. I felt she was throwing out too much, too quickly, but was unable to suggest an alternative. She tried to convince me that atheism was the only option, and offered me books on existentialism and psychoanalysis that had convinced her to throw religion out. She said our God-fearing family was behind the times to the tune of 150 years, and she added, "All thinking people are atheists now." I was reminded of her comment recently when, stuck in traffic, the car ahead of me had a bumper sticker that read: "I think, therefore I am—an atheist."

But soon after making this shift to atheism, my sister went mad, suffering from paranoid schizophrenia for the rest of her life. I could not help linking the two phenomena in some way, although I was never quite sure of the connection. Was there a causal link, or was it mere coincidence? Our family and its ancestral lines (one side Irish, the other English/French) had been religious for centuries, and I imagined that one could not suddenly throw out this legacy or orientation without consequences. But the fact that her paranoia expressed itself in delusions of a supernatural kind made me think that when religion is denied, it projects itself into the world in distorted ways. The mystic and the paranoiac are both responding to nonhuman reality, the one spiritually, the other psychotically. I often think that what happened to my sister is happening to society at large: it once had a spiritual orientation, it has ditched it in favor of materialism, and it is going mad.[3] This is what fundamentalists think as well, but they are approaching it in a different way, with formulas I don't like.

We have to make allowances for the spiritual in our time, and if we can no longer believe in the "big nouns" (God, Holy Spirit, and so on) that expressed spirit in the past, we have to find new ways to define or point to it. If the traditional images of God have become unbelievable, as they have for countless people, this means our old images are useless, but it does not mean the sacred is dead or no longer exists. It

Personal Introduction

means we lack convincing ways of calling it into being. Science and education have changed our understanding of the world, and the notion that spirits, demons, and gods stalk the world in the ways described in scripture has to be revised. I smile at the alacrity with which I once believed that God walked with Adam and Eve in the cool of the evening.[4] But we can't just annihilate the old myths and live in a flat, spiritless world. We are composed of spiritual as well as physical forces, and these have to be respected if we are to live properly. One of the challenges is to invent new images of the sacred, lest we slide into the void of nihilism. But no one could argue that the myths of the past will suffice in their present form. They can no longer be interpreted as literal accounts of real events, and in this regard fundamentalism represents a serious regression.

As a university student, I had a short phase as an atheist that lasted for about a semester. I tried this partly to impress my professors, who were all atheists. Indeed, university study is an induction into the atheistic mindset. My family lived in Alice Springs, central Australia—a thousand miles from the nearest university—and so I had to live away from home, in Adelaide. When I returned home during vacations, I told my father what I had been studying. In my philosophy class, I was taught that God did not exist, never did exist, and never could exist. My father went ballistic hearing this news, and said he would not financially support me in my study, and I should leave the university if the pursuit of knowledge led to a loss of faith. I understood his fury but did not share it. If so-called "faith" can exist only in a state of ignorance, if it cannot dialogue with knowledge, I wanted no part of it. Again, I did not have the language that I needed at the time. If I had had the language, I would have said that knowledge can destroy belief, but not faith.

Atheism did not suit me, nor did the university mindset that preaches this doctrine today. I am a spiritual person by nature, and if my father had known me better he would have realized this. I would say I am "religious," if the term is understood in its original meaning, deriving from the Latin *religio*, meaning to "bind back" or "reconnect." My life has been about trying to bind back to the sacred, and I see myself as following the path of *religio*. But the term religion generates confusion and one has to use it advisedly. Today this term is conflated with the current forms and beliefs of religions, many of which I cannot accept. I inhabit a different universe to the churches and belong to a "religionless" religion, as the scholars who have influenced me in recent years, such as Derrida, Caputo, and Kearney, would say.[5]

Beyond Literal Belief

I accept that there are spiritual forces in the world, but these are not to be interpreted literally, and insofar as religions are systems of literal thinking I cannot accept them. Spiritual forces are beyond our range of comprehension, and as soon as we attempt to describe them we enter the field of culture, which is governed by metaphor. Derrida said, "The history of metaphysics, like the history of the West, is the history of metaphors."[6] I agree, but this need not lead to nihilism or loss of faith. Metaphors are all we have, and we need to treasure them, and deepen our appreciation of them, which is what I am doing in this book. There are realities beyond metaphors, but we can only *know* them through metaphors that are transparent to the transcendent. Many fail to understand this point of view, believing that if religions are metaphorical this means they are false. As a culture, we have a long way to go before we grasp this point. Our prejudices derive from centuries of rational indoctrination, which have taught us that things are only true if they happened in time and space, as historical events.

Despite my university degrees and scholarship, I remain true to my family of origin and its need for faith. I still share my family's longing for God, even though they could not possibly accept my criticisms of their understanding of God. The God whom they believe in has long since exploded for me, and this is so devastating that I rarely use the word "God" in my university teaching, lest students think I am advocating a belief which has disappeared from my world as well as theirs. The word "God" is difficult, since it carries much literal and historical baggage. But there is, and must be, a new way to speak of God. I like what Paul Tillich did in his attempt to rescue God for modernity. He said God is not a supernatural being, but Being Itself.[7] God is not a man or person, but a depth or quality of existence; a personification of what is sacred.

God is the proper noun for mystery, and does not point to an object in space. Nor does God point to anything known, as tradition has asked us to believe. Tradition has tried to put a familiar face on mystery and protect us from the fact that the finite can never perceive the infinite. All attempts to describe God are provisional, relative. God is a metaphor for what is purposive in creation. The mystics have long known this, and have tried to say so. The institutions, on the other hand, have pretended that God is a person who "looks over us." Institutions have not been able to bear the uncertainty of not knowing. They hoodwink many good and uneducated folk, such as my family members. But when God is called upon in times of trouble, and does not respond in

Personal Introduction

the supernatural ways that we have been led to believe, such folk lose their belief, because there was never an interventionist God to begin with. Western religion, with its infantile images of God, has set up the conditions for widespread and pervasive atheism.

I have never been able to take on uneducated belief, nor have I been able to accept educated disbelief, making me an outsider in both camps. I have a critical mind that refuses blind belief and a receptive heart that is open to faith. Much of my writing has attempted to bridge the gap between the belief of my background and the disbelief of my academic training.[8] I have spent a lifetime searching for a middle ground, an alternative to naïve belief on the one hand, and educated nihilism on the other. We deserve something better than these options, and I would hope that the future will deliver something new along these lines. Intelligence and faith need to be brought together, but it has not yet happened in Western civilization. Or rather, it has not happened in the mainstream, in public view, but it has happened in the mystical sub-traditions.

At university I specialized in literature, and it was during my years as a student that I began to wonder if the Bible were not a form of literature, perhaps a form we still do not know much about. Why did people assume that the Bible was history and should be read as fact? Why not a work of poetry or myth, in which stories were used for the purpose of teaching about the spirit? I had these thoughts in the early 1970s, and it has taken me until now to formulate them in a book. Forty years I have pondered these possibilities, and during this time I have wondered why many have not wanted to discuss these issues. On the one hand, believers find the proposition to be offensive, as they assume I am implying that the Bible is nonsense and I am devaluing the word of God. On the other hand, most nonbelievers can't be bothered to think about the Bible at all, since they are sure it is unreliable history and have ditched it.

But why is there such a dismissive approach to these texts? If they are sacred, as claimed, then we should continue to reflect on their meaning. To view the writings at face value, as history or fact, may be mistaken. The miracles and wonders might not be intended to be read as facts, but as symbols or metaphors of a level of significance inherent in what is being narrated. My view of miracles is often mistaken for atheism by those who don't understand where I am coming from. To me, there are two actions needing to be performed as we come to terms with religious statements. The first is to bring doubt and suspicion to religion and the way it has been presented. We cannot swallow the creeds or dogmas whole, and to that extent, I am similar to the disbelieving types who fill our universities and halls of learning. But there is a second action to be performed: after doubt and suspicion, we need to ask, What were these stories all about? What did they, and what could they, mean? We can't believe them in their literal form; but what if we regard them as myths? How might we bring new value to them?

Robert Johnson reports that an American schoolteacher once asked her class, "What is a myth?" A young boy raised his hand and replied: "A myth is something that is true on the inside, but not true on the outside."[9] I met Johnson numerous times during his lecture tours, and knew what he was thinking when he recounted this story. It is a profound story, and I have used it as an inspiration in writing this book. Contrast this boy's wisdom with the silliness of celebrity Joanna Lumley, who has no understanding of the "inside" life of myth. Lumley was brought up in the Christian tradition, and in contrast to what she calls her "dear friend Richard Dawkins, who believes in nothing," Lumley is at the opposite end of the spectrum, since she "believes in virtually everything."[10] Celebrity believers and celebrity atheists are not to be trusted. They are both on the wrong track. Lumley says her passion was to search for the remains of Noah's Ark:

> It's so familiar to us all, from the animals going in two by two and the dove of peace, and the olive branch and the rainbow. But who was Noah, and what was the Ark and what was it made of? When and why did the flood happen? It has fascinated me all my life, and I'm going in search of the truth.[11]

She is asking all the wrong questions. It never seems to occur to this celebrity that the truth of Noah's Ark might be found in symbol and myth, not in history and geography. It is not found "out there," but "in here," as we reflect on its symbolism. The notion that it narrates a literal flood and a literal Ark is fanciful, and yet this actress "would never be so ill mannered as to insist that it is a myth."[12] Myth has lost so much respect in our world that to refer to a story as a myth is impolite.

Canadian writer Tom Harpur puts it well when he says:

> Mention "myth" or "mythology" to the average person, and he or she will assume you are speaking of remote, insubstantial, irrelevant matters. In our culture, the word is synonymous with, at best, fairy tales and, at worst, outright lies and deception. If you pay attention, you'll

be amazed at how often you'll read or hear someone say, "It's only a myth." It is of paramount importance that this disastrous distortion and misunderstanding be met head on.[13]

With this negative understanding of myth, how is religion ever to get back on track and announce to the world that its stories are primarily myths? Public opinion declares myths to be untrue, since they appear to conflict with reason. But this is only on the surface. If we peel back the outer layer and look at what they mean, they are true, as the schoolboy surmises. What they *denote* is false (fictional), but what they *connote* is true (spiritual). But most of us in the West see only the outside layer, which is believed or disbelieved, according to temperament and background. The inside truth is ignored by believers, like Lumley, who only grasp the external layer of myth, and by disbelievers, like Dawkins, who assume that myths are delusional.

Believers and nonbelievers don't seem to realize how similar they are. Both are looking at the outside husk. Both are misreading myths, and drawing opposite conclusions. Joseph Campbell puts the dilemma in memorable terms:

> Half the people in the world think that the metaphors of their religious traditions are facts. And the other half contends that they are not facts at all. As a result we have people who consider themselves believers because they accept metaphors as facts, and we have others who classify themselves as atheists because they think religious metaphors are lies.[14]

This points to the widespread confusion in the modern world. In a semi-facetious manner, Campbell says "myth might be defined simply as "other people's religion," by which he means that few followers of a tradition are prepared to see their religion as mythology.[15] Myth, believers say, is what others have, whereas they have the truth, often claimed to be absolute truth, and literalized as historical truth. Campbell offers a serious but shocking definition of religion as "misunderstood mythology." He says "the misunderstanding consists in the interpretation of mythic metaphors as references to hard fact."[16]

Several factors contribute to this misunderstanding. One is the lack of imagination in religious adherents, who find sacred stories so arresting they assume them to be historical. Another is the emphatic mode in which scriptures are written, which encourages readers to take them at face value. A further problem is that such texts were written long ago, when mythos,[17] not factual reporting, was the favored mode

xxiii

of writing. Finally, religious institutions do little to prevent adherents from reading texts literally, and often encourage this kind of reading. The churches have constructed themselves as bastions of literalism, and are destined to continue their downward course, since most modern people cannot abide their point of view. The receptive heart will not accept what the thinking mind rejects. This has been a dilemma in my own life, and I have received criticism from both sides: scholars tend to find me too religious, while the religious find me not religious enough.

Ironically, to present an interpretation of religion that might be acceptable to our age, I have upset a number of people who are settled in their beliefs. I don't belong to their fold, and they know it. Along the way to completing this book, I have presented numerous talks in which I have tiptoed around people's sensitivities, not wanting to create too much disturbance. I am not a fighter by nature, and I don't want to "fight" for this cause. I want people to understand the nature of religion as mythological discourse, and increase the appreciation of this discourse. I don't see myself as doing anything startlingly new; after all, the argument of this book is that scripture was deliberately written in a mythological mode and has been misinterpreted for centuries. If I am perceived as a radical, it should be in the true meaning of this term, where "radical" derives from the Latin *radix*, meaning "roots." I see myself as going back to the roots of religion and trying to understand it from this perspective.

Inevitably, what I will write in this book will shock some readers. This gives me no pleasure, and I shudder to think that I might be responsible for some "losing their faith," as the saying goes. But if faith is constructed as belief, it is hard to see how such disturbance can be avoided. According to Bishop Spong, a radical in the field, the possibility that such revelations might offend those with traditional pieties is unavoidable:

> To suggest that these miracle stories might not be literally true engenders shock, is greeted with fear and not infrequently creates anger. That emotional response is sometimes mistaken for either zeal or firm conviction. It is neither. It is an expression of the primal anxiety of a self-conscious creature manifesting itself, as the religious security system of yesterday begins its inevitable slide toward death.[18]

I am not entirely sure of my audience. Those with traditional pieties tend to avoid "modern" ideas, viewing them as anathema. Such people tend not to read many books anyway, as they believe they already possess the truth. On the other hand, those who have dispensed with religion don't see the point of rescuing it at this late stage. But I can only hope there is an audience in between the ardent believers and despisers of religion. I think there is, and hope such an audience will grow once the field is laid out and explained in language they can understand.

But what some will find shocking has been commonplace in academic circles for at least two hundred years. The philosophers Hegel, Strauss, Feuerbach, and Nietzsche in the nineteenth century were well aware of the mythological nature of religious statements. In the twentieth century, psychoanalysts Jung and Freud were writing on this subject. Later, theologians began to take note, including Tillich, Bultmann, Tracy, and more recently, thinkers such as Karen Armstrong, Dominic Crossan, and Eugen Drewermann have made important contributions. But little of this has filtered down to the general public, or to the religious institutions, which saw these thinkers as dangerously modern. Part of the problem is that the "case" for the metaphorical reading of scripture has still not been put in an accessible form. Much of this work is locked away in academic tomes and scholarly papers that the general public would not read. Therefore, in this book I aim to simplify what has been known in scholarly circles for some time. My originality, if such it is, is to provide my personal stamp on an existing field.

There are some leading lights in the churches who are on the same page as me. As well as John Spong in New Jersey, there is Alan Jones in San Francisco and Richard Holloway in Scotland. There are many others, but I haven't had the opportunity to meet them. In the company of clergy, I am reluctant to raise this topic, as I am greeted with disapproval, and such clergy seem to think it is their duty to put me right by trotting out the party line. It is a sad state of affairs. Richard Holloway, former Bishop of Edinburgh, wrote in *How to Read the Bible*:

> Unimaginative literalists have destroyed the reputation of the Bible by insisting on [its] factual truth rather than encouraging us to read it metaphorically.[19]

There are "unimaginative literalists" on the other side of the fence. We have the celebrity atheists, Richard Dawkins, Sam Harris, Christopher Hitchens, who are literalists coming from the disbelieving fraternity.[20] They and a host of others are trying to wipe the horizon of religion and telling us the world is better off without it. Although the new atheists come out of a post–9/11 context and are concerned with warmongering fundamentalism, they do not differentiate between good and bad religion, or realize that what they are rejecting is a misreading. They want to throw out religion, but I want to renew it by reconnecting it with its roots in mythos. Nevertheless, some will not see any difference, and I will be accused of destructive activity because I question the frame in which religion is conceived. Be that as it may, and despite the possibility of being misunderstood, I have to press on with the task, which is vital to rediscovering the integrity of our spiritual lives.

My greatest fear is not offending traditional pieties but encouraging people to accept the metaphorical approach and then having them decide that scripture is a tissue of lies. One has to battle against a flood of prejudices to get people to understand that religious metaphors are meaningful. As a youth, I used to be haunted by the song of Aretha Franklin and Bobby Darin: "It ain't necessarily so, the things that you're liable, to read in the Bible, it ain't necessarily so."[21] The song is right and wrong. The things in the Bible "ain't necessarily so" if read literally. But if read as metaphors, they are true, as faith has asserted. These metaphors are not empty, they are not arbitrary, but point to spiritual realities that need to be respected. I want us to see beyond surfaces, to the connotations behind the stories. In this way, we conduct *midrash* in the modern age, where midrash is seen as the recovery of truths in a tradition that is failing to speak to the modern world.[22]

The task today is to switch from literal to metaphorical thinking, and not fall into the gap between them. I am anxious that many will fall, and have fallen, into the gap. The disbelieving majority has already done this. When my daughter was a teenager, I saw she was outgrowing her religious beliefs and tried to explain the metaphorical approach. She later said it destroyed her faith, and this made me realize that this way is fraught with problems. Still, I see signs that some will get the point, and this inspires me. I see no other way to renew faith than to dissociate it from belief. Mine is the faith of the nonbeliever, the faith of those who cannot believe in impossible events. However there will come a time when we can redefine belief, when the current battles have been fought and won and we can understand belief in a different way.

As a young adult, most of my friends abandoned Christianity and moved across to Eastern pathways, Buddhism mostly, but also Hinduism and Taoism. I was interested in this turn to the East, but I could not join them because I felt there was treasure in the Judeo-Christian tradition that had not yet been discerned. People were throwing out this heritage too quickly, and pointing this out did not make me popular.

I did not wish to shift to the East merely because it was fashionable, with the allure of exotic practices and remarkable philosophies. I have always felt that the West is sitting on a treasure trove that is not understood. But the dead hand of convention keeps this wisdom from us, locked up in what Jung called "sacrosanct unintelligibility."[23] If we could overcome convention, and the instruction to read things literally, the West might experience a renewal of its own, and Westerners might find wisdom closer to home.

Notes

1. *The Cloud of Unknowing*, authored by an anonymous writer of the late fourteenth century, in Clifton Wolters, ed., *The Cloud of Unknowing and Other Works* (Harmondsworth: Penguin, 1978), p. 136.
2. 1 Corinthians 13:11.
3. I explore the connection between spirituality and mental health in *Gods and Diseases* (Sydney: HarperCollins, 2011; London and New York: Routledge, 2013).
4. Genesis 3:8.
5. See for instance my essay "Jacques Derrida: The Enchanted Atheist" in *Thesis Eleven: Critical Theory and Historical Sociology* (London: Sage), 110, 1, June 2012, pp. 3–16.
6. Jacques Derrida, *Writing and Difference* (Chicago: University of Chicago Press, 1978), p. 353.
7. Paul Tillich, *Theology of Culture* (Oxford and New York: Oxford University Press, 1959), p. 61.
8. This was the personal context of my book *The Spirituality Revolution* (Sydney: HarperCollins, 2003; London and New York: Routledge, 2004).
9. Robert Johnson, *We: Understanding the Psychology of Romantic Love* (1983; New York: HarperOne, 2009), p. 2.
10. Joanna Lumley, speaking of her film *The Search for Noah's Ark*, in *The Age* (Melbourne), 6 March 2014, p. 7.
11. Joanna Lumley, narrator, *The Search for Noah's Ark*, Matt Bennett, director; Rebecca Harris, producer; Burning Bright Productions, UK, December 2012.
12. Lumley, *The Age*, p. 7.
13. Tom Harpur, *The Pagan Christ: Is Blind Faith Killing Christianity?* (Sydney: Allen & Unwin, 2005), p. 7.
14. Joseph Campbell, "Metaphor and Religious Mystery" (1985), in Eugene Kennedy (ed.) *Thou Art That: Transforming Religious Metaphor. The Collected Works of Joseph Campbell*, Vol. 1 (Novato, CA: New World Library, 2001), p. 2.
15. Joseph Campbell, *The Inner Reaches of Outer Space: Metaphor as Myth and as Religion* (1986; Novato, CA: New World Library, (Novato, CA: New World Library, 2002), p. 27.
16. Ibid.
17. *Mythos* (sometimes *muthos*), Greek for sacred story or tale, will be further discussed in future chapters.
18. John Shelby Spong, *Jesus for the Non-Religious* (New York: HarperOne, 2007), p. 66.

19. Richard Holloway, *How to Read the Bible* (London: Granta Books, 2006), p. 5.
20. Richard Dawkins, *The God Delusion* (London: Bantam Press, 2006); Christopher Hitchens, *God is Not Great: How Religion Poisons Everything* (New York: Hatchette Book Group, 2007); Sam Harris, *The End of Faith: Religion, Terror and the Future of Reason* (New York: W.W. Norton & Co., 2004).
21. Aretha Franklin and Bobby Darin, "It Ain't Necessarily So," in their 1959 album, *That's All*. The lyrics were by Ira Gershwin and music by George Gershwin for the 1935 opera *Porgy and Bess*. In the opera it is sung by Sportin' Life, a drug dealer who expresses doubt about the veracity of religious statements.
22. The Jewish term "midrash" is described by S. Aarowitz as "the attempt to penetrate into the spirit of the text, to examine the text from all sides, to derive interpretations not immediately obvious, to illumine the future by appealing to the past"; in *The Jewish Encyclopedia* (London and New York: Funk & Wagnalls, 1925).
23. C. G. Jung, "A Psychological Approach to the Dogma of the Trinity" (1942/1948), *The Collected Works of C. G. Jung* (hereafter *CW*), 11, § 170.

1

Miracles as Imagination

The symbolic language of myth will always be degraded into a language of the tangible. Every epoch has the critical task of correcting such perversions.
— Karl Jaspers[1]

Mythos and History

There are elements of history in scripture, but the miraculous moments with gods, angels, devils, and other visitations are metaphors pointing to the presence of spirit in human experience. Such moments of presence are personified as supernatural "beings" according to the conventions of myth, which we today do not understand, and tend to either dismiss as nonsense or believe literally. Many secular people assume scripture writers were deluding themselves by seeing things that did not exist. Many religious people assume scripture writers were taking eyewitness accounts of supernatural happenings. Neither is true. Scripture writers were engaged in literary conventions and tropes that today's believers and unbelievers fail to appreciate. Religion is literature and art that has been distorted by literal readings.

If modern poets, visionaries, or novelists write about their experience, and use myth or legend to amplify their thoughts and feelings, we do not assume they are talking about literal gods if they draw on Greek, Roman, or Hebrew mythology. On the contrary, we assume they are using mythic figures symbolically to amplify themes or visions. Then why do we read "the good book" in such a narrowly dogmatic way? Imagination has to be brought to bear on holy scriptures, so we can read them correctly.

Religious stories are to civilizations what dreams are to individuals. They are symbolically encoded messages from the depths of the human soul. Just as it would be inadvisable to interpret our dreams literally, in which case we would get into all sorts of trouble with the real world and human relationships, so we miss the inner meaning of scriptures by unimaginative readings. They are only loosely related to "reality" as we understand it. They demand reflection, contemplation, and an understanding of symbolic language. If we bring imagination and knowledge to bear on religious stories they can come to life in unexpected ways. At the same time, this metaphorical turn brings with it the advantage that religion loses its arrogant and absolutist sting, allowing us to combat the violence and discord to which literalism gives rise.

The metaphors of religion do not appear in a cultural vacuum. History and myth work together: there are historical occurrences that trigger metaphors to describe their inward meaning. Unless history has been turned into myth, the significance of historical events is not realized. As T. S. Eliot said: "history is a pattern of timeless moments."[2] Events by themselves do not establish truth. These events "mean" something, "want to say" something, and their timeless truths can be communicated only in metaphor. In the case of the gospels, the fact of Jesus' existence (which I do not doubt) triggered the myth of the Christ who is eternal. The fact of his ministry, its emphasis on love and compassion, triggered the myth that he was God's only begotten son. The fact that his disciples felt that his spirit still dwelt among them after the crucifixion triggered the myth of the resurrection, and so on. Metaphor and history work together to weave sacred history. Metaphor draws out the spiritual significance, while history acknowledges that certain events took place in time and space. But for too long, we have treated the significance as fact; a simple but fatal error.

The churches have failed to understand that the scriptures are a mixture of mythos and history, not pure history. I use the Greek term "mythos" advisedly. This term means sacred story, whereas the modern term "myth" has been debased and refers to falsity. We can revert to the English word "myth," but only after we have familiarized ourselves with the proper meaning of the term and its Greek origins. It is impossible to call for a recovery of myth, or more respect for myth, if the word itself subverts all attempts to restore value. The debasement of the term is part of the crisis we face in trying to recover the meaning of religion. Western intellectual history has virtually undermined the platform upon which religion stands.

In recent times, partly as a defense against critical thinking, some churches have pretended that the Bible is primarily historical. The Bible is aware of history, to be sure, but "being aware of history and being historical are different things."[3] Northrop Frye admits that "the

Miracles as Imagination

degree to which the Bible does record actual events can perhaps never be exactly ascertained." The Bible looks at first like a historical narrative, but this impression is misleading, as Frye makes clear:

> The historical narrative in the Bible is not really a history but a *mythos* or narrative principle on which historical incidents are strung. The narrative of the Bible is much closer to poetry than it is to actual history, and should be read as such.[4]

This is scandalous to naïve believers who imagine every word is historical. Frye is adamant that the Bible is least historical when it comes to the miracles and wonders, which have to be read as sensational symbols of the life of the spirit, its quest to "overcome" our finite nature and material conditions. To take the miracles literally is to misread the Bible and end with a belief based on falsity. Such belief has almost nothing to do with faith, and does not give faith a chance to mature, confining it to childhood ideation.

Some scholars within the church attempt to preserve the cherished sense of history, as well as admit to the presence of myth. A case in point is George Caird, who was professor of exegesis of holy scripture at the University of Oxford. In *The Language and Imagery of the Bible* he said the metaphorical element does not invalidate the church's claim that scripture is a narrative of historical events.[5] Caird claims that "the New Testament lays great emphasis on the actuality of the events it records."[6] He then contradicts this by saying "at certain points the gospel tradition has been embellished with new detail and even new events."[7] But at what points are the tradition embellished? He does not say. He admits that "bare facts are never significant in themselves, but only when brought into relation with a tradition and seen in a framework of interpretation."[8] He places us in a whirlpool of competing claims. Frye is correct when he says fact is subordinate to myth in the Bible, and I suspect Caird agrees but is afraid to say so. As a conservative, Caird hedges around this fact, as he wants to toe the line and not create ecclesiastical disturbance. It is all very well for him to say that real events are "elevated" above the ordinary by literary devices, but only if the reader/believer is made aware that the Bible's miraculous moments are to be read in the light of history-told-as-myth.

If we say scripture represents sacred history, emphasis has to be placed on "sacred" rather than "history." Caird is regarded as a pioneer of the metaphorical approach, but his conservatism destroys his courage and necessitates the rise of strong voices like Armstrong, Crossan, Frye, and Spong after him. His findings are muffled in a highly scholastic style, almost as if he did not want to be understood by the average reader or by those sitting in the pews. His exegesis of scripture made it apparent that the conventional readings of biblical language have been naïve in the extreme, but he has an uncanny ability to fudge this point and end up saying little that is memorable. He was sitting on dynamite but did not want to bear witness to any explosions. He wanted to come back to church next Sunday and not change a word of any of the claims made by creeds, dogmas, and liturgies.

The history of Christianity is a history of errors. It has mistaken belief for faith, mythology for theology, and poetry for doctrine. The result is that a good religion has been ruined by its advocates, who got so caught up in literalism that its essence was lost. Its essence is more humble, yet more profound, than most believers have been able to realize. If we strip away the literalism, a real religion is left for us to appreciate—perhaps for the first time. But as this religion has presented itself to the world, it has adopted a fake appearance that most educated people have been unable to accept. When we reject this façade, we think we have rejected religion per se, but not so. We have only rejected the packaging of unimaginative churchmen. Baptist minister Harvey Cox tells of his crisis when he saw through the charade of his tradition. He almost lost everything, until it dawned on him that to confuse "belief with faith is simply a mistake": "We have been misled for many centuries by the theologians who taught that 'faith' consisted in dutifully believing the articles listed in one of the countless creeds they have spun out."[9] His healthy skepticism is what saved his faith.

When religion adopted a literalist frame it set itself against reason and allowed itself to be taken down by scholars. As Eugen Drewermann writes:

> We won't give religion a solid foundation by seeking the truth of mythical texts in a place where it can't be found: in the external world. Anyone who insists on this sort of logical confusion as an article of faith will involuntarily play into the hands of atheism and irreligion, instead of getting closer to the real point of the mythical traditions.[10]

A new tradition of celebrity atheists responds to the mysteries of the Bible with contempt, dismissing them as lies. Most atheists consider themselves more intelligent than believers because they have seen through the deception. This comes across in the interview style of

Miracles as Imagination

Richard Dawkins and others, who talk to religious people as if they are morons. But the celebrity atheists rarely stop to wonder if what they are rejecting is the essence of religion. Indeed, one could say that what atheists are rejecting—literalism and idolatry—*must* be rejected by intelligent persons. Atheism has an important role to play, not only in society but in the formation of faith. I commend atheism insofar as it strips back religion and rejects the ways in which it has been misrepresented in the past.

The crisis of atheism is that it not only strips back the false overlay, but it goes further and denies there is anything of value in religion. We need to question the dogmatic claims, but not destroy the interior life of religion, which contains the best of what it means to be human. There is too much unraveling, an orgy of destruction, without attention to preserving what is worthwhile. In this regard, we have only just begun the great adventure of our time: sifting the chaff from the wheat, and preserving what is life giving and precious. Insensitive deconstruction can be seen as an early stage of faith, the stage in which faith tries to shrug off the burden of literalism.

We are faced with a conundrum in which those who believe in the Bible, and those who attack it, are caught by the notion that it is a historical document. Believers read scripture as good history, a depiction of things that happened, while unbelievers see it as bad history, a cooked-up version of events. Both are making errors and failing to ask the right questions. The Bible is an amalgam of myth and history. Some of what we read has historical credibility but the wonders and miracles are mythical images.

The Miracles of Jesus

The miracles of Jesus can be read as metaphors of the significance astir in the events of his ministry. I don't believe there were any supernatural miracles performed by Jesus, as claimed by tradition. To assume there were such miracles is a misunderstanding of the mythic mode in which the texts were operating. It is, rather, a case that the apprehension of what happened to people in their responses to Jesus was such that writers—and oral traditions—were inspired to proclaim that "miracles" had occurred. It was "as if" he cured people of their maladies and sicknesses, "as if" he brought the dead back to life. Spiritual vision overrules ordinary perception; or as we might say today, poetry is more profound than prose. Yet we live in a world of prose, where poetry is discounted or misinterpreted.

Beyond Literal Belief

Jesus gave inspiring talks to thousands of people, and large crowds were nourished by his teachings. Perhaps this "spiritual nourishment" was expressed, two thousand years ago, as a wonderful event in which people *seemed* to receive supernatural blessings. There are two miraculous feeding stories in Mark and Matthew. In Mark, a crowd of four thousand gathered on the Gentile side of the Sea of Galilee, and Jesus took "seven loaves" and "a few small fish," and distributed them to the starving masses, who had been with him "three days" with "nothing to eat."[11] At the end of the feast, there was so much food left over that his disciples gathered "seven baskets full."[12] Matthew records this same event in similar terms,[13] but introduces a second miraculous event on the Jewish side of the lake. In this case there were five thousand people who were fed with "five loaves of bread and two fish."[14] Jesus blessed the food and distributed it to the five thousand, after which "the disciples picked up twelve basketfuls of broken pieces that were left over."[15] The rational response to this is: "This cannot have happened as reported; it is a lie." The believer says: "This did happen, it is a miracle, and praise be to you, Lord Jesus Christ!"

I cannot agree with the believer or unbeliever, because these are literary interpretations of real events. The miracles have nothing to do with belief as such, but are literary appreciations of the significance of the gatherings beside the lake. You either appreciate the poem, or you do not. We are in the realm of mythos,[16] which in this case is based on history, but not reducible to it. The stories are parables, and the miraculous feedings must be seen as interpretive signs, not facts. It was "as if" Jesus had fed the crowds with bread and fish, "as if" they went away satisfied and full. Everything here is metaphorical: their "hunger" signifies their need for spiritual sustenance, and the three days without food signifies a phase without the blessings of God. The words of Jesus were received like loaves and fishes to those who were starving. Everyone went away renewed in their faith. If cameras had recorded these events, there would have been no miraculous feeding in any literal sense, but cameras could hardly record the fulfillment of a satiated spirit. The believer and unbeliever are right and wrong: there was no such thing through the eyes of common sight, but there was such a thing, if viewed through insight. Myth opens us to this uncertain, risky place in which we either see the point or we don't. But the point can't be verified, only conceded.

What the literal reading of these tales ignores is that the miraculous feedings are examples of the Jewish tradition of midrash. Or to be more

Miracles as Imagination

precise, they are examples of Haggadic midrash. Haggadah, one of the three major forms of midrash, refers to the interpretation of a story or an event by relating it to another story in sacred history. This is what literary studies calls "intertextuality," and this was hardly invented yesterday. Midrash is an ancient Jewish practice that says everything to be venerated in the present must be connected with a sacred moment in the past. Since the writers of scripture want to show that Jesus is as great as Moses, or greater than him insofar as Jesus completes the reconciliation of humanity and God, they proclaim Jesus performs acts similar to those of Moses. The children of Israel were starving as they escaped from Egypt and wandered through the wilderness. Moses asked God to rain an unlimited quality of bread upon them so their well-being and confidence could be restored. They gathered this bread or manna dew into countless baskets.[17]

The miraculous feeding stories of the gospels follow this pattern and express a line of continuity between Moses the liberator and Jesus the redeemer. These stories preserve cultural memory in the present and point to the holiness of Jesus by a method of literary affiliation with the past. The prophets Elijah and Elisha were also said to have had the power to produce a food supply that was bountiful.[18] Just as the great Jewish leaders fed the starving people and catered to their needs, so the new leader, Jesus, is able to perform these acts in the imaginations of first-century Jewish writers and oral traditions. But what is "performed" operates primarily in the literary imagination, as that is the place where religious memory is preserved in these "religions of the book." An interesting detail is that Moses caused birds of the air and swamps (quail and poultry) to satiate the children of Israel,[19] whereas Jesus commanded fish to be distributed to his people. This suggested that the new era of Jesus would be symbolized by the sign of the fish, indicating that this was not a repetition of the past but a departure from it.

In his ministry Jesus was said to heal the sick, make the blind see and the deaf hear. He cured lepers and cast out demons from those who were epileptic or mentally ill. Two thousand years ago, might not these have been metaphors as well? The metaphors are no longer appropriate for our time, because we no longer see epilepsy and mental illness in terms of possession by evil spirits. But in Jesus' time, this is how mental illness was perceived, and thus the metaphors used to express his healing powers are in accord with the attitudes of his time. Today we might say: he made me feel complete or a better person, or my psyche feels renewed. Whatever the expressions of today, we would no longer say that he cast out demons or exorcised spirits. But the effectiveness of a charismatic healer is often in the eyes of the beholder, not in the objective witness of what has taken place.

With regard to our spiritual well-being, we often require skilled teachers to make us see the spiritual significance of our lives. It is typical for us to be *blind* to the spirit, to fail to *hear* its sound, not to be open to its call. We are not whole in body, mind, and spirit, but live partial lives that require healing. When someone gifted is able to make us aware of what is not perceived, might not this be characterized as a gift of sight, sound, or health? Similarly, in terms of the Lazarus story, if one is "dead" to the spirit and unable to perceive its call, might not the new awareness of the presence of spirit be depicted as a "return to life," a coming back into the world after one has been shut inside a mental tomb? The Lazarus story can be read as a parable about bringing a person back to spiritual life, after a period of spiritual death.[20] Again, believers will affirm that Jesus called Lazarus out of the tomb and brought him back to the living, and skeptics will say it could not have happened. Both are missing the point, which is made possible through myth.

Metaphor and Its Hazards

But it was not just the thirty or forty miracles performed *by* Jesus that could be seen this way. The miracles performed *on* Jesus by the Spirit, the wonders of the virgin birth and physical resurrection, could be viewed in this same light. In fact, the sequence of events in the gospel stories could be read as a string of metaphors that most have not understood as metaphors. These ideas gestated in me over years, and eventually I began to see there were other ways of approaching scripture. One did not have to believe these things and be burdened by convictions that ran against the grain of intelligence. Nor did one have to take a stand against them and deprive oneself and others of a spiritual life. One could receive these stories in a new way, as we might poems or mystical writings. Perhaps this is what the "words of God" ask of us, not the literal acceptance of these words, but that the inspiration behind the words are of the spirit. The Bible was written in a code language that few had cracked, a symbolic register that was systematically misinterpreted.

Over decades, I read a number of theologians in the hope of finding out something about the metaphorical—which ends up being mystical—approach to scripture. To my amazement, most sidestepped this issue and existed in a kind of bubble of their own making, full of comforting clichés about religion but overlooking the fact that the modern mind finds these statements implausible. Some theologians have faced the mythic nature of biblical language. These would include Paul Tillich and Rudolf Bultmann on the Protestant side, and Dominic Crossan and my near-namesake David Tracy on the Catholic side. But such theologians are rare. It seems that most are caught in a spell cast by the church and its authority. They are certain that the miracles are "true." This did not impress me, because it showed tradition was trapped in an ideology, which might be called historical positivism. Theologians spoke in reverent tones about the "revelation" of God's work in the life of Jesus, and central to this was his ability to perform miracles and have miraculous acts performed on him.

In recent years I have brushed up against a new tradition referred to as "progressive Christian thinkers." This tradition includes such radical figures as Donald Cupitt of Cambridge, Lloyd Geering of New Zealand, Francis Macnab of Australia, and Gretta Vosper of Canada. They appear to be saying what I am saying, that the miracles are metaphors. They see through the charade of historicity to the metaphorical, but this does not go hand in hand with increased respect for the metaphorical. To this group, inspired by Bultmann, the existentialist, miracles are "just metaphors," and can be discounted as literary decoration, having no intrinsic value in themselves. Quickly I discerned my difference from this tradition, and why I could not join them: I had respect for the miracles, and they did not. The miracles <u>are not empty</u>, but full of significance if we can turn to them with the right attitude. The metaphors stand for something and point to something. Perhaps my literary background and training in symbolic thinking predisposed me to a respect that these theologians could not muster. No one asks if a poem by William Blake is based on a true event, if his "Sick Rose" is based on a real rose, or if the "worm" inside the rose is factual. Who cares about this? The fact is that his "Sick Rose" is a great poem, and that is all we need know.

The lack of historical foundation in the Jesus miracles does not destroy their significance, if we are viewing them through the eyes of mythos. But for "progressive Christians," once the game of history is over, the magic ends. Metaphors for them are mere allegories, not full of suggestive power. They are viewing them through logos, not mythos. For me, the magic begins once we rediscover the miracles as metaphorical. This is because I could never "believe" them as purported facts in the first place, and as such they were far-fetched and easily dismissed. But once I adjusted my perception, and understood them through the mythos mode, they came to life and made new claims on my imagination. Progressives lack an appreciation of poetry, and their problem is not one of faith so much as illiteracy. They are tone-deaf to the literary quality of scripture and cannot perceive the spiritual life of metaphors. They cannot perform midrash, if by this term we mean the rescuing of spiritual significance of old sacred stories that no longer speak to the modern world.

Preserving the Spiritual Meaning

By far the best of the progressive thinkers is Bishop John Shelby Spong, who seems like the others but is not one of them. Spong is an intellectual who is skeptical of the claims of religious tradition. He could not "believe" in the miracles as presented by church piety. He states his position boldly:

> I do not believe that miracles, understood as the supernatural setting aside of natural causes, ever happen. I do not believe that the miracles described in the New Testament literally occurred in the life of Jesus of Nazareth or that of his disciples.[21]

Like Spong, I cannot abide a religion based on supernaturalism and the whole concept of literal miracles is repellent to me. With relief I discovered that Spong is not progressive in the sense of wiping away the supernatural so that nothing is left. He is not like Bultmann or Cupitt, who explode the myths and get rid of everything. He is a modern thinker, but trying to reclaim what is essential. He strives not only to debunk, but to reimagine the miracles as metaphors.

What stirs my imagination is Spong's quest to find alternative ways to read the miracles:

> Must we today be committed to the historicity of these first-century miracle stories? Or is there another way that these dramatic acts can be understood in our day? Was there perhaps another way to understand them even when they were originally written?[22]

This question is what interests me. Are miracles to be read as real events, or as symbols of a level of significance astir in these events? Are they metaphors, no longer perceived as such, that seek to highlight the spiritual significance of what took place? Are they poetry and wisdom, rather than incursions of a supernatural kind? Spong argues that they were not eyewitness accounts of what happened, but were "added later as part of the interpretive debate that swirled around Jesus." He doubts that they were viewed at their origins as events that occurred in history:

> Were these miracles even then recognized as prophetic interpretive signs designed to address questions of meaning? Is it possible that what first-century people thought of as a miracle would be to us today not a supernatural invasion at all, but an internal process of spirit?[23]

If this is true, we don't have to reject these statements, but need to understand them in their first-century context. The miracle is a literary device[24] used by first-century writers to talk about significance, but they did not see these miracles as "supernatural invasions," or as "the supernatural setting aside of natural causes." If this is true, we can find a connection between how we think today and the religion of the past, without having to reject early wisdom as out of date and unbelievable. Our incomprehension of religion has nothing to do with faith as such, but is a problem to do with literary style and conventions.

Spong gives us hints as to how we might close the gap between our minds and those of the past. He says scripture writers employed supernatural language to describe the movements of spirit because this language had been used in the Jewish writings and was seen as "good enough" to use in the descriptive accounts of Jesus:

> The problem faced by the disciples was: how were they going to talk about their experience of Jesus? They solved the problem by searching the Hebrew scriptures for God language, and when they found it they wrapped it around Jesus—not because these words described things that actually happened, but because they were the only words big enough to make sense out of their experience. So the disciples used the narratives of miracles to demonstrate the presence of God in Jesus.[25]

Scripture writers were inventing miracles to describe what they felt about Jesus and his authority. As Spong put it, "miracles represented the only way first-century Jewish people could stretch human language sufficiently to allow them to communicate what they believed they had encountered in Jesus." But for us this convention has backfired:

> Today that first-century supernatural language not only blinds us to the meaning of Jesus, but actually distorts Jesus for us.[26]

We are repelled by the literary devices that early writers used to endear readers and the faithful to Jesus. That is why we have to do something about it, and confess that the old-time religion needs to be revised, according to modern understandings of truth and representation. If we don't rescue the spirit of Jesus from the old forms, his spirit will be lost. Already Jesus has become "little more than a fading memory, the symbol of an age that is no more and a nostalgic reminder of our believing past."[27] Rescuing his spirit from the burden of cliché and platitude is the task I have set myself, along with others who feel called to this work of reparation.

In my opinion, if we don't change religion, it will implode. Thus to what extent are the "conservatives" conserving anything? They are overseeing the demise of a tradition. They would rather risk the death of the tradition than find the courage to change. The churches cling to what they call their "revealed and unchanging truth," yet without change there can be no future. Despite the actions of some religious leaders, most traditional forms of religion are destined to collapse in the near future. What will happen after this collapse? Spong is convinced that we are already "living at the end of the Christian era." We face "the death of Christianity as it has been historically understood."[28] Nevertheless he has "a lively hope that a new Christianity can grow out of the death of the old supernatural forms of yesterday's Christianity."[29] To achieve this we need "to get beyond the literalism of a premodern world," and reshape religion so we can be "both believers and citizens of the twenty-first century."[30]

Spong often uses this term "believer," but I am unhappy with it. I don't like belief, but I respect faith. In fact, most of what Christians "believe" Spong has jettisoned anyway, so I am uncertain why he persists with the term. I think the less we believe the better, but faith is a different matter. The point of faith is that one is filled with a sense of the sacred that does not require evidence. If faith requires proof it isn't faith, but *belief in impossible events*, such as a virgin birth or a physical resurrection. Faith is the heartfelt reception of spiritual realities, and an acceptance that the expression of those realities require symbols. Such symbols hint at transcendent realities of spirit, and faith intuits the realities to which the symbols point. Every religious tradition, in its own way, gropes toward the mystery of God. Overwhelmingly, faith has been fused with belief and misinterpreted by institutions that seem to want to keep people in a state of spiritual sleep.

Peter Todd suggests that those who read scriptures literally "lack an evolved symbolic function," and this "lack," which is not just a personal but a cultural lacuna, has to be addressed.[31] Children read scriptures as fairy stories, but adults ought not. There are adults who prolong their childhood beyond the required period and deceive their intelligence by taking stories literally. There are a growing number of adults who reject the stories as lies and see them as delusional. The challenge facing religions is to overcome naïve belief while not falling into a slump of despair once we realize that what have been taught as facts are metaphors. I will have more to say later about the dangers of falling into the gap between beliefs we can no longer sustain and a faith to which we might aspire.

Notes

1. Karl Jaspers, "Myth and Religion" (1953), in Joseph Hoffmann, ed. and Norbert Guterman, trans., *Karl Jaspers and Rudolf Bultmann, Myth and Christianity: An Inquiry into the Possibility of Religion Without Myth* (1954, New York: Prometheus Books, 2005), p 32.
2. T. S. Eliot, "Little Gidding" (1942), in *Collected Poems 1909–1962* (London: Faber, 1965), p. 222.
3. Northrop Frye, "History and Myth in the Bible" (1975), in Alvin A. Lee and Jean O'Grady, eds., *Northrop Frye on Religion, Collected Works of Northrop Frye*, Vol. 4 (Toronto: University of Toronto Press, 2000), p. 13.
4. Frye, "History and Myth," pp. 14; 17.
5. G. B. Caird, *The Language and Imagery of the Bible* (London: Duckworth, 1980), p. 201.
6. Caird, p. 215.
7. Caird, p. 214.
8. Caird, p. 202.
9. Harvey Cox, *The Future of Faith* (New York: HarperCollins, 2009), p. 18.
10. Eugen Drewermann, *Discovering the God Child Within: A Spiritual Psychology of the Infancy of Jesus* (New York: Crossroad, 1994), p. 24.
11. Mark 8:2.
12. Mark 8:3–9.
13. Matthew 15:29–38.
14. Matthew 14:17.
15. Matthew 14:17–20.
16. *Mythos* (sometimes *muthos*), Greek for sacred story or tale, will be further discussed in future chapters.
17. Exodus 16:1–8.
18. 1 Kings 17; 2 Kings 4.
19. Exodus 16:13.
20. John 11:1–57.
21. John Shelby Spong, *Jesus for the Non-Religious* (New York: HarperOne, 2007), p. 54.
22. Ibid, p. 54.
23. Ibid, pp. 67–68.
24. Ibid, p. 94.
25. Ibid, p. 69.

26. Ibid, p. 95.
27. Ibid, p. 9.
28. Ibid, p. 7.
29. Ibid, p. xiv.
30. Ibid, p. 55; p. 54.
31. Peter Todd, *The Individuation of God: Integrating Science and Religion* (Wilmette, Illinois: Chiron Publications, 2012), p. 102.

2

Religion as Metaphor

Taking it seriously does not mean taking it literally.
— Jung[1]

The Literary Mode of Scripture

Nonliteral thinkers like Spong and Drewermann have not arisen out of the blue but have built on a long-standing tradition that has been arguing for two hundred years that scripture ought to be read metaphorically. Most of this thinking has emerged from German-speaking countries, but in England Matthew Arnold was instrumental in getting this debate started in the 1870s. In the early 1800s, Hegel and Schelling were claiming that mythology and symbol are the keys to religion. In the mid to late nineteenth century, Strauss, Feuerbach, Schopenhauer, and Nietzsche were building on their arguments. Freud suggested that religion was metaphor, but he meant this as an attack on religion; it fell to his student Jung to convert this realization into a positive opportunity for faith. "Religion as myth" became a slogan for the atheists, who saw this as a way of discrediting religion and proving its irrelevance to the modern world. The atheists were half right, but got the wrong perspective on this matter, making it difficult for scholars like Jung, Spong, and Drewermann to rescue a positive message from this new realization.

Drawing on this background and discoveries in classical studies, Alvin Kuhn said: "Myth was the favorite and universal method of teaching in archaic times."[2] In their first-century context the scriptures were written in the favored mythic mode of the time. It is ludicrous to suggest that these writings, apart from others, were aiming for historical accuracy. Historical reporting was not seen as appropriate for sacred narratives, nor was it seen as revelatory or interesting. It wasn't used because it could not capture the presence of God in creation. Because of the confusion in the public mind about the nature and purpose of scripture, scholarship has emphasized that the biblical writers were not *intending* to deceive. In a brilliant encapsulation of the conundrum, Dominic Crossan writes:

> My point is not that those ancient people told literal stories and we are now smart enough to take them symbolically, but that they told them symbolically and we are now dumb enough to take them literally. They knew what they were doing; we don't.[3]

This should be written up on the walls of churches, schools, religious education classes, and theological institutes. Most people have no idea what Crossan is talking about, and this is due to a lack of education in communities of the faithful. Spong said the same thing when he indicated that the major elements of the Jesus story are mythical, and that "even originally they had no literal substance."[4] Scripture writers were not "recording events," nor were they "telling lies for God," as one of my academic colleagues put it.[5] They were telling figurative stories to grasp the depth of our relationship with God. If we say that the metaphorical approach is "new," it is nothing more than an optical illusion. There is nothing new about grasping what was intended in the beginning.

Before Crossan and Spong, Caird investigated what biblical writers meant in what they said. Where theologians went astray, he said, was to "assume that the biblical writers had minds as pedestrian as their own."[6] He argued that "the biblical writers were not only skillful handlers of words but were also well aware of the nature of their tools."[7] He refuted the notion that these writers were naïve primitives who were "imagining things" that had not happened. They knew they were writing in the modalities of myth. Caird argued they were self-conscious in their use of language and claimed "linguistic awareness is always a better working hypothesis than primitive mentality for understanding the sacred texts."[8] Even a writer as astute as Matthew Arnold could not understand that biblical writers might be deliberately employing myth and metaphor:

> The first Christians misunderstood Jesus and had the multitude's appetite for miracles, the multitude's inexact observation and boundless credulity. They it was who supplied the data which Christian theology took from them without question, and has ever since confidently built upon. But trained, critical, indifferent minds, which knew what evidence was and what popular beliefs were, could not but be struck with the looseness in the joints of the Christian belief, with the slightest of evidence for its miraculous data.[9]

Arnold was a fine Victorian poet, and even he could not identity metaphor in the scriptures. He mistook it for "inexact observation and boundless credulity." If a poet cannot spot metaphor, what chance have others got?

We need to read religious stories in the manner in which they were intended. If this seems challenging it is because our culture is suffering from amnesia and cannot remember the modalities of the past. Northrop Frye wrote:

> When the Bible is historically accurate, it is only accidentally so: reporting was not of the slightest interest to its writers. They had a story to tell which could only be told by myth and metaphor: what they wrote became a source of vision rather than doctrine.[10]
>
> The Bible is, with unimportant exceptions, written in the literary language of myth and metaphor.[11]

The narratives were written as vision but are misread as doctrine. If we awaken our capacity for poetry and ambiguity, we might be able to regain some of their original meaning. As Frye put it: "Myth is paradoxical and says both 'this happened' and 'this can hardly have happened in precisely this way.'"[12] The basis of myth is the metaphorical "as if." Myth presents things *as if* they happened this way, although we know they did not. But to the poetic eye, the imagination, they might have happened this way.

Since the Bible is written as myth, we cannot assume a correspondence between its words and history. Because readers want the scriptures to be "true," they apply the standard of truth that they most readily understand. But this was not how truth was understood two thousand years ago. The Bible is written in code, and the code is not Dan Brown's *Da Vinci Code*,[13] or any other popular fantasy that has been put forward in recent times. John Allegro claimed that the Bible was written in code and could be unraveled by referring to the effects of hallucinogenic mushrooms.[14] The idea of a "code" seems to inspire many silly and improbable theories. But the Bible's code is symbol and myth, with roots in the Hebraic, Egyptian, and Hellenic traditions.[15] If we read the German philosopher Ernst Cassirer, we can restore dignity to the idea of a code language, which has become distorted by pop culture. Cassirer points out that the modern mind tries to understand the products of myth at a literal level, and this does not get us far. He says myth can only be understood if we approach it "from within":

> Instead of viewing the contents of mythical consciousness from the outside, we wish to understand them from within. Thus myth

> becomes mystery: its true significance and depth lie not in what its configurations reveal but in what they conceal. The mythic consciousness resembles a code which is intelligible only to those who possess the key to it—that is, for whom the contents of this consciousness are signs for something "other."[16]

Myth does not yield its meaning through its denotations, but through what it points to, hints at, or connotes. The denotations are "preposterous nonsense," but the connotations are priceless.[17] The meanings have to be decoded, dug out, searched for. The images have to be interpreted, and they can only be interpreted according to the knowledge that is available at any point in time. The myths exhaust all attempts at interpretation and are never explained away. The myths remain, whereas interpretations come and go. This must be so, as myths deal with enigma and mystery, which we can never fully understand, but nor must we get impatient and throw them out.

Myth does not point to itself, but to something "other." It is a finger pointing at the moon, and we don't understand the moon by obsessing about the finger. Myth points away from itself, and if we do not realize this we are locked out of religion and unable to appreciate its meaning. "Myth is a sacred story which is not scientifically true but contains religious truth."[18] When we appreciate this, we are on our way to making sense of religion, perhaps for the first time. But there is a hurdle: "The meaning of myths in religious stories is very different from a popular understanding of myth."[19] Myth in popular language means lies, illusion. Myth in religious stories means a window into eternity. We have been corrupted into believing that there is only one kind of truth, which puts symbolic truth at a disadvantage. Once the realm of symbolism opens up, we see a new world of possibilities. Kevin Treston argues that if we read the gospels literally, we miss their purpose: "When religious stories are understood as factual accounts of what happened, they lose their essential religious meaning."[20] Thus we have to reverse conventional opinion. Instead of a literal reading being the "religious" one, we need to see that only a metaphorical approach yields the genuinely religious meaning.

Myth is a doorway into another kind of consciousness. We need patience and reflection to understand this, and these are missing in our busy world. There is a great difference between fact and truth. Myth provides us not with facts of history but with truths of spirit.

Religion as Metaphor

These truths never "happened" in time or space, but they are true for all time, as Frye explains:

> Mythos... tells us of events that are real, not in the sense of having happened just like that, but in the sense of being the kind of thing that is always happening.[21]

The Bible is not "world history," but "holy history" which tells us the story behind appearances. It uses symbols and myths to convey this meaning. Nineteenth-century scholars assumed that myth was bad science. James Frazer defined myth as mistaken notions of natural phenomena,[22] and Max Müller said mythology is a disease of language.[23] Such views reflect the prejudices of the time: "truth" can only be what occurs in demonstrable facts. But the Bible is a work of mythopoesis, a combination of myth and poetry. Its language is primary and cannot be reduced to bad science or mangled history. Only in our time are we beginning to understand how primary mythopoesis is. It is the most ancient form of art, but it is art that embodies the sacred and tells of the divine. But even "art" does not quite work as a descriptor, insofar as we see art today as secular. It is more primary than art, reflecting a time in which art and religion were one. William Blake gets it right when he refers to the Bible as "The Great Code of Art."[24]

It takes considerable effort to read the Bible.[25] The notion that anyone can pick it up and understand it without prior learning is wishful thinking. "The Bible demands a literary response from us."[26] Caird argues that we need to know what sort of language we are dealing with before we can understand the Bible.[27] Nietzsche said one cannot talk about sacred texts without assuming a scholarly approach, because one needs to think "by means of mediating abstractions."[28] Although simple folk can experience the grace of God—and possibly have more access to it than intellectuals—as soon as we touch on the "words of God" we enter the field of culture and need to be aware of complexities. There is no such thing as an "unmediated" experience of God's words, and when I hear preachers claim that we have to "return to the gospel message," I can only wonder what they have in mind. There is no contact with truth except through a cultural context. The uneducated cannot read sacred texts unaided, not unless they are gifted with poetic intelligence. They cannot read them as they might read articles in newspapers. If they do, the stories are nothing more than fairy tales. The nearest equivalent to the scriptures today would be visionary poetry or mystical writings.

Beyond Literal Belief

The early church fathers were not literalists and had a sophisticated understanding of symbol. The theologian Origin (185–254) said scripture was a symbol, and its words and stories merely the outward "images of divine things."[29] While the early church councils moved in a literal direction, intellectuals in the early church were philosophically minded and did not counsel literalism. But there was a strong turn toward literalism when Christianity was made a state religion, and this was reinforced at the time of the Intellectual Enlightenment. For survival reasons, religion wanted to keep pace with science in its emphasis on empirical fact, history and rationality. It did not want to be left standing as "myth" in a world that had come to value logos and reason. In so doing, religion lost its soul and the ground of mythos that makes religion meaningful.

In recent times literalism has received a boost from evangelical fundamentalism, which is a reaction to the "liberal" direction of theological colleges, which were trying to introduce the idea that scripture could be read in nonliteral ways. Religion seems to take one step forward and two back, and in our time literalism is rife in the popular domain, while the theological colleges seem to be sidestepping the main issue and losing themselves in intellectual inscrutability.

Scholars who speak out about literalism are ostracized by churches or have to leave their posts at theological colleges. There are many examples of this throughout history: David Strauss was offered a pension to remove him from his post at the University of Zurich even before he started his teaching duties. Bruno Bauer was removed from his position at the University of Bonn; more recently Eugen Drewermann has been prevented from teaching. The best and brightest minds are persecuted by churches that want to cling to literalism. Strauss, Bauer, and Drewermann point out that not only are the main events of scripture fantastic and implausible, but the gospels contradict each other in astonishing ways, indicating that historical accuracy is not the desired end. But these "aberrant" minds are simply returning to what early Christians always knew. Instead of complaining—as modern readers do—about the contradictions of scripture, Origin praised God for their existence, for they prevent us from falling into literalism. Karen Armstrong writes: "The glaring anomalies and inconsistencies in scripture forced us to look beyond the literal sense."[30] Origin believed that God had planted these "stumbling blocks and interruptions of the historical sense" to make us look deeper. These "impossibilities and incongruities present a barrier to the reader and lead him to refuse to proceed along the pathway of the ordinary meaning."[31]

Biblical criticism has shown that "the gospels are to be read not as faithful eye-witness accounts of Jesus' life but as carefully sculpted versions of that life, arranged to suit different interests, personalities and factions within the years of early Christianity."[32] Moreover the gospels were written in the last third of the first century and "were put into their current form slowly over a period of three hundred years."[33] The earliest of the gospels, Mark, appeared about 70 CE, forty years after the crucifixion. Matthew and Luke were written in the 80s and John closer to 100 CE. The further away we move from the actual years of Jesus' life, the more florid and mythical the gospels become. There is more literary construction in the Bible than has been understood. In treating the Bible as inerrant truth, believers assumed they were treating it with respect. But if treated with full respect, the Bible would be seen as a mix of mythos, political construction, and institutional treatise. Hopefully, after one takes all that into account, there can still be some sense of the divine light that might shine through these socially constructed grids.

The Bible deserves to be read in the literary genre in which it was written. It is not a text that gives a list of objective facts or manual for living. It is a source of myths and metaphors that point in the right direction, but it is not the stuff of doctrine or law. Frye says, "We have to move from the historical and doctrinal to the poetic and literary in getting a better understanding of the Bible." The two-millennia-old New Testament has still not been read correctly. Frye suggests that "real literary criticism of the Bible, in the sense of a criticism that takes seriously its mythical and metaphorical aspect, has barely begun."[34]

Myth, Metaphor, and Jesus

The life of Jesus provided the impetus for the New Testament's mythopoetic creativity. The gospels and letters of the apostles set to work weaving threads of imagination and hyperbole around this singular and outstanding figure. So much myth has been wrapped around Jesus that the historical person has virtually disappeared. This is not, however, because a historical figure did not exist in the first place, as a great many skeptics have believed. I do not doubt the existence of a real Jesus, but I adopt the view that the representation of this figure in the gospels is not historical but mythological. This has caused some to draw a distinction between the Jesus of history and the Christ of theology. We know little about the former, but I concur with Jung that "this Christ of St Paul's would hardly have been possible without the historical Jesus."[35]

My reading of Jesus is not to be confused with the tradition known as the "Christ myth theory." This so-called "mythicist" view uses "myth" in a negative sense, as make-believe. It began in the eighteenth and nineteenth centuries, and its early proponents included the French historians Charles Dupois and Constantin Volney, and German philosophers David Strauss and Bruno Bauer. In recent times, its advocates include John Allegro, Christopher Hitchens, and G. A. Wells.[36] This tradition is atheistic, and seeks to discredit the biblical tradition. It detects myth in the Bible and jumps to the conclusion that everything that contains myth is false. It reads scripture with rationalistic prejudices and insists that if the Bible is to have credibility it ought to be factual. It lacks imagination and is illiterate when it comes to literary genres and linguistic modalities. In my view, this "mythicist" approach has done a great deal of harm, and made it difficult for writers such as myself who acknowledge the presence of myth but still want to affirm faith and a historical dimension to the stories.

To me, Jesus existed as a historical figure, but most of the representations of his life and ministry are mythological. I share this view not only with Jung, Crossan, and those already mentioned, but also with anthropologist James George Frazer and classicist G. R. S. Mead.[37] I do not believe that the recognition of the mythical dimension leads to atheism, skepticism, and nihilism. In fact, I think quite the opposite: the acceptance of myth leads to a deepening of faith and a profound appreciation of what the biblical writers were trying to express. They were writing of a transcendental order that is impossible to convey through fact and description. They used metaphor and myth to grasp the deeper significance of what happened in Jesus' life, not to record what happened on the surface. If we fail to understand this, we are approaching the texts with a mean spirit and in bad faith.

The gospels offer *interpretations* of events using the language of myth. They do not set out to distort or tell lies. As the wily fox says in Saint-Exupéry's *The Little Prince*, "It is only with the heart that one can see rightly; what is essential is invisible to the eye." Truth requires the elaboration of facts and the use of metaphor. We might say that the lens of a camera cannot do justice to levels of meaning that are beneath the surface. There are different ways of seeing reality: through the physical eye and through the imagination. It is the eye of insight that the Bible privileges above external seeing. If we say this second eye "lies," it is because we are ignorant of the meanings it can reveal. As Van Gogh said, there is a level of truth that is "truer than the literal truth."[38] The cynical call this distortion, but they have no feeling for metaphor and no appreciation of spirit.

The Italian writer Vittorio Macchioro put the situation this way:

> There is no denying that only by means of myth does our experience of the sacred become concrete and communicable. Myth is necessary for religious history.... It cannot be dispensed with, since the divine, the mysterious, the ineffable cannot be expressed except by imagination, that is, by myth.[39]

This is what the consciousness of our civilization fails to understand. It judges truth according to what literally took place. It does not respect myth or understand its function. But in the past, our standards of determining truth were reversed.

Thus the New Testament does not say that Jesus was born out of wedlock to an unmarried Joseph and Mary, but says it was a virgin birth announced by angels and ordained by God. It says this because Jesus grew up to demonstrate such love and mercy as to suggest that his origins must be divine. Such an inspired life was not only the will of human beings or social circumstance, but must have been the will of the divine. If eyewitness reports had recorded the birth of Jesus there would have been no angels, no wise men from the East, no guiding star or holy signs. It would have been an ordinary event, the birth of an illegitimate son to a somewhat startled Joseph and Mary. The "cosmic" symbolism has been added by tradition. The more removed the gospels are in time from the life of Jesus, the more elaborate are the narrative depictions. The scholars tell us that Jesus was most likely not Mary's first child, his birth did not take place in Bethlehem, and nor did it happen on December 25.

Jesus was a master of metaphor, and when he taught of the kingdom of heaven he used parables or extended metaphors. He knew that the world of spirit cannot be described directly but only indirectly through symbol. Heaven is not a "place" to be visited but a state to be experienced. This should have given us the clue as to how his life would be depicted by writers of scripture. They would employ his methods to describe his life and work. Dominic Crossan grasps this in *The Power of*

Parable: How Fiction by Jesus Became Fiction about Jesus.[40] Metaphor and spiritual life are inextricably linked. In Revelation 11:8 the meaning of the word "spiritual" is "metaphorical." Paul used metaphor constantly in his letters, especially when he wrote, "I live yet not I but Christ lives within me."[41] Whenever we are being religious we are immediately in the realm of metaphor.

The word "metaphor" comes from the Greek *meta*, a "passing over," and *phorein*, to "move or carry." Metaphors carry us from ordinary to "meta"-thinking. They allow us to describe things unknown by referring to things that are known. They enable us to "cross over" to spirit, to see what might not be seen by ordinary sight. That is why metaphors, not facts, are the central agency of spiritual awareness and religious teaching. Jesus' ministry was about developing an appreciation of the nonliteral. He taught uncomprehending followers about the power of imagination to reveal the realm of spirit. It was only a nonliteral awareness that gave access to the kingdom. The truth claims of scripture do not depend on a correspondence with physical reality but on a correspondence with spiritual reality.

Blake used the phrase "Jesus the Imagination," and saw imagination as the vehicle of revelation. He was not worried about the metaphorical layerings upon the figure of Jesus, but on the contrary saw the role of Jesus in precisely these terms: to grant us the gift of metaphorical seeing, or what Blake called "double vision," which, he claimed, is synonymous with being saved, as in "saved" from literalism and idolatry. As soon as we trust in the life of the imagination, we are saved from materialism, literalism, and the ego-bound state. The purpose of imagination is to enable us to get inside the *mythos* mode and its pattern of seeing. Logos cannot get us there; imagination is the doorway to the other side of experience. If we enter through its way, we allow the "reality" of illusion to work its magic on us. If we remain caught in the modality of logos, we cannot get drawn into the images or discern their truth.

Literal Thinking as Idolatry

The spiritual is ultra-natural, not supernatural. It comes to us from the depths of the soul, not from other worlds. Yet one of the consequences of literalism is that the spirit is felt to descend from above, to be the handiwork of an external being who stands outside us. This is what happens when we take the mythic images of scripture concretely: it alienates spirit from the soul and makes it seem far away. When sacred language is read literally, everything is removed from the soul and seen as supernatural discourse about figures who inhabit a different realm. The Bible is then read as a series of divine interventions in history, and God becomes a kind of fairy-tale character in the sky who occasionally performs miracles.

This is an alienating view of the world and turns God into a cartoon figure, a superman who uses "his" powers to alter history. Such a reading sets up the conditions for a host of disappointments. People develop the false expectation that God can continue to act in this way, intervening in history and setting things in order when they get out of hand. When things go wrong, people pray earnestly for God to intervene and set them right, and the history of petitionary prayer is based on this view. If God does not act in the expected way, at the right time, people get angry and suppose that God has betrayed them. If "he" does exist, he is said to be brutal, unkind, and no longer an omnipotent father. This image of God, although easily arrived at, sets up the conditions for a collapse of faith. The idea of an interventionist God has been disastrous for religion, because no such God ever existed, and if we embark on a journey of faith with this in mind we will be disillusioned. This is not God but an idol, and idols block our way to the sacred.

Norman Brown claims literalism promotes idolatry. In *Love's Body* he says:

> Literalism is idolatry, taking shadows for reality; taking abstractions, human inventions, unconscious projections of the human spirit, as autonomous powers; letting the metaphors go dead, and then, when dead, bowing down before them, taking them literally.[42]

Literalism kills spirit because it takes the mythic forms as fact, failing to see that such forms cannot encompass the spirit of God, which is beyond form. As soon as we impose form on spirit we have trapped it in a narrow container. This is why the second commandment is a warning against images: "Thou shalt not make unto thee any graven image, or any likeness of any thing that is in heaven."[43] No "likeness" can be made, because nothing that we can know is "like" anything in heaven. Spirit is beyond form, and the Islamic faith is virtually the only one that takes this commandment seriously. Christianity carried on as if this commandment did not exist; it generated countless forms, and was happy to bow down before them. The West created likenesses, and always will, because the West can only know God by forming images. These images help us forge a relationship with the eternal, but we overlook the fact that they are against biblical law because they generate untruth.

Whenever we fashion such likenesses, we should say to ourselves: these might help us in our faith journey, but these images are not factual, they are not God. It is this strategic devaluation of our own creations that is not found in the West, and thus the West is constantly plagued by the specter of idolatry. We are too in love with our own creations. If we can learn to understand that our images are ephemeral, we are on our way to a mystical understanding. But we cling to our created forms, in which case they are no longer "icons" but idols that enslave us. Once we create idols we are cut off from God, because God is wholly other, or at least, that which is other than our anthropomorphic images. Icons are serviceable—and disposable—because they are translucent to the divine and allow us to see beyond them.

Literalism brings spiritual death because as soon as images become fixed, we are no longer transported. Our images are no longer allowed to be metaphorical; in Brown's terms, they "go dead." The "passing over" or *meta-phorein* does not take place if the metaphors are regarded as the powers themselves. Clergy who fail to understand this are not leading their congregations into spiritual life but into illusion; and this happens all too frequently. We can only be carried over to the transcendent if the imagination remains alive, and if we can see there is "more" than what our metaphors have revealed.

Religion as Unconscious Poetry

Although Matthew Arnold did not fully recognize that the biblical writers were deliberately employing myth, he did recognize that religion evoked a feeling response in readers that was closer to poetry than history. He wrote in "The Study of Poetry":

> Our religion has materialized itself in the fact, in the supposed fact; it has attached its emotion to the fact, and now the fact is failing it. But for poetry the idea is everything; the rest is a world of illusion. Poetry attaches its emotion to the idea; the idea *is* the fact. The strongest part of our religion today is its unconscious poetry.[44]

Although religion views itself as "fact," and fact is "failing it," it can still function as unconscious poetry. What continues to draw people to religion is the way in which it evokes archetypal images that represent the life of the spirit. It is a linguistic system that enables people to enter into the living spirit and understand its nature. Religion often works in spite of itself, Arnold is saying, because the poetic content is present, even if it is presented in a distorted, literal form. Jung would put it differently: the archetypal power of its images shines through, even though those images are not comprehended.

In "Dover Beach," an elegy on the decline of religion, Arnold declared that the "sea of faith" was at ebb tide, and one could hear its "melancholy, long, withdrawing roar."[45] He believed this was due to the supernaturalism that had attended religion from the beginning, which was now palling in modern times. As an educationalist and inspector of schools, Arnold noted that educated people throughout England were turning away from religion as if from bad taste or inferior science: he said "the veil of the preternatural, which is now its popular sanction, should . . . be given up."[46] He saw the demise of supernatural religion as an opportunity for poetry and imagination to assert themselves and reclaim their ancient charm over the mind:

> More and more mankind will discover that we have to turn to poetry to interpret life for us, to console us, to sustain us. Most of what now passes with us for religion and philosophy will be replaced by poetry. . . . Our religion, parading "evidences" such as those on which the popular mind relies now . . . are but the shadows and dreams and false shows of knowledge. The day will come when we shall wonder at ourselves for having trusted to religion and philosophy, for having taken them seriously; and the more we perceive their hollowness, the more we shall prize the "breath and finer spirit of knowledge" offered to us by poetry.[47]

Theology and religion are infantile in their privileging of a supernatural worldview, and just as humanity grows out of supernaturalism and accepts the nature of reality as it is, so religion will be left behind as a relic of the past. But as mentioned earlier, Arnold was too imbued with the nineteenth-century attitude to understand that religion could be conscious, not just unconscious poetry. He was religious himself, but read the miracles as bad reporting and unreliable observation. He was closer to the spirit of our time than he could have known, and all we have to do is get rid of his jaundiced response to religious language and value it for its hyperbole and metaphor. It will not be "replaced by poetry," because it is poetry. It has to be reclaimed as literature, which is, after all, what Arnold stood for.

Pious Fraud

Keats declared that religion is a pious fraud.[48] It is a strong claim, and for years atheists and anti-religious have used this statement out of context. The fact is that Keats had huge reverence for Jesus, and yet he contrasted Jesus' ministry with that of the institutions that operate under his name. Keats wrote:

> Jesus was so great a man that though he transmitted no writing of his own to posterity, we have his mind and his sayings and his greatness handed to us by others. It is to be lamented that the history of [Jesus] was written and revised by men interested in the pious frauds of religion. Yet through all this I see his splendour.[49]

Like Arnold after him, Keats felt that the sacred fire had gone out of religion and poetry could do a better job of rekindling the spirit. But what do we think today about the claim that religion is a pious fraud? For Keats, the fraud was evident in the fact that religion read its stories literally. In this he seemed more advanced than Arnold, who did not quite grasp the poetic intentions of scripture.

With reference to Christian scriptures, the nineteenth century historian of religions Godfrey Higgins wrote:

> I have become quite convinced that almost all the ancient histories were written for the sole purpose of recording a *mythos*, which it was desired to transmit to posterity, but yet to conceal from all but the initiated. The traditions were made subservient to this purpose, without any suspicion of fraud; and we only give them the appearance of fraud when we confound them with history. Real history was not the object of their writing.[50]

Higgins makes a wonderful point. Ancient writings made history *subservient* to mythos, and this was done without intending any fraud: "We only give [ancient writings] the appearance of fraud when we confound them with history." Fraud emerges when we take them literally, which was Keats' point. Fraud is the result of misreading the content and purpose of these works. One could say that all naïve and uncontextualized readings of scripture engender falsity.

Higgins goes on to say that "our priests have taken the emblems for the reality,"[51] which is to say that the traditions based on these writings have unwittingly inculcated and perpetuated deceit. Ironically, this deception has been conducted in an atmosphere of reverence and awe. Higgins concludes his two-volume study of this topic with these words: "I contend that it is philosophical to hold in suspicion all such histories, and unphilosophical to receive them without suspicion."[52] In 1836 Higgins expressed surprise that any intelligent person could fail to see that

> almost every part of Genesis is enigmatical or a parable. The system of concealment and of teaching by parable is the most marked characteristic of the religion. I suspect that there is not a sentence in Genesis which is not consistent with good sense if its true meaning could be discovered. I feel little doubt that such a passage as that of God wounding Jacob in the thigh, and his failing in his endeavor to kill Moses at an inn, are wholly misunderstood. The Genesis was considered by most if not all of the ancient Jewish philosophers and Christian Fathers as an allegory. For persons using their understanding, to receive it in a literal sense was impossible; and when we find modern Christians so receiving it, we only find proof that with the mass of mankind reason has nothing to do with religion.[53]

What I appreciate about Higgins' approach is that he can see there is "good sense" in scriptures, "if its true meaning could be discovered." Instead of attacking scripture for being incoherent, he turns his venom upon those who fail to discern its meaning.

Another vigorous critique comes from the outspoken, but little known, scholar of religions Alvin Kuhn. Kuhn can barely contain his contempt for a religious tradition that has misread its sacred documents:

> The most calamitous of all blunders was the mistaking of religious myth for factual history; this unbelievable stupidity, prolonged over centuries, cannot escape being laughed at for centuries more.... Religion is still steeped in the crassest forms of dark superstition, and this has been due to the miscarriage of ancient symbolism.[54]

Kuhn wrote a number of books in which he outlined the nature of myths, their role in religion, and how they have been misread across centuries of Christian teaching. He was ahead of his time, and anticipated the positions of Armstrong, Campbell, and others before the revival of respect for myth in psychoanalysis.

Kuhn reversed popular prejudices about myth and reality. To him myth is the true record of experience and surpasses the facts of history:

> What was known of old ... is that the myth as employed by ancient illuminati in Biblical scripture is not fiction, but the truest of all history. The myth is the only true narrative of the reality of human experience. It is the only ultimately true history ever written. Real as history is, it is finally less true than myth. Myth is always and forever true; actual history is never more than an approximation of the truth of life.[55]

Kuhn is writing in the spirit of Van Gogh and the latter's assertion that there is a truth that is truer than literal truth. He invests in hyperbole to make his point, and the notion that myth is "the truest of all history" is perhaps going too far. But I have welcomed his insights, even if they are eccentrically expressed.

In *The Lost Light*, Kuhn argues a case for the spiritual function of myth:

> The ancients regarded it of far less importance to catalogue the occurrences of objective history than to dramatize its inner "spirit." The outward actions of humans are in the main trivial, because they constitute in the end only a partial and ephemeral account of whole verity. Ancient literature aimed at something infinitely higher and more universal. It strove to depict in the myths and dramas the eternal norms of life experience, which would stand as truth for all men at any time in evolution. The myths were cryptographs of the great design and pattern of human history.[56]

Kuhn anticipates the approach of Northrop Frye, especially in his handling of the miraculous as a mythic genre in which we are asked to suspend judgment to enter a larger kind of truth:

> Religious myths are fables of events which, as events, never happened. The aim was never at any time to deceive anybody. It was never imagined that anybody would ever "believe" them. Nevertheless the myth was designed to tell truth of the last importance. Its instrument was fancy, but its purpose was not falsehood, but sublime truth. Outwardly it was not true, but at the same time it portrayed full truth. It was not true for its "characters," but was true for all mankind. It was only a myth, but it was a myth of something. It used a false story to relate a true one. While it never happened, it is the type of all things that have happened and will happen.[57]

The modern debate about myth shifts the ground of religion from history to literature. This shows that metaphor and symbol are the real carriers of the sacred. This flies in the face of Western prejudices and stands on its head the notion that something can be true only if it happened in time and space. It demolishes the arrogance of a tradition that has prided itself on its basis in history.

The Greatest Story Ever Sold?

Philosophers and scientists have long been aware of the crisis of religion. Does religion admit its truths are metaphorical, raising a storm of protest from believers, who would scream that there has been a centuries-long fraud? Or does it continue the pretense that it is historical fact, and perpetuate lies? It is stuck between these equally difficult positions, neither of which will yield comfort to billions of believers. But religion should call an end to the hoax. The philosopher Schopenhauer gets it right when he says:

> When the Church says that, in the dogmas of religion, reason is totally incompetent and blind, and its use to be reprehended, this attests the fact that these dogmas are allegorical in their nature, and are not to be judged by the standard which reason, taking all things *sensu proprio* [as strictly true], can alone apply. Now the absurdities of a dogma are just the mark and sign of what is allegorical and mythical in it.[58]

The "absurdities" in religion are "the mark and sign of what is mythical in it." Schopenhauer is saying that the symbolic contents of religion are "absurdities" if viewed as facts. A century later Einstein made the same point:

> It is this mythical, or rather this symbolic, content of the religious traditions which is likely to come into conflict with science. This occurs whenever this religious stock of ideas contains dogmatically fixed statements on subjects which belong in the domain of science. Thus, it is of vital importance for the preservation of true religion that such conflicts be avoided when they arise from subjects which, in fact, are not really essential for the pursuance of the religious aims.[59]

Einstein believes that religion ought not compete with science when it comes to descriptions of physical reality. The actual domain of "true religion" is myth and symbol, and so long as religion keeps to this domain, and understands what it is doing, "conflicts with science" will be avoided. Scientists and philosophers are trying to be kind to religion when they make these statements. Einstein does not want collisions to occur, as he knows that religion will come off second best. Then why do the churches want us to read myths as facts, reducing them to absurdities?

Some of the greatest minds in the churches have been aware of the mythic nature of the dogmas. But they have only been prepared to make indirect references to this problem, so as not to disturb the supernatural overlay that has been constructed by theology to make the "greatest story ever told" appealing to the superstitious masses. St Augustine, St Thomas Aquinas, Cardinal Newman have been too intelligent to allow the mythic structures to pass without comment. Augustine hints at the mythic nature of the Bible by declaring that "God is a poet and speaks to the world in metaphors, symbols and parables."[60] Cardinal Newman said the Christian revelation is "poetical" in nature, and "it presents us with those forms of excellence in which a poetical mind delights."[61] Perhaps more daring than any is this from the father of the medieval church, Thomas Aquinas:

> Holy Scripture fittingly delivers divine and spiritual realities under bodily guises. It delivers spiritual things to us beneath metaphors taken from bodily things.[62]

Spiritual realities are "delivered" under bodily guises. This is what is going on in the figurative language of scripture. But note that Thomas does not say there was no physical resurrection or virgin birth, only that "spiritual things" are conveyed to us "beneath metaphors taken from bodily things." He does not have the courage to say outright what our age has to say: that to take these metaphors literally is an aberration and a travesty of religious meaning.

Intelligent minds inside the churches have often pointed to these problems. But such people use vague and opaque language to make their point. They say "God is a poet," but fail to say we should not read his poems literally. They say the spirit uses bodily imagery, but do not warn that these images are not to be seen as idols. They say narratives "delight the mind" but do not say they confound the senses. Points are made by sideways allusion rather than direct statement. There are exceptions to this rule, as found in Bishop John Spong or Bishop Richard Holloway, but these are constructed as "radicals" who are ignored. The churches engage in tiptoeing around issues so as not to disturb the slumber of billions who take figurative language literally. Consequently, angry scholars such as Dorothy Murdock have referred to Christianity as a "conspiracy" and "the greatest story ever sold."[63]

Have we been deceived by religion? Like the long-suffering Job, many today want to say to religious authorities: "Is it on God's behalf that you argue dishonestly, or in his defense that you allege what is false?"[64] The scriptures do not mislead, but the teachers of scriptures mislead. Insofar as there has been this abject failure in the response to scripture, and insofar as this has characterized organized religion for centuries, then, yes, there has been deception. By claiming to be fact or history, religion has become a false comfort to believers, while it is regarded as a laughingstock by others. But these others are now the majority in our secular societies. Secular people are starving for spiritual nourishment, but they cannot take on conventional religion for all these good reasons.

Notes

1. C. G. Jung, "The Transcendent Function" (1916/1957), *CW* 8, § 184.
2. Alvin Kuhn, quoted in Tom Harpur, *The Pagan Christ: Is Blind Faith Killing Christianity?* (Sydney: Allen & Unwin, 2005), p. 17.
3. John Dominic Crossan, *Who is Jesus?* (Louisville, KY: Westminster John Knox Press, 1996), p. 79.
4. John Shelby Spong, *Jesus for the Non-Religious* (New York: HarperOne, 2007), p. 31.
5. Ian Plimer, *Telling Lies for God* (Sydney: Random House, 1994).
6. G. B. Caird, *The Language and Imagery of the Bible* (London: Duckworth, 1980), p. 271.
7. Caird, p. 193.
8. Caird, paraphrased by D. R. De Lacey, "The Language and Imagery of George Caird," *Vox Evangelica* 13 (1983): 79–84. Available at: www.biblicalstudies.org.uk/pdf/vox/vol13/language_lacey.pdf.
9. Matthew Arnold, in his Preface to *God and the Bible* (1875; London: Smith, Elder & Co., 1897), p. xvi.
10. Northrop Frye, paraphrased by Johan Aitken, in his Foreword to Frye's last work, *The Double Vision: Language and Meaning in Religion* (Toronto: University of Toronto Press, 1991), p. xii.
11. Northrop Frye, *Words with Power* (Ontario: Viking, 1990), p. xiv.
12. Frye, *Words with Power*, p. 72.
13. Dan Brown, *The Da Vinci Code* (Garden City, N.Y.: Doubleday, 2003).
14. John Allegro, *The Sacred Mushroom and the Cross* (Hodder & Stoughton, 1970).
15. A good case is put by Alexander Jacob in *Brahman: A Study of the Solar Rituals of the Indo-Europeans* (Berlin: Georg Olms Verlag, 2012), that the Christian story is a historicized and Judaized version of the Egyptian myth of the dying and resurrecting god, who descends into the underworld (Osiris) and emerges as the light of the world (Horus).
16. Ernst Cassirer, *The Philosophy of Symbolic Forms*, Vol. 2, *Mythical Thought* (1925; New Haven and London: Yale University Press, 1955), pp. 37–38.
17. Jung, "A Psychological Approach to the Dogma of the Trinity" (1942/1948), *CW* 11 § 170.
18. Kevin Treston, *Emergence for Life, Not Fall from Grace* (Melbourne: Mosaic Pres, 2013), p. 133.
19. Ibid, p. 18.
20. Ibid, p. 18.
21. Northrop Frye, "History and Myth in the Bible" (1975), in Alvin A. Lee and Jean O'Grady, eds., *Northrop Frye on Religion, Collected Works of Northrop Frye*, Vol. 4 (Toronto: University of Toronto Press, 2000), p. 20.
22. James Frazer, Introduction, *Apollodorus, The Golden Bough* (Cambridge, Mass.: Harvard University Press, 1921), p. xxvii.

23. Max Müller, *Lectures on the Science of Language*, 5th edition (London: Longmans, 1866), p. 12.
24. William Blake, annotation to his engraving of the Laocoön, in David V. Erdman and Harold Bloom, eds., *The Poetry and Prose of William Blake* (Garden City, N.Y.: Doubleday, 1965), p. 271.
25. A point made by Richard Holloway in *How to Read the Bible* (London: Granta Books, 2006).
26. Frye, "History and Myth in the Bible," p. 22.
27. G. B. Caird, *The Language and Imagery of the Bible* (1980; Grand Rapids: Eerdmans, 1997).
28. Friedrich Nietzsche, *The Birth of Tragedy*, R. Speirs, trans. (1882; Cambridge: Cambridge University Press, 1999), p. 108.
29. Origin, *On First Principles*, in G. W. Butterworth, trans., *On First Principles* (Gloucester, Mass.: Peter Smith, 1973), 4.2.9.
30. Karen Armstrong, *The Case for God: What Religion Really Means* (London: The Bodley Head, 2009), p. 97.
31. Origin, *On First Principles*, in G. W. Butterworth, trans., *On First Principles* (Gloucester, Mass.: Peter Smith, 1973), 4.2.9.
32. Andrew Harvey, *Son of Man: The Mystical Path to Christ* (New York: Jeremy P. Tarcher, 1998), p. 4.
33. Ibid.
34. Frye, "History and Myth in the Bible," p. 17.
35. Jung, "Concerning Rebirth" (1940/1950), *CW* 9, 1, § 216.
36. See for example, G. A. Wells, *The Jesus Myth* (Chicago: Open Court Publishing, 1999).
37. G. R. S. Mead, *Did Jesus Live 100 B.C.?* (1903; New York: Cosimo, 2005).
38. Vincent Van Gogh, Letter (1888), in Naomi Margolis Maurer, *The Pursuit of Spiritual Wisdom: The Thought and Art of Vincent Van Gogh and Paul Gauguin* (Cranbury, NJ: Associated University Presses, 1999), p. 31.
39. Vittorio D. Macchioro, *From Orpheus to Paul: A History of Orphism* (New York: Holt, 1930; reprinted New York: Lightning Source Incorporated, 2003), p. 218.
40. John Dominic Crossan, *The Power of Parable: How Fiction by Jesus Became Fiction about Jesus* (New York: HarperOne, 2012).
41. Galatians 2:20.
42. Norman O. Brown, *Love's Body* (New York: Random House, 1966), p. 222.
43. Exodus 20:4.
44. Matthew Arnold, "The Study of Poetry" (1880), in M. H. Abrams, ed., *The Norton Anthology of English Literature* (New York: W. W. Norton & Company, 1987), p. 2171.
45. Arnold, "Dover Beach" (1851), in Margaret Ferguson, Mary Jo Salter and Jon Stallworthy, eds., *The Norton Anthology of Poetry*, 5th edn (New York: W. W. Norton, 2005), p. 1101.
46. Arnold, *God and the Bible*, p. vii.
47. Arnold, "The Study of Poetry," p. 2172.
48. John Keats, letter to George and Georgiana Keats, 3 May 1819, in Jane Campion, ed., *Bright Star: The Complete Poems and Selected Letters* (London: Vintage Books, 2009), p. 503.

49. John Keats, Letter to George and Georgiana Keats, 3 May 1819. In *Bright Star: The Complete Poems and Selected Letters*. Jane Campion (ed.) London: Vintage Books, 2009), p. 503.
50. Godfrey Higgins, *The Anacalypsis: An Inquiry into the Origin of Languages, Nations and Religions* (London: Longman & Co, 1836; reprinted Digireads.com Publishing, 2007), p. 616.
51. Higgins, p. 366.
52. Ibid, p. 622.
53. Ibid, p. 366.
54. Alvin Boyd Kuhn, *The Lost Light: An Interpretation of Ancient Scriptures* (1940, Lexington, Kentucky: ZuuBooks, 2011), pp. 20–22.
55. Kuhn, quoted in Tom Harpur, *The Pagan Christ*, p. 17.
56. Kuhn, *The Lost Light*, p. 24.
57. Ibid.
58. Arthur Schopenhauer, "The Christian System" in Thomas Bailey Saunders, trans. *Religion: A Dialogue, and Other Essays* (1899; Westport, Connecticut: Greenwood Press, 1973), p. 106.
59. Albert Einstein, "On Religion, God, and Philosophy," in Alice Calaprice, ed., The *New Quotable Einstein* (Princeton: Princeton University Press, 2005), p. 148.
60. Augustine, as quoted in Paul Avis, *God and the Creative Imagination: Metaphor, Symbol and Myth in Religion and Theology* (London and New York: Routledge, 1999), p. 3.
61. Cardinal Newman (1885), quoted in Avis, op. cit., p. 56.
62. St Thomas Aquinas, *Summa Theologiae*, Blackfriars edn (London: Eyre and Spottiswoode, 1964–1981), Ia. l.9 *Responsio*.
63. D. M. Murdock, *The Christ Conspiracy: The Greatest Story Ever Sold* (Kempton, ILL: Adventures Unlimited, 1999).
64. Job 13:7.

3

The Soul's Symbolic Code

*Myth arises from within humanity from a depth of feeling
and conviction untapped, as yet, by human knowledge.*
— *Diarmuid O'Murchu*[1]

Why Myth Matters

Why is myth used in every religious system? What is it that makes symbol and myth indispensable? Why does religion persist in using a code language when our time has no patience with ambiguity and indirection? Why have we lost touch with symbolic discourse? I will attempt to respond to these and other questions in this chapter.

One of the best commentators on these questions is Karen Armstrong, who has done much in recent times to recover respect for religious myth, and to deal with the pitfalls of literalism. Armstrong wrote *The Case for God: What Religion Really Means* as a defense of religion against the attacks of the new atheists.[2] She has no problem with the way in which atheists attack fundamentalism or "bad religion" as it has been called.[3] If anything, Armstrong would chime in with the new atheists and join them in their refutation of literalism, extremist claims about God, and calls to violence to defend what fundamentalists call "absolute truth." But the new atheists are often attacking a straw man: they are trying to get rid of all religion, and condemning it as "evil,"[4] when in fact they are reacting against misrepresentations of religion in its virulent, popular, and often pathological forms.

Armstrong argues that "what religion really means" is that we have the potential to encounter and have a relationship with eternal forces. This side of our lives is not reducible to rational thought. Religion is the language and life of soul and spirit, and this language has to be respected. It is difficult to recover respect for myth because our modern minds make little sense of it:

> Today we live in a society of scientific logos and myth has fallen into disrepute. In popular parlance, a "myth" is something that is not true. But in the past, myth was not a self-indulgent fantasy; rather, like logos, it helped people to live creatively in our confusing world, though in a different way. Myths may have told stories about the gods, but they were really focused on the more elusive, puzzling and tragic aspects of the human predicament that lay outside the remit of logos.[5]

Armstrong does not accuse people for this loss of respect for myth. It is something that has occurred with modernization, one of its unfortunate by-products. We have focused so much on the development of intellect and reason that spirit and soul have fallen by the wayside. This is tragic, but it can be rectified, by rehabilitating the language of myth. In an earlier work, *The Battle for God*, which is one of my favorite texts, Armstrong explains that the civilizations of the ancient world valued mythos more highly than logos. This is why they were more concerned with symbolic imagery than historical reporting.

> Myth was regarded as primary; it was concerned with what was thought to be timeless and constant in our existence. Myth looked back to the origins of life, to the foundations of culture, and to the deepest levels of the human mind. Myth was not concerned with practical matters, but with meaning. Unless we find some significance in our lives, we mortal men and women fall very easily into despair. The *mythos* of a society provided people with a context that made sense of their day-to-day lives; it directed their attention to the eternal and the universal.[6]

She explains that these views have been reversed today. Mythos has been discounted, and logos has achieved ascendancy. Poets and writers of our time carry forward the legacy of ancient times, whether they are aware of it or not. Writers who work with the imagination and creativity focus on that which has eternal and universal importance. The exceptions to this are those writers who aim for historical accuracy. But writers who are looking for universal values rather than concrete details gloss over the particulars in their search for significance.

Armstrong argues that the writers of sacred texts were not concerned with "history" in the way we are today:

> In the premodern world, people had a different view of history. They were less interested than we are in what actually happened, but more

concerned with the meaning of an event. Historical incidents were not seen as unique occurrences, set in a far-off time, but were thought to be external manifestations of constant, timeless realities. Hence history would tend to repeat itself, because there was nothing new under the sun. Historical narratives tried to bring out this eternal dimension.[7]

The task of the ancient writer was not to get lost in detail but to bring out the significance of an event, to find the right myth or symbol for the occasion. The real task was to record the "constant, timeless realities," or as Nietzsche put it, to view experience *sub specie aeterni*, "under the aspect of eternity."[8] Armstrong gives the example of the crossing of the Red Sea to illustrate her point about the interweaving of myth and history:

> Thus, we do not know what really occurred when the ancient Israelites escaped from Egypt and passed through the Sea of Reeds. The story has been deliberately written as a myth, and linked with other stories about rites of passage, immersion in the deep, and gods splitting a sea in two to create a new reality. Jews experience this myth every year in the rituals of the Passover Seder, which brings this strange story into their own lives and helps them to make it their own.[9]

The task of myth is not to falsify history but to deepen our experience of it, and place history in the realm of spirit. Time is elevated by linking it with the timeless. It is myth that allows us to experience the spiritual dimension of history.

Myth as Ancient Psychology

From our point of view, myth can be interpreted as an ancient form of psychology. It is not to the psychology of consciousness that myths refer, but to the "depth" psychology of the unconscious. This is what links myth with psychoanalysis, which goes beyond consciousness to the psychic strata beneath the surface. This is why Freud and Jung sought out myths to ground and amplify their theories of human nature. They sensed that myth would be the resource to turn to if they wanted to know human nature at its depths. Some claim they were not being "scientific" enough, but that is a prejudice of logos thinking. The fact is that there is a dimension of human existence where science in the usual sense gives way to myth, or to what James Hillman calls the "poetics of mind."[10] It is to the poetics of mind that the scriptures address themselves.

Empirical science does not explore the unconscious and scientific psychology in the universities does not even acknowledge that it exists.

The reason is that this deeper realm is not made of a substance that can be analyzed according to the dictates of laboratory analysis and empiricism. The unconscious participates in the realm of spirit as well as matter. It is the liminal space where spirit and matter meet. It points to the existence of spirit in the human, and that is why myth is important in elucidating the hidden aspect of ourselves.

Instead of being regarded as bad science, or primitive descriptions of the world, myth is composed of sophisticated descriptions of what takes place in the inner world. Alvin Kuhn understood this when he said: "Mythology is the repository of man's most ancient science." Mythology is the science of the spiritual life in early humanity and it is a science we have sight of. It is a science we have to learn again, and we can retrieve it by reading mythology and scripture through a psychological lens. Even Northrop Frye, based in the humanities and no advocate of science, argues that to appreciate myth properly, our understanding "needs to be grounded in psychology."[11] Armstrong does not write in the field of psychology either, but she too is alert to the psychological dimension of myth:

> The various mythological stories, which were not intended to be taken literally, were an ancient form of psychology. When people told stories about heroes who descended into the underworld, struggled through labyrinths, or fought with monsters, they were bringing to light the obscure regions of the subconscious realm, which is not accessible to purely rational investigation, but which has a profound effect upon our experience and behaviour.[12]

She says the mythological stories were *not intended to be taken literally*. It was not the intention of writers of myth to be read in a literal way, nor was it the intention of those who wrote a "mixed" medium of parable and history, as in the Jesus story, to have their metaphors removed from mythos. According to Kuhn, "Never did intelligent people believe [literally in their myths]; they believed what they represented, symbolized, adumbrated."[13] If this is true, a great many followers of religion are "unintelligent" according to Kuhn.

In another study, Armstrong argues:

> Myths were not understood as primarily factual stories. They were designed to help people negotiate the obscure regions of the psyche. A myth was never intended as an accurate account of a historical event: it was something that had in some sense happened once but that also happens all the time.[14]

The Soul's Symbolic Code

The point of myth was not to "believe" it but to live by its lights and adjust one's behavior to its wisdom. The point of myth is to "show us how to live more richly and intensely, how to cope with our mortality, and how to endure the suffering that flesh is heir to." "If we failed to apply it to our situation, a myth would remain abstract and incredible."[15] This is our situation today, she argues: we no longer live by myths, at least, not consciously, and as such they appear "abstract and incredible." We don't know to what they refer and a great many people deem them to be irrelevant, while religious people think of them as histories. In the past, however, religions were not abstract systems of knowing, but were stories to be lived, enacted and embodied in daily life:

> From a very early date, people re-enacted their myths in stylised ceremonies that worked aesthetically upon participants and, like any work of art, introduced them to a deeper dimension of existence.[16]

She is speaking as a historian of ancient civilizations and pointing out that, in their context, religions were dramas or rituals of the soul, and not "dogmas" to be abstractly presented to the mind. The function of mythos is that it teaches us how to live, and in particular, how to live "under the aspect of eternity." They describe our experience for us, insofar as our experience is open to the divine.

Armstrong argues that if Western culture wants to get back on course, and not deviate further from our religious impulse and its need for universals, it must recover the art of reading mythological language. If we want to rediscover our bearings we have to recover respect for mythos as a carrier of truth. She goes as far as to say that unless history has been transformed into myth it does not, properly speaking, become "religious" at all:

> One could say that unless an historical event is mythologized in this way, and liberated from the past in an inspiring cult, it cannot be religious. To ask whether the Exodus from Egypt took place exactly as recounted in the Bible or to demand historical and scientific evidence to prove that it is factually true is to mistake the nature and purpose of this story. It is to confuse *mythos* with *logos*.[17]

Armstrong shows herself to be psychologically astute in her understanding of the function of mythos. She argues that mythos is important not only for religion and culture but for mental health:

> The mythos of a society is rooted in what we would call the unconscious mind. Because of the dearth of myth in our modern society,

we have had to invent the science of psychoanalysis to help us to deal with our inner world.[18]

This is the basis of Jung's depth psychology, about which more will be said later. Jung argued that if we are deprived of myth the psyche is unable to express its most profound longings. As a result, for want of a story to contain the soul, we suffer neurotic disorders because the soul is unexpressed. When the soul is unable to discover its meaning, it goes mad. Meaning is the bread and wine of its existence, and soul has to find meaning to fulfill itself. The ego, on the other hand, seeks power, status and identity, but soul has a requirement of meaning that our present age is unable to deliver.

When Mythos became Logos

Armstrong is concerned that religion has become derailed. It has lost its grounding in mythos and pretends to be a kind of logos. She is unsure when this happened precisely, and we still need more research into this question. When did mythos become confused with logos? I would say it happened early, probably in the first century when the churches were in their nascent period. Some argue it happened in the fourth century, when Christianity was made the state religion of the Roman Empire. Kuhn is an advocate of this view, and claims that when the truth of Christianity was appropriated by the power of Rome, it lost its soul and paraded as historical fact.[19] He believes that power always lays claim to facts and history, whereas mythos or story is a far more humble form of discourse, and power brokers do not like it. The truth is that religion in the West has probably moved in and out of this confusion. The mystics and poets have always seen it as mythos, from the start, whereas the theologians and systematizers have claimed that "their" religion was history.

Armstrong's view is that the drive toward logos, always present in religion, was accelerated by the intellectual enlightenment and rise of science:

> During the sixteenth and seventeenth centuries, a period that historians call the early modern period, Western people began to develop an entirely new kind of civilisation, governed by scientific rationality and based economically on technology and capital investment. Logos achieved such spectacular results that myth was discredited and the scientific method was thought to be the only reliable means of attaining truth. This would make religion difficult, if not impossible. As theologians began to adopt the criteria of science, the *mythoi* of Christianity were interpreted as empirically, rationally and historically verifiable and forced into a style of thinking that was alien to them.[20]

The Soul's Symbolic Code

This makes a lot of sense: religion was forced to redefine itself as history by the spirit of the time. How could theologians withstand the impact of science and still claim that myth had any value when it was rapidly being discredited? Since the logocentric packaging of religion was already present in the fourth century, the early modern period would have intensified this process, and by the time myth was devalued, religious leaders would have turned gleefully to the historical hypothesis to bolster their tradition. This question about how and when religion was turned into history will be further explored in the next chapter. But I applaud Armstrong for her groundbreaking thought, and appreciate her one-line summary of the crisis:

> We have not been doing our practice and have lost the knack of religion.[21]

Or, as Cassirer put it, we are "observers who no longer live in it [mythos] but reflect on it."[22] It seems that religious myth is best "lived in," and perhaps this is the appeal of fundamentalism, which encourages people to recapture the idea of living *inside* a mythos, not observing it from without. But we can't do this today without forfeiting our minds. Ritual, which leads us into the interiority of myth, is probably the safest way to capture this interiority without losing our minds.

The intellect is at home in logos, but the soul lives and breathes mythos. The sacred cannot be picked up on the logos frequency, and that is why we have "lost the knack of religion." Many clever people in society are atheistic and oblivious to the sacred. To pick up on the sacred requires intuition and that is something that is enabled through enactments of mythos. The sacred can send out its signals, but our rational receivers are unable to respond. Consequently in the modern world we live in a flat landscape, without the verticality of spirit, and this is a crisis of our own making. It is not that "God is dead," but we are dead to God. Our culture generates spiritual atrophy because we only know how to function on logos.

The Ancestral Mind

Moving from religious philosophy to depth psychology, I would like to explore mythos as a language of psyche.

To understand myth is to learn another language. It is a very old language but new to us. The mystery is that it operates subliminally and impresses itself on us from below. It does not arise from our conscious thought but operates semi-autonomously. It speaks from psychic depths we do not understand and can only guess at. It is little wonder that, before the discovery of the unconscious, this language was felt to come from the "gods and spirits" of the netherworld. An intelligence in the unconscious speaks to us, even today, in myth and symbol, and we can only marvel at this strange phenomenon. We encounter this language as foreign, something belonging to early childhood, the disturbed world of schizophrenia, or prehistoric humanity with its rites and ceremonies. It is both distant and close, as we have contact with this voice in our dreams and fantasies.

It is as if we have an ancestral part of the mind, which is present but not the product of conscious intention. Modern people claim to have outgrown the world of myth, since we see ourselves as civilized and rational. But just as an "inner child" continues to haunt the psyche of the adult, so an ancient dimension of life continues to dwell in the modern person. Jung contends that:

> It is not only primitive man whose psychology is archaic. It is the psychology also of modern, civilized man, and not merely of individual "throw-backs" in modern society. Every civilized human being, however high his conscious development, is still an archaic man at the deeper levels of his psyche.[23]

Is it that the psyche contains traces of earlier evolutionary stages, going back to the dawn of time and the origin of the species? This may be the case, but I am not an evolutionary biologist and cannot pass judgment on this hypothesis. Rather, it seems that, regardless of whether this atavistic legacy can be scientifically proved, there is something within us that continues to speak in the language of mythos.

We may not use the language of myth, but the psyche does. Mythos is its native tongue, its symbolic code. We need no elaborate experiments to establish this fact. All we need to do is think of last night's dreams, and the dreams we have every night, that bear a striking resemblance to the productions of myth, fairy tale, folklore, and religion. This language goes on all the time, in the hinterland of our consciousness. Our dreams are rarely complete or whole myths, but contain fragments or echoes of myth, as if emanating from the same primordial source as myths and religions. If we reflect on this, it is enough to make the most skeptical person develop a sense of awe and reverence. Evidence of a spiritual heritage is apparent every day and before our eyes. All we have to do is tune in to the psyche and listen to its frequency. The impulses that drive mythic formations are found in every culture of the world, and especially in those we call "indigenous." But the mythic life is preserved in modern religions: "Religious thought keeps alive the archaic state of mind even today, in a time bereft of gods."[24]

Jung says the spiritual forces that generate these myths "appear as involuntary manifestations of unconscious processes whose existence and meaning can only be inferred."[25] He does not believe these manifestations are the results of external perception, or that myths are primitive attempts at scientific explanations of the world. Speaking of the Dreaming of Australian Aboriginals, he writes:

> It is not the world as we know it that speaks out of his unconscious, but the unknown world of the psyche, of which we know that it mirrors our empirical world only in part, and that, for the other part, it moulds this empirical world in accordance with its own psychic assumptions. The archetype does not proceed from physical facts, but describes how the psyche experiences the physical fact, and in so doing the psyche often behaves so autocratically that it denies tangible reality or makes statements that fly in the face of it.[26]

The language of myth is primary; it does not reflect the world, but molds the world into its own image. In Jung's view, consciousness emerges from this primal background, and is an ever-present origin, as Gebser put it.[27] It cannot be outgrown, cast off or superseded. It is the template from which life emerges and will always emerge.

Mythos, Soul, Eternity

Jung explores the psychology of what he calls "primitive mentality," and argues that archetypes—or universal patterns—are present in the myths and rituals of indigenous people. He claims these patterns have not been passed from culture to culture through external transmission but have arisen spontaneously from the collective unconscious. He disputes the notion that myths are "allegories" of external experiences, a view which is still prevalent in the social sciences. He reverses this theory and sees myths as self-revelations of an original or a priori psychic structure:

> The primitive mentality does not *invent* myths, it *experiences* them. Myths are original revelations of the preconscious psyche, involuntary statements about unconscious psychic happenings, and anything but allegories of physical processes. Such allegories would be an idle amusement for an unscientific intellect. Myths, on the contrary, have a vital meaning.[28]

The "vital meaning" is psychological and spiritual—both at once—and Jung argues against any so-called "scientific" reduction of archetype and myth to external factors. Science is weirdly "unscientific" in its avoidance of psychic reality. It does not want to admit that humanity has a soul, that we are spiritual beings with links to a universal mind that is greater and more encompassing than the human mind. Indeed, the connection to universal mind, through myth and ritual, is for Jung the very nature and substance of the human soul:

> Not merely do [myths] represent, they *are* the psychic life of the primitive tribe, which immediately falls to pieces and decays when it loses its mythological heritage, like a man who has lost his soul. A tribe's mythology is its living religion, whose loss is always and everywhere, even among the civilized, a moral catastrophe.[29]

In relation to Aboriginal cultures, we can see he is accurate in his diagnosis of the cultural life of tribal groups. Since the devastating impact of colonization, Aboriginal people have been struggling to maintain their integrity and well-being, not only because their land has been stolen and traditions decimated, but because their mythology or Dreaming has been destroyed by imperialism and the imposition of Christianity. Jung says "there is nothing more fatuous than the attitude of the missionary who pronounces the gods of the 'poor heathen' to be mere illusion."[30] To the colonizers, the Dreaming was a bizarre set of infantile attempts at describing reality, but in fact it represented the soul of the people. As the above passage makes clear, when the soul is disturbed, a people falls to pieces. One does not need psychology to reach this conclusion, since in Proverbs we read: "Where there is no vision, the people perish."[31] Mythology is not a series of random stories or fantasies, but the fabric of the soul.

Myth can be seen as a narrative attempt to develop a creative relationship with the cosmos. Its concern is not time as such, but the timeless world of archetypes that form the basis of our spiritual lives. Again, in relation to Aboriginal cultures, Jung writes:

> In so far as the forms or patterns of the unconscious belong to no time in particular, being seemingly eternal, they convey a peculiar feeling of timelessness when consciously realized. We find similar statements in primitive psychology: for instance, the Australian word *aljira* means "dream" as well as "ghostland" and the "time" in which the ancestors lived and still live. It is, as they say, the "time when there was no time." This looks like an obvious concretization and projection of the unconscious with all its characteristic qualities—its dream manifestations, its ancestral world of thought-forms, and its timelessness.[32]

Myths are stories that enable us to participate in sacred time. They oppose the profane world and seek to move beyond it to forge a link with eternity. In Christian mythology, the nearest we have to this is the prayer: "As it was in the beginning, is now and ever shall be, world without end. Amen." These are not mere words; they represent an attempt to forge a connection with the infinite. People of faith are transported to that greater reality on the wings of these prayers.

The religious studies scholar Roger Schmidt put it well when he wrote:

> Myths deal with cosmic time and exemplary time, rather than historical time.... Cosmic time stands outside history, beyond the reach of eye-witnesses and is thus inaccessible except through the imaginative and revelatory dimension of sacred expression.[33]

Myths serve the function of generating the sense of an "eternal life," which is a healing medicine for the psyche, insofar as it stems the anxiety that arises when we contemplate our mortality and transitory existence. But when we grasp the fact that myths are not entirely human inventions, but are the psyche's attempt to build a spiritual world of its own, we are on the road to recovering the respect for myth needed in the contemporary world. Myths are "self-portraits of what is going on in the unconscious, or statements of the unconscious psyche about itself."[34] This allows us to understand that myths are not just about the past, but about our lives, and especially about the health and welfare of the soul.

Mythos in Art and Entertainment

When mythic impulses disappear in religion, or get dried up or rigidified by dogma, they seem to find new outlet in the arts and humanities. These impulses are, however, hampered by such literary modes as realism and naturalism, because mythic impulses can only express themselves in figurative and hyperbolic forms. In modern times they have found expression in such stylistic modes as surrealism, expressionism, primitivism, neo-romanticism, imagism, science fiction, and magic realism. It is the archetypes, and their need for expression, that keep the creative arts alive and looking for new ways to express psychic realities. Cinema and media are based primarily on archetypal impulses, and the most popular and commercially successful productions are the ones that most powerfully represent what is in the unconscious life of the time.

The renaissance of these arts and visual expressions indicates that the mythic life is just as active now as it was in the past. However, because our time does not respect the workings of the sacred, we downgrade archetypal expressions to "entertainments," since this is the only way they can be packaged in secular culture. In traditional cultures *all* expressions of mythos are endowed with religious importance, and there was no such thing as "entertainment." Although our entertainment gives these archetypal expressions form and public display, at the same time this packaging of the soul is a denial of their power and authority. On the one hand we flock to the movies to see the latest blockbuster and how it handles archetypal themes, but on the other we are able to dismiss the contents as "only a movie." In this way the modern ego regains its control over these products, and can defend against them even as it responds to their aesthetic appeal.

While our scientific rationality has driven myths and religions to the wall, we find ourselves drawn to countless mythic productions of our postmodern age. We engage in a kind of Freudian return of the repressed, and what is driven out by our imperial consciousness returns in downgraded form in movies, entertainments, games, novels, fantasy, and science fiction. These productions tell stories that are the same as those that are told in sacred scriptures and traditions, and we note such parallels but don't pay much attention to them. We are more interested in technological questions, in special effects, computer-generated imaging, and the illusion of three-dimensional narratives. We are more interested in what is novel about our entertainment, not in what is ancient or archetypal. The archaic "works" on us, but we are self-hypnotized in a technological dream.

Mythos as a Structure of Thought

The work of Cassirer is densely textured and at times impenetrable. It operates at a high scholarly level that few can appreciate. But I want to note that the second volume of his monumental *Philosophy of Symbolic Forms* is given over to the proposition that "myth is a form of thought."[35] This should set us on the right track to understanding why the soul speaks in mythic language. Cassirer insists that myth is a "symbolic form" that, like language, is a means of responding to our world. But unlike language, which is influenced by the logos of the mind, myth speaks of a more primary level, which is nonintellectual and based in image and symbol. It is the emotional, unmediated language of experience. Literature which draws on the wellsprings of mythic consciousness will reveal the "dynamic of the life feeling" that gives depth and meaning to our world.[36]

In his work on mythos and psyche, *Symbols of Transformation*, Jung puts forward a theory of "two kinds of thinking."[37] He argues that although logos governs our daily lives and interactions, mythos is always present, often behind the scenes and frequently undetected. He differentiates between directed and nondirected thinking. Directed thinking is also referred to as logical or conscious thinking, and nondirected thinking has four other designations: fantasy, dream, mythic, or archaic thinking. Directed thinking operates under the influence of logos, while dream thinking expresses the life of mythos. Jung developed his theory of two kinds of thinking almost a hundred years before the work of Karen Armstrong, but she seems to have arrived at the same theory, through the history of religions rather than depth psychology. In Jung's view, the inability of modern consciousness, including religious consciousness, to understand mythos has a long background. It is as if an ancient modality of mind, which was pronounced in ancient times, has shriveled up and atrophied in our own.

Directed thinking appears to be under conscious control, while nondirected thinking is not something we do but something that happens to us in unguarded moments. The psyche appears to "think," if we can be permitted this expression, along mythic or archaic lines, as we find in such phenomena as unconscious fantasies, daydreaming, night dreams, and visions. Jung points out that "the goal of [dream thinking] does not seem to be how to understand the real world as objectively and accurately as possible."[38] The psyche produces images spontaneously, and these "should not be taken literally, but must be interpreted according to their meaning."[39] Elsewhere he states: "one must not take them literally, but must surmise a hidden meaning in them."[40] This "meaning" refers not to the outside world, but to an internal reality that he perceives as psychological and spiritual. Not all dream thinking has spiritual significance, but only that which can be said to arise from the collective unconscious, also called the objective psyche. This meaning is "hidden" because our normal sight focuses on externals, and symbolic meaning points to an internal order of being.

Jung argues that directed thinking is the form of mental activity favored by our modern world, but archaic thinking is still present in our psyche but has fallen into the unconscious. The modern prejudice is that we are more advanced than the peoples of the past, who "wasted" their time on the productions of fantasy and legend. Jung is a champion of the thinking of the past and writes:

> It would be a ridiculous and unwarranted presumption on our part if we imagined that we were more energetic or more intelligent than the men of the past—our material knowledge has increased, but not our intelligence. We have become rich in knowledge, but poor in wisdom. The centre of gravity of our interest has switched over to the materialistic side, whereas the ancients preferred a mode of thought nearer to the fantastic type.[41]

What is misleading is his term "fantasy." Many would agree that archaic peoples were concerned with fantasy, and that is why their thinking is irrelevant. It is a pity Jung could not find a different word to express the mental activity of the psyche, due to the prejudice built up around the term. Perhaps he could have used the term "imaginal," as employed by Henry Corbin, who differentiates the imaginal from the "imaginary," to avoid the undervaluation found in the word "fantasy." Terms such as fantasy, imaginary, fictional, etc. are synonymous with "useless" in our vocabulary, since such terms do not point to what is seen as real. We have moved so far "to the materialistic side" that we no longer recognize the sources of spirit, and are no longer responsive to its language. We have "become rich in knowledge and poor in wisdom"—almost an epitaph of our age.

Mythos Downgraded

Jung reflects on the paradox that the highest aspect of human nature, our capacity to reach toward eternity and touch the cosmos, is relegated to the lowest levels of experience. Mythic fragments are "found" in the paranoid fantasies of psychotic patients, in the crass advertisements of commercial industries, in comic books and colloquial expressions. A world that has experienced the "death of God" has experienced the death of mythos as a meaningful discourse. Thus Jung recommended that the interested enquirer had to search in the rubbish dumps of modernity for the clues to our lost spiritual life. We need to fossick around for shards of myths and legends that can be found in the grounds of cultural forms now dead. It is precisely in what modernity throws out that the gems of wisdom are found.

We imagine that defunct myths point to the metaphysical objects of superseded belief systems, but according to Jung they point to the deepest dimensions of our experience:

The Soul's Symbolic Code

> Where and when does anything take place to remind us even remotely of phenomena like angels, miraculous feedings, beatitudes, the resurrection of the dead, etc.? It was therefore something of a discovery to find that during the unconscious state of sleep intervals occur, called "dreams," which occasionally contain scenes having a not inconsiderable resemblance to the motifs of mythology. For myths are miracle tales and treat of all those things which, very often, are also objects of belief.[42]

Remnants of myths are found in the dreams and fantasies of normal people, but they are dramatically revealed in the visions and psychic eruptions of the insane:

> Dreams, fantasies, and psychoses produce images to all appearances identical with mythological motifs of which the individuals concerned had absolutely no knowledge, not even indirect knowledge acquired through popular figures of speech or through the symbolic language of the Bible. The psychopathology of schizophrenia, as well as the psychology of the unconscious, demonstrate the production of archaic material beyond a doubt. Whatever the structure of the unconscious may be, one thing is certain: it contains an indefinite number of motifs or patterns of an archaic character, in principle identical with the root ideas of mythology and similar thought-forms.[43]

It is indicative of the devaluation of mythos in modern times that it was championed by alienists who rediscovered it in the "psychopathology of schizophrenia." The most valuable form of language known to the soul, which has been called "God's forgotten language,"[44] was so discounted that it was found in the junk heaps of mental refuse and insane ramblings.

The prevalence of mythical thinking in indigenous cultures, and in the early childhood of moderns, led to the notion that consciousness becomes "modern" and mature only when it renounces this kind of thinking. Psychoanalysts have found remnants of archaic thinking in the modern mind, but in most cases it has been pathologized as negative and unreliable. In *The Interpretation of Dreams*, Freud noted the prevalence of mythical thinking in dreams and commented:

> What once dominated waking life, while the mind was still young and incompetent, seems now to have been banished into the night.[45]

"Young and incompetent" expresses Freud's prejudice about this kind of thinking. This prejudice is what makes Freud's work dated and unhelpful today, when we are trying to move toward a post-secular culture in which spirit and soul can be revived. Karl Abraham similarly found archaic thinking in the modern psyche and wrote that "the myth is a fragment of a superseded infantile psychic life of the race."[46] Eugen Bleuler dismissed mythical thinking as "autoerotic" and "autistic."[47] Everywhere we turn in the psychoanalytic literature, we see mythical thinking undermined as pathological.

Jung insisted that the presence of mythos in the modern mind is not a sign of poor adaptation. In response to Abraham's assertion that myth is infantile he wrote:

> One must certainly put a large question mark after the assertion that myths spring from the "infantile" psychic life of the race.[48]

Mircea Eliade gets it right when he says mythos is not "a stage in the history of consciousness but a content in the structure of consciousness."[49] It will always be with us because it is fundamental to our psychic structure:

> The unconscious bases of dreams and fantasies are only apparently infantile reminiscences. In reality we are concerned with primitive or archaic thought-forms, based on instinct, which naturally emerge more clearly in childhood than they do later. But they are not in themselves infantile, much less pathological. To characterize them, we ought therefore not to use expressions borrowed from pathology. So also the myth, which is likewise based on unconscious fantasy processes, is, in meaning, substance and form, far from being infantile or the expression of an autoerotic or autistic attitude, even though it produces a world-picture which is scarcely consistent with our rational and objective view of things.[50]

The devaluation of mythic thinking is related to the prejudice that such thinking is subjective, having no reference to anything objective. However, Jung argues that the West is limited in its understanding of objectivity. There is not only an objective world "out there," but an objective world "in here." Paradoxically, not everything arising from the subject is "subjective," because at the depths of our subjectivity is an objective psyche. This level expresses itself through the subject, however, and can be confused with subjectivity. This is linked in his thought with the existence of spirit and soul:

> There is no real ground for assuming that [mythic thinking] is nothing more than a distortion of the objective world-picture, for it remains to

be asked whether the mainly unconscious inner motive which guides these fantasy processes is not itself an objective fact.[51]

If we fail to see this objective life, we cut ourselves off from spirit and meaning. What may appear to psychiatry as autoerotic, autistic, or defective may be the sources of revelation and mystery. By misreading these sources we pathologize them and lose their meaning. Hence spirituality can be annihilated not only by literalism but by medical reductionism.

Myths, Dreams, Religions

Jung argues that mythic thinking is inherited in the structure of the brain. I am not sure of this, because I am not qualified in science. I would imagine that Jung is on shaky ground, but I am interested in his speculations, which are colorful if not scientifically convincing. Jung claims that ontogeny, the development of the individual, recapitulates phylogeny, the development of the species:

> All through our lives we possess, side by side with our newly acquired directed and adapted thinking, a fantasy-thinking which corresponds to the antique state of mind. Just as our bodies still retain vestiges of obsolete functions and conditions in many of their organs, so our minds, which have apparently outgrown those archaic impulses, still bear the marks of the evolutionary stages we have traversed, and re-echo the dim bygone in dreams and fantasies.[52]

This gives ammunition to his critics. If mythic thinking is similar to the "obsolete functions" of bodily organs, scientists can say we have outgrown this "antique mind" and should let it go. Jung would reply that antique thinking is not dead but found in the activity of the psyche. He believed that archaic thinking has to be reintegrated into consciousness and respected. His critics would demand proof that such thinking is an expression of soul, and there the argument becomes circular and self-defeating. Either one adopts the view that this activity is meaningful, or one does not. It seems to be a question of faith as much as science, and although Jung felt he was providing the scientific framework his detractors were not convinced.

Jung did not develop this idea in intellectual isolation. He was borrowing from Nietzsche:

> In sleep and in dreams we pass through the whole thought of earlier humanity.... What I mean is this: as man now reasons in

dreams, so humanity also reasoned for many thousands of years when awake.... This atavistic element in man's nature still manifests itself in our dreams, for it is the foundation upon which the higher reason has developed and still develops in every individual. Dreams carry us back to remote conditions of human culture and give us a ready means of understanding them better. Dream thinking comes so easily to us now because [it] ... has been drilled into us for immense periods of time. To that extent, dreaming is a recreation for the brain, which by day has to satisfy the stern demands of thought imposed by a higher culture. From this we can see how *lately* the more acute logical thinking ... has been developed, since our rational and intellectual faculties still involuntarily hark back to those primitive forms of reasoning, and we pass about half our lives in this condition.[53]

Nietzsche says that "as man now reasons in dreams," so humanity reasoned in the past when awake. One can see where Freud drew some of his ideas. Dreams are extremely difficult to understand. This is not because they are subject to an internal "censor" that hides unsavory things from our morality, as Freud conjectured. Rather, dreams are speaking to us from an ancient past, from an ever-present structure that we can only understand with great difficulty.

This is why we struggle to understand the scriptures of the ancient world. They speak from the world of mythos, and in our logocentric society we hardly understand what they are saying. But the effort is rewarded, because in trying to reach into the mythical structures of scripture we are at the same time digging up the structures of our own minds. We then realize that the scriptures are speaking to us, and not merely of the ancient world. Although the work of excavation is time-consuming, it has enormous spiritual value. As we engage in this archaeological project, we are transformed. Jung encourages us not to become defeatist, but to continue in the hope that there is buried treasure in the field:

> What was once strong enough to mould the spiritual life of a highly developed people will not have vanished without trace from the human soul in the course of a few generations.[54]
>
> [In mythical thinking] the mind is brought into contact with the oldest layers of the human mind, long buried beneath the threshold of consciousness.[55]

Today some think the products of the "oldest layers of the human mind" are incoherent babble. But an earlier age valued these productions as

Something Continues to Speak

In an interview with the *New York Times* Jung used the term "the two million-year-old man" as a metaphor for the ancestral psyche:

> Together the patient and I address ourselves to the two million-year-old man that is in all of us. In the last analysis, most of our difficulties come from losing contact with our instincts, with the age-old unforgotten wisdom stored up in us. And where do we make contact with this old man in us? In our dreams.[57]

Metaphors such as these can be misleading, and many Jungians get derailed by Jung's suggestive language. Obviously there is no two-million-year-old man inside us. But this metaphor appealed to Jung, and he thought that personifying the psyche enabled us to form a relationship with its contents. He advised his students to approach dreams from the perspective of getting in touch with the ancient source of wisdom:

> Go to bed. Think of your problem. See what you dream. Perhaps the Great Man, the two million-year-old man, will speak. In a cul-de-sac, then only do you hear his voice. The urge to become what one is is invincibly strong, and you can always count on it, but that does not mean that things will necessarily turn out positively. If you are not interested in your own fate, the unconscious is.[58]

Jung is careful not to link our reconnection with mythos with unreal expectations of happiness. But he is right to argue that such contact is a minor miracle. We have to trust the unconscious to show the new direction. Since mythos has been lost to consciousness, we are forced to turn to dreams with hope and an anticipation of discovering our fate. The qualities and values of mythos, which include meaning, direction, orientation, destiny, and connectedness have been lost to our world. We are forced to turn to the night world, in the hope that our instincts will not fail us. We are indebted to the generosity of the unconscious, even though we have abused mythos in our daily life.

The language of myth is "indigenous" to the psyche, and no amount of modernization will get rid of it. It is how the psyche speaks. The notion that we can outgrow mythic thinking is one of the fallacies of the modern era. We can no more afford to dispense with it than we can with our souls:

> One can withhold the material content of primitive myths from a child but not take from him the need for mythology, and still less his ability to manufacture it for himself. One could almost say that if all the world's traditions were cut off at a single blow, the whole of mythology and the whole history of religion would start all over again with the next generation. Only a very few individuals succeed in throwing off mythology. Enlightenment avails nothing, it merely destroys a transitory manifestation, but not the creative impulse.[59]

Even if enlightenment tried to banish myths and symbols, the history of religion and myth "would start all over again with the next generation," because such language is endemic to the psyche. Something within us continues to speak. We can destroy the "transitory manifestations" of myth, but not its original impulse.

Notes

1. Diarmuid O'Murchu, *The God Who Becomes Redundant* (Dublin and London: The Mercier Press and Fowler Wright Books, 1986), p. 32
2. Karen Armstrong, *The Case for God: What Religion Really Means* (London: The Bodley Head, 2009).
3. See Peter Vardy, *Good and Bad Religion* (London: SCM Press, 2010).
4. Christopher Hitchens, *God is Not Great: How Religion Poisons Everything* (New York: Hatchette Book Group, 2007).
5. Karen Armstrong, *The Case for God: What Religion Really Means* (London: The Bodley Head, 2009), p. 3.
6. Karen Armstrong, *The Battle for God: Fundamentalism in Judaism, Christianity and Islam* (New York: Alfred A. Knopf, 2000), p. xiii.
7. Armstrong, *Battle for God*, p. xiv.
8. Friedrich Nietzsche, *The Birth of Tragedy* trans Shaun Whiteside (1872; London: Penguin, 1993), p. 111.
9. Armstrong, *Battle for God*, p. xiv.
10. James Hillman, *Re-Visioning Psychology*, 2nd ed. (1975; New York: Harper Perennial, 1992), p. 2.
11. Northrop Frye, *Words with Power* (Ontario: Viking, 1990), p. xiii.
12. Armstrong, *Battle for God*, p. xiii.
13. Alvin Kuhn, in Tom Harpur, *The Pagan Christ: Is Blind Faith Killing Christianity?* (Sydney: Allen & Unwin, 2005), p. 19.
14. Armstrong, *Case for God*, p. 3.
15. Ibid.
16. Armstrong, *Case for God*, p. 4.
17. Armstrong, *Battle for God* p. xiv.
18. Ibid, p. xiv.
19. See the next chapter in which Kuhn's argument is explored in the context of the deification of Jesus.

20. Armstrong, *Case for God*, p. 6.
21. Ibid.
22. Ernst Cassirer, "Mythical Consciousness," in *The Philosophy of Symbolic Forms*, Vol. 2, *Mythical Thought* (1925; New Haven and London: Yale University Press, 1955), p. 38.
23. Jung, "Archaic Man" (1931), *CW* 10, § 105.
24. Ibid, § 138.
25. Jung, "The Psychology of the Child Archetype" (1940), *CW* 9, 1, § 260.
26. Ibid.
27. Jean Gebser, *The Ever-Present Origin* (1949; Athens, OH: Ohio University Press, 1986).
28. Jung, "Child Archetype," § 261.
29. Ibid.
30. Jung, "The Aims of Psychotherapy" (1931), *CW* 16, § 111.
31. King James Version, Proverbs 29:18.
32. Jung, "Psychological Commentary on 'The Tibetan Book of the Great Liberation'" (1939/1954), *CW* 11, § 782.
33. Roger Schmidt, *Exploring Religion* (Belmont, CA: Wadsworth, 1980), p. 127.
34. Jung, "The Psychology of the Child Archetype," § 262.
35. Ernst Cassirer, *The Philosophy of Symbolic Forms*, Vol. 2, *Mythical Thought* (1925; New Haven and London: Yale University Press, 1955).
36. Cassirer, p. 38.
37. Jung, "Two Kinds of Thinking," in *Symbols of Transformation* (1912/1952), *CW* 5, § 4–46.
38. Ibid, § 24.
39. Ibid, § 44.
40. Ibid, § 4.
41. Ibid, § 23.
42. Jung, *Aion* (1951), § 66.
43. Jung, "Psychological Commentary on 'The Tibetan Book of the Great Liberation,'" § 782.
44. John Sanford, *Dreams: God's Forgotten Language* (1968; New York: HarperOne, 1989).
45. Sigmund Freud, *The Interpretation of Dreams*, in *The Standard Edition of The Complete Psychological Works of Sigmund Freud*. Volume 4 (1900; London: Hogarth Press, 2001), p. 567.
46. Karl Abraham, Abraham, Karl 1909: "Dreams and Myths: A Study in Folk Psychology," in Hilda C. Abraham (ed.) *Clinical Papers and Essays on Psychoanalysis* (1909; London: Hogarth Press, 1955), p. 36.
47. Eugen Bleuler, *Dementia Praecox: or, The Group of Schizophrenias*, ed. Joseph Zinkin (1910; New York: International Universities Press, 1950), p. 6.
48. Jung, "Two Kinds of Thinking," § 29.
49. Mircea Eliade, *The Quest: History and Meaning in Religion* (1969; Chicago: University of Chicago Press, 1975), p. i.
50. Jung, "Two Kinds of Thinking," § 38.
51. Ibid, § 37.
52. Ibid, § 36.
53. Friedrich Nietzsche, *Human, All-Too Human* (1878), trans. R. J. Hollingdale (Cambridge: Cambridge University Press, 1996), pp. 24–7.

54. Jung, "Two Kinds of Thinking," § 35.
55. Ibid, § 39.
56. Ibid, § 5.
57. Jung, "The Two Million-Year-Old Man" (1936), in William McGuire and R.F.C. Hull eds., *C. G. Jung Speaking* (London: Picador, 1980), p. 100.
58. Jung, "A Talk With Students at the Institute" (1958), *C. G. Jung Speaking*, p. 335.
59. Jung, "Two Kinds of Thinking," § 30.

4

Jesus the Metaphor

All that we see is vision, from generated organs gone as soon as come, permanent in the imagination, considered as nothing by the natural man.
— *William Blake*[1]

Imagination and Reality

Blake saw Jesus as the imagination. By this, he meant that the story of Jesus enables us to see into the life of the spirit: the Jesus story opens a window to the soul. For Blake, soul and spirit were realities, and not merely, as contemporary parlance puts it, "figments of imagination," a phrase used when practical people want to reduce something to nothing. As with the word "myth," which today means lies or illusion, "imagination" has been downgraded to refer to that which is not real. Spiritual reality is indeed not "real" in the sense of physically existent, and spirit and soul are not objects of sense perception. But they are real in the sense of being more real than what we call "reality." Little wonder that earlier ages believed spirit and soul "descended" from heaven, and were "visitations" from another world. They are not visitations from above, but aspects of this world. They are only "above" in a metaphorical sense, in terms of being above ordinary perception.

Blake recognized that sacred metaphors are "considered as nothing by the natural man." By "natural man" he meant the person in whom imagination had not awoken, the man or woman who only grants reality to what is physically real. Many of us fit into this category. I have met many people who have said they only like reading "true" stories, because the others are "made up." But only the "made-up" ones can access the deeper truth. The "natural man" thinks otherwise. It is the prevalence of ordinary perception that has thrown us into the spiritual dark ages. We are not attuned to spiritual reality, and our education does little or nothing to aid this development. In ancient societies the "natural" person is the one who is uninitiated, who has not gone through the trials of initiation into spiritual vision. Today even our religious institutions are divorced from the spiritual. Blake despised the churches and saw them as institutionalized versions of natural thought. In his time, the churches had already "modernized," that is, turned poetry into purported history and fact. He said he could not attend churches, as the sermons were profane. It was like listening to someone trying to explain mystical poetry in the language of moralistic prose.

Blake argued that the churches were blasphemous insofar as they did not understand the metaphorical language of spirit, and insofar as they claimed to represent God and spirit in society. Blake protested that

> The outward ceremony [of religion] is Antichrist.[2]

If religion could not understand the first principle of spiritual life, which is that spirit speaks in metaphors, what was the value of such traditions? Blake, like Keats and Wordsworth, wanted to tear away this charade and start again with a new, spiritual understanding of Jesus. To reduce Jesus to a conjurer or magician who performs tricks is a cheap and nasty reduction of this singular figure. Indeed, the devil himself asked Jesus to perform tricks, and Jesus refused to do so. It is for this reason that the poets, who attempt to defend the spirit in all times and places, are often at odds with ecclesial traditions.

Blake was astounded by the literalism of religion, and felt it to be a disease of the soul, an inability to see religion for what it is: a system of metaphors and symbols that transport us to transcendent dimensions of this world. But this does not happen automatically; we have to be in the right frame. Only if we employ our imaginations can scripture enable the flight of spirit. Once the imagination is functioning, we don't need the miracles to be literally true, because as soon as we perceive their meaning they have performed their function. Miracles are for those who don't see spirit always already at work. In this sense, everything is miraculous, and we don't need historical miracles to make this apparent. It is the presence of spirit that opens our lives to the miraculous in the ordinary. Nowadays biblical miracles are alienating because we don't see the world as possessing a supernatural layer. With imagination, we are capable of seeing the miraculous in the ordinary but supernatural miracles running counter to nature are dismissed as fantasies.

Blake claimed that religion has brought us to this impasse. Religious literalism did two things: it reduced the stories to absurdities, and set up religion for atheistic rejection. And it obliterated the spiritual meaning of religious stories, which might never be grasped by way of ordinary perception.

If we understood our poets correctly, we would not need books like this one, which seek to counter the impulse to literal thinking. I have sometimes felt that poets like Blake and Keats are our only way into religious truth. The official religious channels have <u>obscured the spiritual dimension</u>, and only poets and imaginative thinkers are our reliable guides to the world of spirit. Theologians speak in an obscure manner that most ordinary mortals cannot understand. Ministers and priests are unreliable, unless they have a special gift for imagination, which is something their training cannot give them. They either have it or they don't: we can't put in what God left out. A crucial way into spiritual insight is the reading of literature. Religion can kill off the spirit if it is delivered in the usual way, with miracles presented as facts and <u>stories as moral messages.</u> But literature, art, and music are "royal" roads to the spirit. Therefore, we need to read the life of Jesus as a <u>parable of the spirit, not as a demonstration of doctrine.</u> Reclaiming Jesus for life, rather than manipulating his image for ideological purposes, is an urgent task of our age.

Fear of Myth

With all that we know about scripture, poetry, and mythos in the Bible, it is strange that religious authorities continue to claim that the key moments in the Jesus story are historical. I don't think we can say that the gatekeepers of Christianity are dumb or unintelligent, as most of them are highly educated and intellectually developed. There is something else going on that is not about intellectual training.

First, there is an <u>incredible fear of myth as a genre.</u> Christians have always hated myth; indeed historically they distinguished their own faith from "pagan" religions by referring to the latter as "myths," whereas their faith was said to be "historical." As Northrop Frye notes:

> For Christian scholars since New Testament times, poetry and fables were what other religions had: they had the "truth."[3]

Christians have been conditioned to believe that myth is false, and to get from this position to one in which myth can be respected is difficult. This prejudice has existed for centuries and is hardly going to change overnight. It shows the extent to which Christianity has capitulated to

Western prejudices: instead of defending mythos as the mode of faith, it attacked mythos and promoted itself as logos.

Religious authorities continue to berate scholars who point to the mythical nature of the Christ story. Indeed, the notion that the Christ story is historical has itself become an "article of faith." Despite all evidence to the contrary, the notion that it is historical is a "belief" that separates the faithful from those who are nihilistic or destructive. With such a colossal bulwark against truth, it is hard to see how reason can prevail. In his paper on "Reason and Revelation," Theodor Adorno wrote that religious tradition will cling to its historical framing of the Jesus story,

> because it knows that its claim on the material-concrete content could not be set apart without being damaged. As soon as it relinquishes its objective content, it is liable to evaporate into pure symbolism, and this strikes at the very life of its claim to truth.[4]

This important point will be taken up in a later chapter. Suffice it to say that religion can still have "objective content" without the historical construction. It can still have content without it being "material-concrete." But the fear in Christians is that if the mythical dimension is exposed, they will consider their religion fraudulent. Such is the disrespect with which myth and metaphor are held.

Christian leaders will fight to the bitter end to defend their religion's claimed historicity. They will fight, but they will not win, because the amount of evidence to the contrary is overwhelming. Instead of working with scholars like myself who are trying to improve the status of myth, and reclaim the credibility of religion, they will stick to their position and frown on myth. I'm afraid the wheels of history will roll over them, because as Arnold said, "fact is failing it [religion],"[5] and the religious have no option but to reconsider myth. The fight will be long and hard, but the presence of "strong religion," fundamentalism, and reactionary attitudes are signs that the battle is being lost, and some are becoming desperate to prop up a collapsing system. Psychoanalyst Alfred Adler would refer to this as a "masculine protest," by which he meant that a failing position engages in a rearguard, aggressive action to assert its power.[6] The louder it protests, the more can we be sure it is going down.

The Secret Life of Us

Second, there is another source of resistance. This, I believe, is less conscious but no less real. If the Christ story is revealed as myth, and does not point to historical fact, to what else does it point? Skeptics will say it points to nothing, just fantasy. I disagree. The story points to us, not to our outward or external lives, but to our internal or hidden lives. One could say that the Jesus story is about the secret life of us, but it is a secret that is guarded with fierce tenacity. The secret is that the "life" of Jesus is not a historical narrative about a person, but a story about the life of the human soul. That "life" never happened as claimed, but it nevertheless happens continually in the soul. Armstrong writes: "A myth was never intended as an accurate account of a historical event... but it is something that happens all the time."[7] Bernie Neville echoes this: "Myths are not about the past; they are about the now."[8] Insofar as religion has emphasized the historical dimension of its story, it has conspired against the soul, within which all myths take shape. As William Blake put it: "Thus men forgot that all deities reside in the human breast."[9] This does not mean that the gods are not real, only that their forms are invented by imagination.

Myths are movements of soul that are too large to be contained by the conscious mind. They well up spontaneously from the unconscious and impress themselves on writers and artists. In ancient times, such inspired writings were said to be the "words of God." Myths are vitally important, because without them we would have no access to the narratives of the soul. They are priceless to civilizations. Myths might be defined as archetypal configurations of spirit, as they impact on the psyche. Mythology is what we refer to today as psychology. But not academic psychology, that sterile discipline that strives to be an exact science. Rather, mythology finds its parallel in depth psychology, the study of mind that takes the unconscious into account, and takes it seriously, as a wellspring of information about the psyche—in the Greek sense of "soul." Myths well up from this obscure region like dreams, and like dreams they must not be taken literally.

Personifying

A key feature of myths and dreams is that the archetypal contents of the psyche are personified. They do not express themselves as abstract principles, ideas, or philosophical equations, but express themselves as persons. We don't dream about ideas, concepts, or formulas; we dream of figures. We dream of people, animals, and the dead, and these narratives are saturated with archetypal images. We interpret dreams by realizing that the people in our dreams are aspects of ourselves, and part of the task of interpretation is trying to figure out which aspects they represent. In the same way, the new archetype that arose at the beginning of our common era, the archetype in which God and man become one, was activated in the psyche and attached to the figure of Jesus. One might say that the historical Jesus was virtually lost in the archetypal motifs that were attributed to him by common fiat. What was found in Jesus were the characteristics of spirit: it does not have a normal birth, and it does not have a normal death. Jesus carried these attributes for us, and still carries them for many today.

Once archetypal images attach to persons, it is hard to pry them apart from their object of focus. Psychoanalysis refers to this as "projection," and it is particularly tenacious because it is unconscious. We don't knowingly "project" these images upon persons; rather, this happens to us, in an involuntary act of the soul. For instance, someone we hate may well be irksome to ourselves and others, but the intensity of our hatred comes from within. There is an element that is particularly bothersome in ourselves that we find "mirrored" in someone else. It is all the more difficult to recognize this element when it involves having to accept that we are not quite what we would like to be. What we hate is present in ourselves: it is a moral challenge to our sense of identity.

Jesus was a "depth psychologist" in this regard:

> Why do you observe the splinter in your brother's eye and never notice the plank in your own? How dare you say to your brother, "Let me take the splinter out of your eye," when all the time there is a plank in your own? Take the plank out of your own eye first, and then you will see clearly enough to take the splinter out of your brother's eye.[10]

Jesus opposed the "natural" man and his unreflective impulses. Nothing is more "natural" than to find someone else objectionable, when the trait that we criticize is crying out to be recognized in ourselves. This viewpoint is never popular and can never be so since it asks us to accept what we do not want to know. But sages of all times have kept emphasizing this point, since we can get so caught up in our rightness that we fail to see the dynamics we project onto others. Each wise person who arises in history and gets murdered for his or her wisdom, such as Jesus or Socrates, puts up a mirror to our dark side and asks us to recognize ourselves in the alter ego that it brings to awareness.

Perhaps "projection" is the wrong term, because it implies a willful action. We are no more responsible for our projections than we are for our dreams.[11] Both of these psychological activities happen to us, and all we can do is experience them and become aware of them. Once archetypal images find an object, they tend to stick. This attachment is said by analysts to be a veritable force of nature, and it takes considerable effort to separate the archetypal contents from their carrier.

Spirit Personified in Jesus

This is what happened with the figure of Jesus: his ministry so nearly approximated the new archetype of the god-man that this archetype became fused with him. Those who came under the sway of his influence were convinced that he was God incarnate, the "only Son" of the Father,[12] the embodiment of the Holy Spirit. There was no separating Jesus from the Christ, the human person from the archetype of spirit. Today we have to separate these things if we are to survive in a humanist and pluralistic world.

The fusion of archetype and person reaches its climax in the gospel of John, where Jesus is a historical person with a real existence, and, at the same time, a preexistent divine being outside or beyond history. Thus John's Jesus can say to the assembly of Jews:

> Your father Abraham rejoiced at the thought of seeing my day; he saw it and was glad.[13]

The uncomprehending Jews, who are made to play the role of literal thinkers in John's gospel, reply: "You are not yet fifty years old ... and you have seen Abraham!"[14] It is here that John's Jesus announces his archetypal status:

> I tell you the truth, before Abraham was born, I am![15]

At this, the Jews "picked up stones to stone him, but Jesus hid himself, slipping away from the temple grounds."[16] This sequence can only be understood if we realize that, for John, or the community of writers calling themselves "John," the historical personage of Jesus is secondary to his "true" nature as archetype. As spirit, he antedates Abraham, Moses, and Jacob. He has become identified with the eternal life of the spirit, and is fused with the image of God.

Scholars tell us that scenes such as this are not historical, and we cannot think literally about this debate, or about "the Jews" at this point. This is a "teaching story," in which objections are raised about the mythic and divine status of Jesus. At the literal level, "the Jews" are correct: this historical person is not the eternal spirit, not one who predates Abraham. But as John perceives Jesus, it *is* correct insofar as Jesus' historical existence has been annulled and replaced by his mythic significance. I would say that both are right and wrong. John is wrong if he fails to notice that a historical figure is being made to carry an archetypal burden. The Jews are wrong if they fail to realize that a historical figure can be invested with archetypal value that surpasses his time-bound existence.

But this debate between Jews and Jesus continues in our time. Through one perspective, the elevation of a historical figure to the status of God is a form of enthusiasm that equates with idolatry. Through another perspective, the archetype of the god-man was constellated at that time and found an appropriate object in the figure of Jesus. In this sense, Jesus is indeed Messiah and Son of God. It all depends on whether we are standing inside the mythos, or outside it. Belief and unbelief are valid responses. In the Mass, when I am participating in the ritual of the Eucharist, I find the idea of Jesus as Messiah completely acceptable. But when the Mass is over, I change my mind about it and think of it as a form of delusional thinking. I become embarrassed by my enthusiasm, by being seduced by ritual. I am one with Jesus and the Jews. This is the paradox of religious thinking; it is both true and untrue at the same time.

Some Christians remain filled with the same enthusiasm that animated the writers of John's gospel. Their belief is so powerful they cannot stand outside it. There is a kind of "possession" involved. They cannot see Jesus through the perspective of "the Jews," in which confusion of archetype and person leads to outrage and stoning of an inflated figure. This is why it is so difficult to ask Christians to see Jesus as a *symbol* of spirit, rather than *as* spirit. Jesus is an archetypal figure, but he is not the archetype. Symbol and object have to be pried apart, so we can mature in our understanding. If we cannot manage this, I think the world is doomed, because fanaticism will make it impossible for people to see the spiritual value of other religions and philosophies. Fanaticism will drive people to violence and oppression. One has to break the "spell" of Jesus upon the human mind to separate spirit from person.

One has to break the spell of Jesus in order to see the Christ-like element of non-Christian people. Tradition encourages us not to do this, which is why tradition has to be changed. Tradition has been caught by the fusion of these entities. It discourages spiritual maturity, and with it, the ability to see Christianity as one tradition of spirituality alongside others of equal value and importance. It is the fusion of spirit and person, the projection of spirit upon Jesus, that has been a negative force in civilization, and made it impossible for many Christians to abide in the knowledge that there are other pathways to God. I will return to the connection between Christianity and violence, which should be a point of reflection for all thinking people.

Ongoing Incarnation

The classical image of Jesus as God is, put simply, wrong. I can understand how theology, or more specifically, Christology, got there, but it is mistaken. Jesus is a spiritual master in whom God's life can be discerned. The reason why he was said to be "God" was because the church has long misunderstood the relation between humanity and divinity. It has kept the two apart, with an abysmal divide between them: God far above, humanity down below. This is the time-honored error that prompted theologians to install Jesus as the Second Person of the Trinity. But as soon as we reconceptualize divinity as a dimension of being that is found at the heart of creation, there is no longer any need for Jesus to be enthroned as God. Rather he becomes an example, a testimony, of what humanity looks like when it appropriates the divine at the core of the human. Jesus did not "bring" God to humans who were otherwise bereft of divine life. He pointed to what was always already present. Wrong assumptions about reality caused theologians to exaggerate Jesus' importance.

Marcus Borg argues in *The Heart of Christianity* that Jesus must be given a "demotion" if we are to understand him anew.[17] I know this will sound obscene to many Christians, but hopefully it will be less obscene after explanation. Borg maintains that Jesus is a genuine spiritual figure, but not quite as holy as tradition wants him to be. Spong, Cupitt, Crossan, and others in this revisionist tradition argue the same position. Robert Price has written an extraordinary book on this subject, both deadly serious and yet astonishingly funny, called *The Incredible Shrinking Son of Man*.[18] Price argues we have to draw Jesus back into the human side, so that, paradoxically, we might experience the presence of the divine in a more intimate way. We cannot afford to lock divinity away in this single figure, or imagine that the incarnation of God was a once-only event, single, absolute, and not to be repeated. Rather, incarnation is to be revisioned as an ongoing and continuous process, occurring everywhere in time and space.

67

A lot of the boasting and fanfare, typical of Christianity once it became wedded to power after 380 CE, has to be wound back, and the inflated claims of the tradition refuted. It is little wonder that Christianity has been reviled by many Jews, Muslims, Buddhists, Hindus, and others, because it has been claiming for centuries that it alone holds the truth and others are dabbling in vanities or shadows. Even diplomatic attempts at "interfaith dialogue" today barely disguise the arrogance of Christians. I have attended many "interfaith" meetings where Christians are as polite as can be, but inwardly they are sure they possess the absolute truth.

Christianity contains a truth, which is why it cannot be brushed aside by secular or religious progress. But its truth becomes false as soon as the idea is literalized and fixated on one person. The powerful idea that Jesus carried for his followers, and eventually for his universal church, was that a new, more intimate relationship to God was possible: "the kingdom of heaven is close at hand."[19] Until the time of Jesus, God was imagined as somewhat distant and remote, removed from human experience. This was not true for Jewish prophets and mystics, who maintained a close and ecstatic relationship with God, but the majority seemed to be somewhat detached from the presence of God, who was thought of as "out there," a God of the universe looking "down" from heaven. What Jesus offered was a radically new, immediate, and democratic "kingdom of heaven," in which even the most humble among us could enjoy proximity to God.

One did not have to be a prophet or mystic to experience this intimacy. Ordinary people, such as fishermen, tax collectors, lepers and prostitutes, could experience the life-giving fullness of the presence. Jesus offered us this proximity in his ministry, and in my view he was offering something original and genuine. It was a new "way" of being, a new modality of experience. He was replacing conventional religion with the spirituality of presence, replacing law with grace. In psychological terms, the archetype of spirit was coming closer to the human, and the responsibilities of this closeness, and the beauty but terror of this proximity, were demonstrated in Jesus' ministry and crucifixion. Jesus was inviting ordinary folk to experience what had previously been reserved for the few.

In John, Jesus says to the Jews: "Is it not written in your law, 'I said, you are gods'?"[20] The allusion is to Psalms:

> I say, "You are gods,
>   sons of the Most High, all of you;
> Nevertheless, you shall die like men,
>   and fall like any prince."[21]

The implication is that humans have divine potential, and can be seen as "sons of the Most High," but despite the connection to divinity, we must live and "die like men," and "fall" like any prince of this world. The divine proximity does not make us gods; we connect with the divine but remain human. This is the paradox that Jesus himself demonstrated in his life, and is dogmatized in the creedal assertion that he is both human and divine. The above phrase "all of you" indicates that this is not just a gift to some, but to all. Jesus sees himself as acting on this promise, bringing it to fulfillment. He indicates that the divine proximity was already evident in Jewish law and is not merely something he has dreamed up in an intoxicated vision. He is showing the rabbis that he is not breaking rules but proclaiming something already present in tradition.

This conversation takes place in the context of the accusation of blasphemy, since he dares to call himself the son of God. In his defense, Jesus is saying we are all sons of God, and thus he is not claiming special status for himself:

> If he [God] called them gods to whom the word of God came, do you say of him whom the Father consecrated and sent into the world, "You are blaspheming," because I said, "I am the Son of God"?[22]

It is unlikely that this conversation ever took place in history. The authors of John are getting carried away by visions of the absolute nature of Jesus. According to many scripture scholars, Jesus' preferred title was "Son of Man," and he never used "Son of God" as a title. Only others used this about him, or in the case of John, put the title in his mouth. But in John we nevertheless get the point that what Jesus is proposing is regarded as blasphemy by the old guard. In the same way, in our world, if anyone dares to suggest that the life of Christ is the secret life of us, we are accused of blasphemy by the old regime. Nothing much has changed; history repeats itself. The established order finds dread and fear in the idea that we are close to the divine. It prefers the divine to be further away, and personified in external figures such as a reified God and a deified Jesus.

In the Sermon on the Mount, and in other places, Jesus extols his followers to love their enemies and pray for those who persecute them,

> ... so you may be sons of your Father who is in heaven.[23]

It is clear that being sons and daughters of God is what we should aspire to. In the Revelation the voice of God is made to say:

> He who [drinks] from the fountain of the water of life ... shall have this heritage, and I will be his God and he shall be my son.[24]

Once again there is no monopoly on the idea of divine filiation. In the gnostic sayings of Thomas, Jesus is explicit about the invitation to all humanity to see ourselves as sons of God:

> If you will
> know yourselves, then you will be known
> and you will know that you are
> the sons of the Living Father. But if
> you do not know yourselves, then you
> are in poverty and you are poverty.[25]

This saying of Jesus makes it clear that divine filiation is our birthright. If we embrace the link with the divine we discover our true nature and will be enriched. Conversely, failure to grasp this affiliation leads to spiritual poverty.

The Messenger as the Message

Ironically, although Jesus came to bring the "good news" that the grace of God was available, and we are all sons and daughters of God, tradition turned the messenger into the message. Instead of announcing a democratic kingdom of God, Christianity made Jesus the embodiment of the proximity he preached. The notion that all are sons and daughters of God goes out the window, and we find Jesus worshipped as the exclusive, absolute, and only begotten son. The finger that points to God becomes God, and thus Christendom blasphemes by misunderstanding the democratic nature of Jesus' message. Tom Harpur encapsulates the Christian misunderstanding as follows:

> The great truth that the Christ was to come in man, that the Christ principle was potentially in every one of us, was changed to the exclusivist teaching that the Christ had come as a man. No other could match him, or even come close. The Dark Ages—and so much more—were the eventual result.[26]

For Harpur, "Christ" is a principle, a presence in the soul, a capacity of our heartfelt interiority, and not a man. To the extent that Jesus embraced the soul and found his interiority, he became Christ, but the term is not exclusive to him. This mystical position was too hot to handle. People could not accept the responsibility Jesus gave them; he was asking us to cultivate personal relationships with God and to know ourselves as God's children.

This is my reading of where Jesus' teaching departs from Christianity. His followers did not "get" it. They still don't get it. And as Harpur suggests, a "dark age" arose—the spiritual and cultural poverty of which the gospel of Thomas spoke. The endowment of spirit, the proximity to God, the sonship to the Father, were too difficult to accept; it was a gift impossible to receive. So we placed it all upon Jesus: he was the Son, not us; he was the Savior, we were not responsible for our salvation. Jung would concede that the "projection" of our divine proximity upon Jesus might have been necessary in the past. Jung suggests that the human mind might not have been mature enough to realize its proximity to the spirit without identifying itself with it. As the human ego negotiates the proximity of spirit, it can become engulfed by spirit, producing inflation or "godlikeness," as the Greeks called it. The Greeks regarded this as the great sin, which they called *hubris*. We see this in schizophrenics who have experienced divine proximity but are unable to cope with it. They "become" God, and identify themselves with the stronger archetype. This is indeed madness, and to be guarded against at all costs.

As the person moves close to the spirit, an appropriate parallel would be a satellite approaching the gravitational field of a planetary body. It is drawn into the influence of the larger body and the results are often disastrous. This "fatal attraction" is clearly what the founders of Christianity had in mind when they set Jesus upon a pedestal and turned us into ordinary mortals, sinners, who could hardly raise a candle to Jesus' light. We are all sons of God, but one son is more divine than others. It is an understandable position in some ways, but it is untenable and has to be overcome. All the children of God have to grow up and become responsible for their salvation. This is why, I believe, Christianity is breaking up today, and has been disintegrating for some time. The old order can no longer work, is no longer effective. Just as Jesus terminated an old Jewish order, so today a moribund Christianity has to be overcome in the same way. There is new wine of the spirit, and the old wineskins can no longer contain it.

It seems propitious to withdraw a projection that has been favored by two thousand years of tradition. The archetype of spirit has been projected upon a messianic figure for twenty centuries, and it seems spirit is no longer interested in maintaining this projection. It is dissolving it, and looking to see how we respond. It dissolves it by revealing to our awareness that the old religious order was based on an infantile understanding of faith: Jesus will save us, we can entrust ourselves to his embrace; he is the shepherd, we the sheep; he has undergone the journey for us, and we need only trust him. Although Jesus tried to dissolve religious rigidity to institute a new spirituality, today we are forced to dissolve a Christian rigidity that blocks the pathway to what Jesus offered. It is the "same old" story, and spirituality is something we are forever losing sight of.

Every spiritual revolution is an attempt to recover a living spirituality from the deadening effect of religiosity. Religion is easier than spirituality, because everything is done at a distance, through clergy and middlemen, through doctrine and the law. The spirit tires of this lack of authenticity and starts to disrupt religious systems to generate change. The cycle of civilization is about maintaining an authentic spirituality in face of the arthritic pressures exerted by lawmakers who think they know how to dispense justice and discern God. The scandal of clerical sexual abuse is only one symptom of the disintegration of the old religious order. When the time comes for a changing of the gods, the system that once provided life-giving meaning becomes toxic and collapses.

The redeemer is not "out there" but "within."[27] Jesus said this to those who had ears to hear.[28] In the same way that we find it nearly impossible to withdraw evil projections and become aware of "the plank in [our] own eye,"[29] so we find it difficult to believe that we might possess the highest good. Today we are called to dissolve our fixation on Jesus so we can do what he commended. Jesus as idol has to be smashed, so we can recover our sense of Jesus as icon, one who points the way to our goal. Christianity has to move on from its projections and journey to a more dangerous place, where each Christian has to forge a personal relationship with God. We have been propelled out of the comfort zone into a difficult place where we have to wrestle with the spirits and angels of our nature. Religion can no longer be used as a defense against spirit. Religion can no longer be a crutch, and the journey of Jesus is no longer a guarantee that we will not have to battle with the demons, devils and satanic figures that he confronted.

An Eastern Moment in the West

We have entered an Eastern moment in the history of the West. It is little wonder that countless Westerners are turning to the East for spiritual direction at this time. The East knows that literalism and idolatry are obstacles to spiritual growth and have to be dealt with ruthlessly and without sentiment. In Zen Buddhism, the popular saying runs: "If you meet the Buddha on the road, kill him." This is a warning against idolatry, obsession, and fixation. The East understands that religion can be used against spirituality, and religion is useless if it serves to distance us from a personal encounter with the sacred. Religion is not treated with the same pious regard that it receives from the faithful in the West. Religion is disposable and can be got rid of if it is seen to inhibit a person or be used as a crutch. Icons are kept as icons, translucent to the divine, and do not "stand for" the divine. The East keeps a watchful eye on the possibility of habit and complacency.

That is why there is the remarkable tradition of the Kalachakra mandalas, in which Tibetan monks who have carefully crafted exquisitely symmetrical drawings made of sand, upturn their works, collect the sand in a silk cloth, and take them to the river to be washed away. Westerners protest that these are great works of art and need to be preserved. But the Buddhist monks laugh at this, as they are responding to a higher truth. Their mandalas are not to be worshipped in themselves, nor are they to become fixed in the mind. The mandalas point the way to an experience of a transcendent order that can never be encompassed. All images are transitory and need to be destroyed. "It's a metaphor," they seem to say to Western observers and "art lovers" who ask for the works to be preserved. In the West we try to cling to metaphors of the sacred, whereas the East lets them go; that produces the typically Eastern mirth, and the West's grim and humorless sanctimony.

The East seems ahead of the West in many ways, and that is why the most important Christian mystics of the last fifty years, including Thomas Merton, Bede Griffiths, and William Johnston, have been in close dialogue with the East. In their journeys into, respectively, Buddhism, Hinduism, and Zen, they recognized that Eastern philosophies know far more about spirituality than we do. In particular, the East has a developed a sophisticated understanding of the inward divinity that is only now beginning to be understood in the West. The Hindu idea of the Atman, often translated into English as "true self" or "god within" is a critical idea missing in the West. We see the self only as ego, and the ego is fallen, sinful, and profane, but the East had the wisdom to glimpse another self "behind" the ego, and mostly hidden from common sight.

Jung used the idea of the Atman as a model for his concept of the Self, a supraordinate entity in the psyche that extends into the nether reaches of the soul, beyond the confines of ego-consciousness. Jung has been criticized by theologians for "divinizing" the self, thus producing what they claim is a religion of narcissism and a deification of the ego. This is strongly evident in the Vatican's recent attack on Jung's work.[30] But Jung is not thinking along Western lines in his concept of the Self, and the theological criticism he has received is ignorant of his Eastern sources, where Atman is not the same as ego. The Atman is the "place" in the soul where time and eternity meet. Atman in Hinduism is related to Brahma, the God of creation. Atman, if you will, is a "fragment" or "spark" of God, a smaller infinity, a humanized representation of God in the person. Atman is what God would look like if it took human form and incarnated in time and space. Atman, in Christian terms, is the mystical or interior Christ, or Merton's "true self."

Gnosticism and Other Heresies

Whenever Westerners have claimed that we have to resist the idolization of Jesus and take responsibility for ourselves, such people have been branded "gnostics" and accused of heresy. Gnosticism saw through the charade of orthodoxy and recognized that its idolatry is not a true religion but one that cuts us off from the spirituality Jesus proclaimed. Orthodoxy refused the gnostic challenge to find divinity within, as well as in all religions and all beings. In blocking gnosticism, and regarding it as a curse, orthodoxy annulled the divine potentials of the human soul and burdened it with an original sin from which it could only be extricated by an outside authority. This was a clever strategy in many ways, as it made Westerners dependent on the church and its ministrations, so that only through the church could individuals find salvation.

The Catholic tradition was quick to proclaim the Latin motto: *extra ecclesiam nulla salus*, "outside the church there is no salvation." This power game is collapsing in our time, as we are becoming aware—partly through our contact with Eastern religions, and through our recovery of Western mystics like Hildegard of Bingen, Meister Eckhart and Julian of Norwich—that the indwelling soul has the capacity to free the human being from illusion, a truth long known in the perennial philosophy but forbidden in the West by clergy. The West has projected all sacredness into one historical revelation, declaring all others spurious, false, or fake, and protecting its truth by issuing threats of hellfire to those who challenge its dominion. Countless gnostics were murdered by orthodox Christianity, and all in the name of a God of love. The Cathars in the south of France were annihilated by the Roman church, and all this to relieve orthodoxy of the burden of discovery of divinity within.

In addition to outlawed gnosticism, there were other heresies in the early church that protested at the rapid rate at which Jesus was promoted to God. Arianism, which derived its inspiration from Arius of Alexandria (250–336 CE) declared that Christ was subordinate to God the Father. Arius argued that Jesus was distinct from God, pointing especially to this gospel passage:

> If you loved me, you would be glad that I am going to the Father; for the Father is greater than I.[31]

Arius' argument was taken seriously at first, and the ensuing controversy forced the early church to organize the first Council of Nicea (325 CE). At that council, however, Arius was pronounced a heretic and his teachings denounced by the congregation of bishops. The official church desperately wanted its spiritual founder to be nothing short of God himself, for political reasons that I will elaborate on in a moment.

After the Arian crisis, Nestorians argued that the human and divine persons of Jesus should be considered separate. This is similar to my emphasis on the separation between ego and soul. Nestorius, bishop of Constantinople, questioned the divinity of the infant Jesus. He thought that too much emphasis was being placed on Jesus as a divine being "sent" from heaven. Nestorius argued that Jesus acquired his divine self at the time of baptism, and not before. The Nestorians believed that at the moment of baptism, Jesus touched divinity and became the Christ. They further maintained that the divine aspect withdrew on the cross, when he cried out, "My God, my God, why hast thou forsaken me."[32] At that moment, Joseph Campbell says, "God did forsake him, and all that died was Jesus again, not the Christ, on the cross."[33] This makes sense because it is by separating the Jesus aspect from the Christ that we can understand the symbolic importance of this figure. He is not a God to be worshipped. He is a holy man who becomes a symbol of what we all must do: balance our human and divine selves, find an equilibrium between them, live the mortal ego *and* the divine spirit.

Absolutism, Violence, and Conflict

When John's Jesus is made to say: "I am the way, the truth and the life; no one comes to the Father, but by me,"[34] this is a powerful statement if read as myth or poetry. But it is dangerous if taken literally. If read outside the context of ritual and poetry, the statement is not only wrong, a distortion of truth, but it is the basis of conflict, violence, and unrest between peoples, races and religions. Indeed this passage from John 14 has long been used as the pretext upon which Christian missionaries have destroyed other faiths, Christian explorers ruined other cultures, and Christian armies marched off to bloody and murderous wars.

But if we understand to whom (or what) the "I" refers, we can see this in a different light. Read metaphorically, we might understand that it is a claim about spirit as archetype, not a human person. John's Jesus is the most "cosmic" and transpersonal of all the gospel accounts. As mentioned, his Jesus is made to say: "Before Abraham was, I am,"[35] and we are made aware that the "I am" cannot refer to a historical person. If this Jesus existed before Abraham, "he" can hardly be a person, but can only be an archetype belonging to the cosmos. As discussed, myth and dream personalize archetypal contents, and this has taken place to such an extent that the archetype of spirit has annulled the historicity of the person. But read literally, John 14 is a call to militarism and triumphalism, such as we have seen throughout the ages—especially the Middle Ages, with its bloodthirsty massacres, crusades, and inquisitions.

The connection between literalism, idolatry, and violence has been researched by a number of scholars. It is shockingly ironic that a religion that preaches peace and fellowship, and defines God as Love, could wreak such havoc that one could be excused for thinking it was a religion of hatred. This is the effect of literalism on any religion: if it takes itself literally, and believes that Jesus is *the* way, truth, and life for all people, not just for Christians. This is one of the most dangerous ideologies the world has ever seen. Numerous scholars doubt that Jesus ever said what John makes him say, but despite the question of authenticity, the statements that are made to come out of his mouth have been inspirational for warmongers, troublemakers, and murderous armies.

However if we deliteralize these statements, and see them as references to the archetype of spirit—found everywhere and in all religions—they become "true." Then we can celebrate that "spirit" has set us free, led us to the divine source, and brought us into redemptive relationship with the eternal. Jesus is the way, truth, and life for those who wish to follow him, but as soon as we apply this to all people it becomes lethal and bizarrely inauthentic.

When Jesus became God

According to contemporary scholars, Jesus did not see himself as God and nor did he view himself as the exclusive "Son of God." Whenever such boasts appear in the gospels, these are viewed as redactions of church authorities, not as quotations from Jesus. According to Andrew Harvey, "the historical Jesus never claimed divinity or unique status; on the contrary, he wanted to empower all human beings, whatever their sex, race or social status, with what he knew to be their essential divine identity so that they could together create a new world, the world of the Kingdom."[36] He continues:

> Modern scholarship makes clear that there is no firm evidence to suggest that Jesus thought of himself as the Messiah, or as the "unique" Son of God: the only title we can safely say he gave himself is Son of Man (as in Matthew 11:19). The Jesus we see in the New Testament and Gnostic Gospels is not always omnipotent or omniscient and does not think of himself as completely divine.[37]
>
> Jesus' message was not about believing in him. Jesus never saw himself in such inflated and exclusive terms and never interpreted his crucifixion as a sacrifice for the sins of the world. Such interpretations represent the visions of later followers, and have nothing authentic about them.[38]

Jesus did not see himself as God, but his followers wanted him to be God. They have "willed" it to be so, by meddling with scriptures, inventing sayings he did not say, attributing doctrinal statements to him that scholars claim came from the early churches. As the Jesus movement expanded and developed in the Middle East, it became subject to increasing intolerance and oppression. According to Dominic Crossan, as social conditions became more inimical to the movement, known as "the Way," the claims about Jesus became more extravagant. John's gospel was written under these conditions when the Way was almost crushed by hostile forces. While the early followers of Christianity remained in the Middle East, it seems likely that some faith communities elevated Jesus to God, while others were content for him to remain prophetic and a great spiritual teacher.

However when Christianity was exported to the West, it seems that Jesus' divine nature became entrenched. At the time when Christianity was established in the West, Europeans had stopped believing in the polytheistic gods of the Greco-Roman world. The Roman Empire was in decline and headed for downfall. It seemed to many that the pagan gods had failed, and they were berated as the work of human invention. If the Empire was to find another religion at this stage, it would have to be a "strong" religion, capable of reinforcing a crumbling empire and shoring up its power. The ethos of the day was impatient with myth and legend: the appearance of a religion from the Middle East, claiming it was based on historical fact, was too good to resist. If its charismatic founder could be said to be God incarnate, so much the better. So it was for these and other political reasons that Emperor Constantine the Great made his adroit decision to commandeer Christianity to bolster his ambitions for the empire.

It is often said that Constantine made Christianity the official religion of Rome, but this is not strictly true. Constantine experienced a personal conversion and ordered that Christians were no longer to be persecuted, referred to today as the "Constantinian turn." He declared the Edict of Milan in 313, which not only awarded tolerance to the new religion but allowed its worshippers to freely evangelize. However, after Constantine, Emperor Julian attempted to revive Hellenistic polytheism and restore the pagan shrines; it was left to his successor, Emperor Theodosius, to crown Christianity as the official religion of state in 380. The process of creating a new imperial religion did not happen suddenly, and there were twists and turns along the way. However, there are vast differences between how theologians discuss this period and how historians represent it.

In his study of this period, *When Jesus Became God*, Richard Rubenstein argues that it was political expediency rather than divine revelation that urged the clergy of the late Roman Empire to turn Jesus of Nazareth into God.[39] In *The Shadow of the Third Century*, Alvin Kuhn adopts a similar approach, arguing that the followers of Jesus had integrity while the fledgling religion was based in the Middle East. But

> ... when the Christian movement passed from the Eastern Mediterranean lands of its genesis and was captured by the churchly authority in the more westerly Roman domain, it suffered a "sea change" which left it completely transformed into something far other than what it was at the outset.[40]

Christianity shifted from a spiritually gifted community to one oriented to militarism, empire, and conquest:

> When the new religion was transported from East to West, it passed from the guardianship and care of a civilization that was still bathed in the genial afterglow of the brightest light of philosophy, and came under the blighting influence of another culture that in the main lacked capacity for spiritual enlightenment, the while it manifested in high degree the talent for world organization.... Christianity was taken up by a culture gifted in extraordinary measure with the power of empire building and by it structuralized into a firm organic body of such coherence that it conquered the Western world.[41]

I don't think things are quite as simple as Kuhn wants them to be. He idealizes the early church in the Middle East, but there were some churches there that had already promoted Jesus to God, and the fourth gospel was written in Patmos, not Rome. But even if Kuhn exaggerates, his basic argument is interesting.

There are mixed opinions about the appropriation of Christianity by Rome. Some theologians and church historians still sing its praises, and see it as a miracle, a sign of the power of Christ to sway the nations and turn the tides of history. God had intervened to bring about his salvific plan. But many scholars, including Harvey Cox, disagree. Cox argues that Constantine imposed "a muscular leadership over the churches, appointing and dismissing bishops, paying salaries, funding buildings and distributing largesse." "But for Christianity it proved to be a disaster: its enthronement actually degraded it." Cox believes that Christianity degenerated from a practice of faith in unseen realities, and the presence of the Spirit, to "a system of mandatory precepts that were codified into creeds and strictly monitored by a powerful hierarchy and imperial decrees." Cox's Protestant prejudices against Catholicism are on display, but I think he has a point. From the open, diverse, tolerant culture of the early church, where differences in faith practices were accepted, Christianity wedded state power, where differences of opinion became "heresy," and "heresy became treason."[42]

While Cox is concerned about faith degenerating into "belief," Kuhn is worried about myth being transformed into "fact." According to Kuhn, Christianity "gained the whole world but lost its soul." The tenets of the faith of Jesus were reversed, and instead of winning soul and losing the world, as Jesus commands, Christianity had twisted its founder's teachings and embarked on a new, sparkling career as "Christendom." The obtuse literalism of the Roman tradition "violated its true sacredness by traducing its structural integrity to nonsense." The Western church proceeded to change all Jewish symbols into facts, which "distorted its truths into ludicrous caricature and baneful forms of error and falsehood." The literalism of the Roman tradition "opened the pathway to the transformation of Christianity into errant Christianism," since such literalism gave rise to "a weird and fantastic delusion of historicized scriptural myths, which has steeped the minds of untold millions in doltish superstition over so many centuries."[43]

The reading of Jesus as the exclusive embodiment of the incarnation of God "strangled the divine instinct in man."[44] The dogma of the Incarnation in the person of Jesus: "brought the entire realm of abstract metaphysical conception down into the world of concrete things, in other words, vicariously represented by a physical person." "The tragedy [is] that the naïve mind takes the symbol for the reality, since its power to see beyond the symbol to a metaphysical reality is feeble. So that to simplify it is to falsify it for the simpleminded."[45] Concrete thinking was designed, Kuhn argues, to win over the naïve minds of the masses. The more "concrete" religion could become, the more it would attract supporters throughout the world. This was a "dumbing down" on a grand scale, and instead of urging people to find within themselves the saving grace of the spirit, they were encouraged to devote themselves to the idolatrous worship of a human being:

> By the time the doctrine of the birth of Christhood in man had been put forth for lowly mental grasp as the birth of a baby on December 25, year one, it was no longer true, but fatally misleading. By the time the crucifixion of the divine had been concretized and historicized as the agony of a body on a wooden cross, it was no longer true, but a delusion and a snare to uncritical thought. Instead of enlightening mankind it would hallucinate him, because his ability to lift it from the concrete to the spiritual sense was non-existent. And by the time the incarnation doctrine had been "made plain" as the descent of God's radiant being into the physical corpus of one man, so that simple minds could see it, it was an outright mockery of truth.[46]

These are harsh and bitter words, but Kuhn is outraged by a process that destroys what we might call the "symbolic attitude." Christ as symbol of the spiritual life in man and woman is lost when he becomes an idol. By elevating Jesus to the level of God, the spiritual process in our lives is literalized to such an extent that we are closed off from our spiritual potentials. When the symbol is no longer translucent, but becomes an idol in its own right, the devotees are no longer transported by it to the divine, but are locked into a cycle of adoration and worship. Our consciousness is not elevated, but submerged in an emotionalism that is found even today in the lives of conservative evangelicals and fundamentalists. This is not, strictly speaking, religion at all, and it is certainly not spirituality.

Onward Christian Soldiers

If religion and spirituality can be defined as the transformative encounter with the divine in our interior lives, in the world around us and in creation, this adoration of a historical person could be said to freeze the spirit and lock it into a state of transference. This keeps the subject subordinate to projection and locked into an infantile state with regard to his or her potential for transformation. But this is only to look at the psychological effects. There are the social effects, which stir people to a sense of frenzied commitment that knows no bounds. If one's own religion contains God incarnate, and this figure is the sole embodiment of the divine, all other religions are seen as second-rate and unworthy. The literalism and absolutism that was promoted in the third and fourth centuries set the scene for a bloody and savage history under the name of a loving God. As Kuhn put it, the Roman doctrine led to "the military Christianity of the Middle Ages, a modification of the religion of the Gospel, directly opposed to its genuine principles."[47]

It is significant to consider that the worldly success of Christianity was born in the midst of warfare and strife. In 312 Constantine had a vision of the Cross before the Battle of Milvian Bridge, and in that instant he promised that if he won the battle he would convert the empire to Christianity: he won and the beginning of Christendom, the fusion of church and state, was underway. We have already considered the next steps in the institutionalization of this religion as the faith of an empire. In the year 380, the Edict of Thesalonica *ordered* all subjects of the empire to profess the faith of the Roman bishops. Hardly an auspicious beginning for a religion that was meant to be based on love and peace. Indeed, the teaching of Jesus was that one should love one's enemies, and this was contradicted at the time of the "Constantinian shift." As soon as Christianity wedded political power, it had blood on its hands. Sociologist Max Horkheimer wrote:

> Anyone who does not see from the gospel that Jesus died in *opposition* to his institutional representatives is unable to read. This theology is the most cruel mockery which ever befell an idea.[48]

Blake put the crisis succinctly when he wrote:

> Art degraded, imagination denied, war governed the nations.[49]

The loss of metaphorical awareness is not just a spiritual problem. When the imaginal is "degraded" or "denied," there are real public and social consequences. War and conflict result when men and women fail to discern the metaphorical nature of their beliefs. If the creeds and dogmas are literally true, the claims they make about the "one true God," the "only Son of God," and the one way of doing things are imposed upon the world in oppressive ways. Respect for others and different forms of truth is lost when one is consumed by the thought that what has been "revealed" in one's own tradition is priceless beyond measure and good for all. Evangelism gives way to triumphalism and oppression. Civilizing morality, tolerance and humanity are eclipsed when religious enthusiasm holds sway.

A literal reading of any religion is an excuse for adherents to enact violence and subjugate others in the name of "truth." This is why Kershner wrote that if the Christian gnostics had prevailed, instead of being defeated by the literalists in the imperial church,

> there would have been no Inquisition and no burning of heretics by either Catholics or Protestants. It was the triumph of the imperialistic God of Tertullian and Augustine which led to most of the later horrors in the history of the Church.[50]

If the Christianity we know today was created by Rome to suit its purposes, this imperialism is still evident today, and the cause of much violence and oppression committed in the name of this "imperialistic God." The philosopher Voltaire made the link between violence, literalism, and absolutism when he famously said: "Men will continue to commit atrocities as long as they continue to believe absurdities." As the world becomes more dangerous and as fundamentalism increases, it is of the utmost importance for humanity to distinguish between a faith that is spiritual, and productive of peace, and one that is warlike and productive of violence.

Jesus the Mirror of Our Projections

Jesus expressed in his life and ministry the "new dispensation" that was constellated at the beginning of our common era. God had been distanced from humanity; or rather humanity had lost sight of God, had "fallen short," and there was an imperative to move closer to the divine. In preaching the gospel of divine proximity, Jesus attracted to himself our projections of the spiritual faculty in the soul that would make this possible. He carried the sacred heart for us, that part of ourselves where we come before the divine and ask for rapprochement and forgiveness. In the East, it is the Atman, and it is placed in the interiority of the person, but in the West we have no such equivalent, and thus for the West Jesus was our interiority personified. We asked Jesus to bear an impossible burden for us, and the West experienced him as Redeemer, Messiah, Second Adam, and God. Undoubtedly he was some of these things in his life, but by the time the gospels were written the real person had vanished beneath layers of archetypal projections.

This idolization of Jesus had the effect of alienating us from our interiority. Identification with Jesus, intensified by doctrine, creed, and ritual, generated the expectation that his achievement of integration with the divine would be ours as well. Evangelicals taught that we were on the brink of a new world, where Jesus would lead human society to glorious redemption. But this was largely a religious illusion, a hallucination, because Jesus was not God and had not changed the nature of reality. Our distance from God remained, and we had to traverse this painful distance ourselves, each in our individual ways. Religion could not substitute for spiritual experience, try as religion might to convince us of this fact.

At the same time as the idolization of Jesus progressed, alienation from the divine was expressed in the increasing militarization of the Christian religion. Not long after the empire had made this religion its official faith, Europe was plunged into the Dark Ages. According to Petrarch, who coined the term, the Dark Ages began in the sixth century and extended to the thirteenth—seven hundred years of darkness. It ushered in cultural decline, social breakdown, population unrest, violence, and inhumanity, all of which indicated that the human soul had not been saved. The church argued that people had not taken Jesus into their hearts, but in the church too there was widespread inhumanity. Throughout this period we see the church engaged in the violation of human rights, disrespect of non-Christians, inquisitions, torture, and brutality. It sanctioned the crusades against Muslims, the persecution of the Jews, the murder of "witches," "gnostics," "heathens," and "dissenters." We find the idolization of Jesus and the brutalization of humanity moving in tandem.

The fact that the Jesus of love and fellowship could be transformed so perversely into a champion of war and violence was evidence enough that the idolization was not working. It was not changing people into followers of Christ; rather, they were molding him into the image of their own base instincts: hatred, fear of the other, lust for conquest. The experiment with Jesus had been a failure, and there could be no redemption by proxy. Individuals had to work toward their own salvation, and societies had to begin the long struggle toward peace and harmony, which truly began to emerge, ironically, with the rise of secular humanism and the Intellectual Enlightenment. The secular West has done a far better job at securing respect, social tolerance, and fairness than religion. Perhaps under secular conditions we can find the freedom to discover the spirituality and compassion that Jesus commended.

Notes

1. William Blake, "Laocoön" aphorisms (1820), *Blake: Complete Writings*, ed. Geoffrey Keynes (Oxford: Oxford University Press, 1976), p. 776.
2. Blake, ibid.
3. Northrop Frye, *Words with Power* (Ontario: Viking, 1990), p. xiv.
4. Theodor Adorno, "Reason and Revelation" (1969), quoted in Hans Kung, *Does God Exist?* (London: Collins, 1980), p. 332.
5. Matthew Arnold, "The Study of Poetry" (1880), in M. H. Abrams, ed., *The Norton Anthology of English Literature* (New York: W. W. Norton & Company, 1987), p. 2171.
6. Alfred Adler, "The Masculine Protest" (1912), in *The Individual Psychology of Alfred Adler* (New York: Basic Books, 1964).
7. Karen Armstrong, *The Case for God: What Religion Really Means* (London: The Bodley Head, 2009), p. 3.
8. Bernie Neville, "Celebrating the Solstice," in Annette Lowe, ed., *Jung Talks: 50 Years of the C. G. Jung Society of Melbourne* (Melbourne: C. G. Jung Society of Melbourne, 2011), p. 175.
9. Blake, "The Marriage of Heaven and Hell" (1793), *Blake: Complete Writings*, ed. Geoffrey Keynes (Oxford: Oxford University Press, 1976), p. 153.
10. Matthew 7:3–5.
11. The allusion is to St Augustine, who thanked God that he was not responsible for his sensuous dreams.
12. John 3:18.
13. John 8:56.
14. John 8: 57.
15. John 8:58.
16. John 8:59.
17. Marcus Borg, *The Heart of Christianity: Rediscovering a Life of Faith* (New York: HarperSanFrancisco, 2003).
18. Robert M. Price, *The Incredible Shrinking Son of Man* (New York: Prometheus, 2003).
19. Matthew 4:17; 10:7; and many parallels in the gospels.

20. John 10:34.
21. Psalms 82:6.
22. John 10:35–36.
23. Matthew 5:44.
24. Revelation 21:6–7.
25. *The Gospel According to Thomas* (New York: Harper & Row, 1959), 80:26–81:4; p. 3.
26. Tom Harpur, *The Pagan Christ: Is Blind Faith Killing Christianity?* (Sydney: Allen & Unwin, 2005), pp. 2–3.
27. Luke 17:20–21; KJV.
28. Matthew 13:9.
29. Matthew 7:5.
30. See the Vatican's attack on Jung's depth psychology in its document: *Jesus Christ: The Bearer of the Water of Life: A Christian Reflection on the "New Age."* Vatican, Rome. Located at: http://www.vatican.va/roman_curia/pontifical_councils/interelg/documents/rc_pc_interelg_doc_20030203_new-age_en.html.
31. John 14:28.
32. Mark 15:34; Matthew 27:46.
33. Joseph Campbell, "Understanding the Symbols of Judeo-Christian Spirituality" (1971), in Eugene Kennedy ed., *Thou Art That: Transforming Religious Metaphor. The Collected Works of Joseph Campbell*, Vol. 1 (Novato, CA: New World Library, 2001), p. 71.
34. John 14:6.
35. John 8:58.
36. Andrew Harvey, *Son of Man: The Mystical Path to Christ* (New York: Jeremy P. Tarcher, 1998), p. xiii.
37. Ibid, p. 6.
38. Ibid.
39. Richard E. Rubenstein, *When Jesus Became God: The Epic Fight over Christ's Divinity in the Last Days of Rome* (New York: Harcourt Brace & Company, 1999).
40. Alvin Boyd Kuhn, *Shadow of the Third Century: A Revaluation of Christianity* (Surrey, British Columbia: Eremitical Press, 1949), p. 32.
41. Ibid.
42. Harvey Cox, *The Future of Faith* (New York: HarperCollins, 2009), p. 6.
43. Kuhn, *Shadow of the Third Century*, pp. 51, 3.
44. Ibid, p. 40.
45. Ibid, p. 45.
46. Ibid, p. 45.
47. Ibid, p. 48.
48. Max Horkheimer, *Decline: Notes 1950–1969*, quoted in Hans Kung, *Does God Exist?* (London: Collins, 1980), p. 325.
49. Blake, "Laocoon" aphorisms, p. 775.
50. Frederick D. Kershner, *Pioneers of Christian Thought* (1930; Freeport, New York: Books for Libraries Press, 1968), p. 87.

5

The Myth of the Virgin Birth

*The myths never speak about anything alien or distant:
ultimately they always deal with our own existence,
insofar as it opens itself to the divine.
— Eugen Drewermann*[1]

The stories at the beginning and end of Jesus' life, the virgin birth, and physical resurrection, are myths. This is obvious to most educated people, but believers—including those who are educated—still like to cling to the notion that they are "true." This is where our language lets us down. One could say that they are true as images, and explore a spiritual truth that is unknown to many. But the ways in which they are true remain hidden and rarely understood except by those who have studied such fields as mythology, depth psychology, mysticism, and poetry. The dogmatic approach to religion does not avail itself of this mystical meaning. It does not even know it is present and fails to recognize it as the true meaning. It looks at scripture through a realistic lens, and is caught in the illusion that this lens is validating, while the mythic lens is seen as undermining. Once we get over this prejudice, we walk in a larger universe, one that makes a lot of sense.

The Dead Hand of Patriarchy

Eugen Drewermann is a former German Catholic priest who has been exploring the inner meaning of the birth and death of Jesus. He came to the conclusion that these events in the life of Jesus are myths, but they are not "merely" myths. He put it this way:

> If these are not *just* images, the world can live on them.[2]

They aren't just images, as they illuminate the way for any true seeker. They are not empty myths, they are myths *of* something. When he decided they were myths, he was aware that many inside and outside the church would mistake his meaning. He called on Rome to understand the stories symbolically so they might become coherent and meaningful for believers today. He was making this plea from a position of faith. His one desire, he wrote, was not to destroy faith but to "bring the confessions of faith into the language of our time."[3] What better way to align a tradition with the time than to confront the issue of literalism and avoid the pitfalls of a banal reading of miracles?

In 1989 Eugen Drewermann was asked to explain himself to his ecclesial authorities, given his nonliteral reading of scripture and doctrine. After an inadequate process of enquiry he was summoned before the Bishop of Paderborn and refused the right to teach or preach. By 1992, after Rome had pondered his "scandalous" reading of biblical "history" (prompting Rome to take renewed interest in Jung's writings, which had inspired Drewermann), his priesthood was annulled, and he was not given the dignity of a fair trial. The bishop acted as prosecuting attorney, presiding judge, and jury. Drewermann felt annihilated by this miscarriage of justice. In a secular world, people would not be treated this way—they would have the right to an unprejudiced trial. If anyone says religious authorities are humane, let this be proof to the contrary. These institutions behave like any extremist right-wing regime. When it comes to challenging its doctrinal literalism, the Roman church is about as "Christian" as the Roman empire upon which its structure is based. The outward show, the religiosity, means nothing.

Can We Be "Moved" By Myths?

Drewermann wrestled with a problem that has occupied my mind for years: how to refute obtuse literalism without at the same time appearing to be destructive of faith and negative toward scripture? The question about how to redeem the tradition or institution itself is too large to take up at this point.

The cards are stacked against any priest who tries to talk sense to authorities on these matters. Such authorities assume subversion and are not prepared to engage in discussions about myth, poetry, or the intentions of the authors of scripture. All of these matters are swept aside, as the church believes it already knows the intentions of scripture, which were to record historical events in the life of the Messiah. Drewermann said these miraculous events are not arbitrarily invented, but are the substance of spiritual experience, expressed in symbolic terms. They are, as it were, "true myths," not to be treated with disrespect.

The Myth of the Virgin Birth

Anyone who makes this claim today, but wants to emphasize that they still have faith, has to engage in a kind of "re-education" of his or her audience and accusers. But as Drewermann found, few of his accusers wanted to find out what he had discovered.

The problem of hermeneutics, or methods of interpretation, is not to everyone's liking, and believers are troubled by it if they feel it will undermine their beliefs. Drewermann is one of the most insightful commentators on the crisis of interpretation. He puts the conundrum clearly:

> For us moderns there is no longer any direct access to the ways mythical narratives think and speak: Whenever we suppose to take them "literally" we misunderstand them. And whenever we try to read them "symbolically," we risk deflating the seriousness of their claims on us and flattening their unconditional validity into something arbitrary and aesthetic.[4]

Believers take the narratives literally and the "enlightened" read them as "mere" symbols, but in so doing reduce them to "something arbitrary and aesthetic." We don't know how to read myths without falling into one kind of error or another. The enlightened think they have a handle on the situation, but their smugness and superiority barely disguise their spiritual poverty. The archetypal images of religion are not abstract or aesthetic but point to profound realities. One can only hope that a new wave of mystical feeling might overtake us, because that alone will save us from fundamentalist error on the one hand and intellectualism on the other. But one fears that we might be too late to save the "seriousness" of the images, as Drewermann puts it. We will have to roll back some of the effects of the Intellectual Enlightenment to allow a mystical attitude to prevail, otherwise the myths will have no meaning and not move us.

Drewermann gets it right when he cries:

> Is there nothing beyond the Enlightenment dichotomy between myth and history?[5]

We need some kind of middle term between myth and history, now that "myth" has been discounted. We cannot afford spiritual truth to be placed in the same category as nonsense, fantasy, or fiction. The Enlightenment, as he surmises, has created this crisis, which is another way of saying that logos has held us to ransom.

The field of Islamic studies has faced a similar crisis. But rather than allow sacred scriptures to be dismissed as "imaginary," Henry

Corbin, professor of Islamic Studies at the Sorbonne in Paris, arrived at the term "imaginal" to refer to the "intermediary" realm in which sacred scripture could be said to be true.[6] "Imaginal" had a connection with "imagination," but was felt to refer to spiritual realities. The imaginal pointed to a kind of "theo-poesis," or a poetry that reveals the actions and nature of God. Corbin differentiated the imaginal from the imaginary, and yet we do not have a similar level of sophistication in Christian studies.[7] Corbin revived the Latin idea of a *mundus imaginalis*, an imaginal world in which images of the sacred were true and thus could be protected from the modern tendency to dismiss them as fictitious. Those with a background in Socrates, Plato, and Neoplatonic philosophy would recognize here the notion of the *eidos*, the realm of "Ideas," which Plato claimed was located in the mind of God. It seems that we need to move in a direction similar to the one Corbin mapped out for Islamic studies, if the sense of the sacred in Christianity is to survive.[8]

Inside the churches there is a clinging to the historical sense of scripture, as if no other approach could make it meaningful. Outside the churches we often meet with the opposite response: people are relieved to hear that they might read the stories symbolically, as their rejection of the biblical tradition was based on their inability to accept "fairy tales" as facts. To hear that they were not intended as historical, but were written as poetic images of spiritual life, can be liberating for people. Tom Harpur writes from this position:

> The spiritual, mythical approach to the Bible and to Christian faith . . . solves the enigmas of Scripture and the Christos story as nothing else can do. Bible stories come alive with amazing new freshness, believability, and power. Our potential for Christhood, and for experiencing the indwelling spirit of God here and now, sounds forth in a clear and relevant message for everyone.[9]

Once we grasp the fact that scripture is not alleged history, but poetic description of the spirit, we can experience something of the exaltation and joy with which Harpur approaches the question of interpretation. These scriptures are not about the remote past, but the present: they are speaking to us, are about us, and are trying to show us our spiritual depths. They are about "our potential Christhood" and "experience of the indwelling spirit of God here and now." That "amazing freshness" is still available, if we are prepared to see that the scriptures are about the fate of the human soul. So when it comes to the virgin birth or resurrection, we can appreciate these miracles as personally relevant:

> Seen in their new light, the rituals of Easter and Christmas, along with Christian symbols such as the Cross and the Eucharist, glow with renewed significance and depth.[10]

I admire his enthusiasm and experience this myself at times, but when I am with believers who think that a mythical approach is a desecration of scripture it is hard to keep this enthusiasm alive.

What is important is to bear in mind that this shift from the literal to the symbolic is a twofold process, involving suspicion and affirmation. We are "suspicious" of the religious statement's factual nature, but we "affirm" its meaning. These two actions are hard to perform at the same time, because the shock (for some) that they are not literally true generates an emotional response and sense of loss, such that it is hard to be upbeat about the possibilities. Harpur speaks of "piercing the literal sense of the Bible to reveal its hidden, mystical inner core," and says this "can free us up and offer new, transformative spiritual vistas and insights."[11] But it is hard to realize this if, for instance, one has spent sixty years of one's life in the literal mode. One needs time to grieve, and the person "enlightening" the believer has to take this on board as a consideration. This is not an intellectual exercise, or a university lesson in hermeneutics. It is the believer's life we are talking about.

Sexual Politics and the Uses of Myth

I recall believing in the virgin birth as a boy. It was sacred, revered, and any suggestion that it was untrue was met with a frowned resistance. Then as a young man at university, I recall moving into reverse gear, and finding the idea repugnant. It seemed to be yet another example of how patriarchal culture sets up unattainable ideals for women about sexuality, purity, and saintliness. The virgin birth seemed to set up a persecutory ideal. When myths are taken literally, the impact on human beings, society, and history can be devastating. During my awakening to sexual politics, the "sacredness" of the image became eclipsed by social realities.

The myth of the virgin birth, assumed to be fact, has damaged women over centuries. If Mary is believed to be a virgin, and "untainted" by sexual relations with a human partner, this established an impossible standard by which women would be judged. The implication was that female sexuality was impure, licentious, and evil, and only a miraculous act by an interventionist (and all-male) God could rescue women from their sinfulness. This gross distortion of women was, in turn, based on a literalized interpretation of an earlier myth. The creation myth of the Hebrews, taken literally by Christians but not always by Jews, constructs Eve as the temptress in Paradise, luring man to his destruction. Adam says to God: "The woman you gave me to be with, she gave me fruit from the tree, and I ate."[12] Eve was believed to be the source of sin, a curse perpetuated down the generational line by all "daughters of Eve."

This generational "evil" was supposedly arrested by the Virgin Mary, whose purity was espoused by patriarchal tradition and finally dogmatized in the Immaculate Conception promulgated by Pope Pius IX in 1854. The notion behind the dogma of Mary's immaculate nature was that God intervened at the moment of her conception, and blocked the generational transmission of original sin. This suited patriarchal prejudices about women, whose "sinfulness" was cancelled by supernatural intervention. The fact that "Eve" never existed as a person, and Mary's "virginity" is a misrepresentation of myth, never occurred to the patriarchs of Christian tradition, who were happy to pretend that myth was fact to perpetuate these obscene views of female sexuality.

The virgin birth has nothing to do with facts, either of the biological or historical kind. The idea that Mary's saintliness somehow atones for the evils of Eve is an invention of the early and medieval church, which we can dispense with. It is interesting to note that the theological emphasis on the virginity of Mary coincided with the emphasis on the condition of virginity among dedicated Christian women in the fourth and fifth centuries. It was also linked with the declaration of Mary as the "Mother of God" at the Council of Ephesus in 431. The heinous results of misreading myth as fact has no more tragic example than the construction of Eve as evil and Mary as saintly in Christendom's sexual politics.

More recently, the patriarchal reading of these stories has been turned on its head by feminist theologians and scholars. Marina Warner, Rosemary Radford Ruether, Marija Gimbutas, and others have argued that the story of Mary's virginity can be recontextualized in terms of matriarchal mythology.[13] There are numerous contexts in which a pagan goddess calls on a god to impregnate her and deliver a child.[14] In the matriarchal systems of pre-Christian times, women sometimes saw themselves as self-sufficient, as not requiring men for the tasks of daily life or even for the task of conception. As Drewermann points out:

> Scenes like that of a virgin's conceiving no doubt derive from a matriarchal world, in which the Great Goddess had no need of a man to awaken fertility and life within her.[15]

The Myth of the Virgin Birth

Such images and scenarios can be found in the matriarchal religions of Egypt, Phrygia, Mesopotamia, and Crete. Ironically, when Mary was declared *Theotokos* ("God-bearer") at the Council of Ephesus, that place was the greatest temple-city in the Near East of the Goddess of Many Names: Artemis, Ishtar, Astarte, Anahit, Aphrodite, and Isis. The cult of the Virgin Mary as the Black Madonna, not only tolerated but encouraged by the patriarchal church, has roots in the matriarchal traditions of Isis and Artemis.[16] A knowledge of mythology and the historical background of the virgin birth can thus completely reverse the view that the virgin birth is a patriarchal image born of a masculine religion. Instead of downgrading women's sexuality, or advocating chastity, it can be read as a celebration of feminine self-sufficiency. If men can "work" the myth to their advantage, so too can women construct the myth according to feminist ideals. While the move from patriarchal to matriarchal interpretation is arresting, there is an even deeper layer that compels attention.

The Myth and Its Background

We need to peel away the layers of distortion around this myth and return to its essential core. The virgin birth points to an inner meaning that few have discerned. It refers to the spiritual process by which the soul comes into being. The soul appears to us as a "miracle"; its birth is not a normal birth and does not require sexual intercourse for it to arise. When viewed in nonliteral terms, the virgin birth makes a lot of sense, insofar as it represents an ancient form of psychology. Jesus, as a symbol of the universal soul, comes "into" the world in a miraculous manner, and the business of sexual politics is a distortion of the deep ground of this myth. It is a myth, not in the sense of an outright deception, but in the special sense of telling a story to explain a spiritual condition using bodily metaphors.

Drewermann argues that we have to stick to the image and interpret it according to its desired intention:

> The mythical genealogy and infancy narrative of Jesus must not be read as fantastic biography but as symbolic description of the character's nature. What the text tells us about the "childhood" of Jesus, does not contain specific reminiscences of his youth. Rather it provides a portrait of his spiritual position and roots.[17]

Jesus is "born of a virgin" as a symbol of his purity, his birth is "attended by wise men" as a symbol of his wisdom; it is "announced by a bright star" and "witnessed by shepherds tending their flocks by night" as a symbol of his cosmic significance and ability to reach the lowliest of people. At this birthplace, animals are present, symbolizing his proximity to nature and innocent life. He is "king of kings" because he represents the triumph of spirit over worldly power, and he "comes from heaven" because his roots are in spirit, not the transitory world. Every detail of the Jesus story accords with a symbolic portrayal of the power of spirit in the human soul that has awoken to its divine potential. Needless to say, if we take each of these details literally we end up with a fairy tale that is divorced from the meaning of the nativity of Jesus.

Bishop John Spong insisted that we should penetrate into biblical imagery to find its spiritual meaning. Spong often announced in lectures and writings that the response to the infancy symbols and miracles ought not be, "Did they happen?"—a logos question—but "What do they mean?," a mythos question. A miracle is not something that happened but something "going on" in what happens. It is a level of significance that makes itself felt in images. The symbolic images draw out and hold a deeper layer of meaning. A miracle such as the virgin birth is not a physical event, but a spiritual significance astir in the event. The "miracle" is its possibility, its inward meaning. Acrimonious debates have taken place about whether the virgin birth did or did not happen, but the acrimony is useless, and energy should be redirected into questions of meaning.

If, in the ancient world, the life of an important historical or legendary figure was narrated by scribes, they would refer to the birth of this figure as "virginal," as a sign of his or her special character. In ancient writings there are at least two hundred examples of historical and/or mythic figures born of a virgin. The Roman Emperor Augustus was said to have been born of a virgin. The idea of such a birth was code for "one who is favored by the gods." According to anthropologist James George Frazer, such births were universal across the ancient world, from Egypt to Turkey to Crete. Many were found in Mesopotamian and Babylonian cultures. In Egypt, every Pharaoh was said to have had a virgin birth, and this was meant as a qualification for his being dubbed "Son of God"—or rather, Son of the Sun God, Ra. In Crete, Turkey, and Sumeria, the dying and resurrecting gods Attis, Adonis, and Tammuz had virgin births. In Greece and Rome, the convention was perpetuated, and there were variations of miraculous births, such as the birth of Aphrodite from the foamy sea and the birth of Athena from the head of Zeus.

The Myth of the Virgin Birth

Frazer's twelve-volume *The Golden Bough* records hundreds of these instances[18] and makes us realize that a virgin birth was an accepted literary trope at the time. It is a way of designating the holiness of a person who impacted the world in a significant manner. It seems that the last of these "virgin births" was Jesus, after which the trope died out. Our cultural memory has conveniently "forgotten" or suppressed the other hundreds of these births, and has enshrined only one of them. Significantly, there is no virgin birth in the earliest gospel, Mark, which was written seventy years after the birth of Jesus. Mark also makes it clear that Jesus had four brothers (James, Joses, Judas, and Simon) and two sisters (unnamed), so he must have felt that the virginal trope was not fundamental to the story he wanted to tell. In Paul's letters, written between 50 and 64 CE, and thus before Matthew, Luke, and John, there is no reference to a miraculous birth. The idea of Mary's virginity was added later, in Matthew, and received its most florid and heightened expression in Luke, which added an "Annunciation" sequence, where Mary's "betrothal" to the Holy Spirit is announced. There is no virgin birth in John, but in that gospel Jesus is divine and a virgin birth is assumed.

According to Spong, the figure of Joseph as the earthly father of Jesus is entirely mythical. He argues that Mary was a single mother, with several children born before Jesus. This was, he said, "a scandal that needed to be covered up," first by the idea that Jesus was born of the Holy Spirit, and second by the notion that he had an earthly patron in the figure of Joseph, the carpenter.[19] In "The Parents of Jesus: Fictionalized Composites," Spong presents a compelling argument that Mary and Joseph have been shaped by myth, and although Mary was a real figure, Joseph was nonexistent and invented only to satisfy the requirements of the story in a patriarchal tradition. Mary was a pregnant single mother, unwed with no partner, and "Once the idea of a virgin birth had become part of the tradition [near the midpoint of the ninth decade CE], there was a need for a male figure to provide the protective cover for the pregnant Mary in that cruel and patriarchal society." Spong continues:

> The virgin birth and the earthly father appear in the tradition simultaneously [around 85 CE]. If there had been no virgin tradition, the character of Joseph would never have been created. I do not believe that a person named Joseph who was the protective earthly father of Jesus ever existed. Joseph is from start to finish a mythological character, created by the author of the gospel we call Matthew.[20]

Spong provides an elaborate reading of the scriptures to support his contention, which we need not repeat here. But in texts in which historicity was never a priority, and only "meaning" counted, it does not surprise me to find that figures never suspected in the past of being mythological are precisely that.

It was while reading Frazer's *The Golden Bough* as a graduate student that I began to realize that the virgin birth I had rejected could be reclaimed as myth. And importantly, it could be meaningful as myth. My objections to religion disappeared once I could see that it was poetry speaking in metaphorical images. The notion that Jesus' virgin birth was historical is absurd once we set it in its context and realize that such ideas were legion. I have commented on the Western world and the ancient Near East, but according to Campbell, "American Indian mythologies abound in virgin births."[21] He claims they are found in most indigenous cultures in the world. Before the study of comparative religion and mythology, none of us had access to this knowledge. Without context or genre we are likely to respond to the birth of Jesus either with credulous wonder or incredulous scorn. Believers see it as a supernatural event that defies reason; unbelievers as nonsense that deserves derision.

Divine Insemination

The extended infancy narrative of Jesus in Luke—the most elaborate in the Bible—is "pure myth," according to Drewermann. He claims that it is meant to be understood as symbolic "by those who share the mythic legacy."[22] In the ancient world, many shared this legacy; today, we have to work hard to recover it. In Luke we are introduced to "the primeval mythologem of the birth of the divine child or the divine king from the blessed virgin."[23] Drewermann argues that the infancy narrative, including the Annunciation sequence with the Angel, and the Magnificat, is based on the Egyptian myth of the birth of the Pharaoh. But the Egyptian context is only one in which an angel or supernatural being heralds the birth of a new god:

> In folktales from all over the world the appearance of an "angel" so often introduces the birth of a divine child.[24]

Angels were standard literary tropes of the ancient world, symbols of a spiritual world that acts independently of human nature. Angels, virgin births, and sons of gods were all "of a piece" in their Middle Eastern context. The mythic nature of these beings and events was self-evident to all who shared these narratives. Myth was accepted as a special kind of truth, as the imaginative vehicle of revelation. But Drewermann, like Kuhn and Armstrong, argues that as the Christian faith relocated to Western Europe, the mythic understanding of the narrative was lost. The West, not known for its spiritual or imaginative genius, took the stories literally and began to distort them.

The myth of the immaculate conception, heralded by the angel Gabriel, seems to derive from much older myth. Gabriel, whose Hebrew name means, "my husband (*gabri*) is God (*El*)," proclaims in Luke:

> The Holy Spirit will come upon you,
> and the power of the Most High will overshadow you;
> therefore the child to be born will be called holy,
> the Son of God.[25]

The background to this is the Greek myth of Leda and the swan, where the god Zeus, in the shape of a swan, has intercourse with a chosen virgin. The offspring of this intercourse is the divine child. W. B. Yeats immortalized this in "Leda and the Swan," in which the erotic compulsion of the god for the virgin is seen as the driving force of creation.[26] In this myth, the swan is Zeus, whose union with Leda produced Helen, the greatest beauty of the ancient world. Another religious myth older than Christianity is found in the Psalms and the liturgy of the synagogue, in which the Hebrew God "overshadows" those he loves. The Hebrew expression, "in the shadow of your wings," refers to the sense of refuge and intimacy between God and his faithful. Although the idea of "overshadowing" is not explicitly erotic, the suggestion is that this is indeed an act of intercourse, which is made powerfully erotic in the poem by Yeats. Schalom Ben-Chorin claims that "to the mind of the ancient world there was nothing scandalous about this."[27]

Nor in these Jewish or Hellenic contexts did this intercourse mean that the one born of this coupling was the one and only son of the Most High. The suggestion was that this coupling could take place often, perhaps countless times, whenever the divine found an avenue to penetrate into the heart of a worthy subject. The motif of the divine penetrating the womb of a virgin is symbolic of the incarnational drive in the Godhead: its sexual-spiritual compulsion to reproduce itself in the core of the person, and transform that person into the likeness of the divine. As Yeats put it, the virgin soul, overcome by the god, "put on his knowledge with his power."[28] The soul is transformed into the likeness of the power that overshadows it.

The idea of the virgin *inseminated* by the divine and giving birth to a "being" who is more than human is a perfect example of what Aquinas referred to as the metaphorical function of scripture, which is to "deliver spiritual things to us beneath metaphors taken from bodily things."[29] Naturally the denotative content of the metaphor is subordinate to its connotative suggestion, and to see the denotation without the connotation is to miss the point. It is not a biological statement, but a spiritual imagining. Speaking of the Annunciation in Luke, Schalom Ben-Chorin writes:

> We are dealing here with a myth, whose generative power must not be underestimated. The idea of the God-man, who is a son of the Most High, is evidently one of the archetypal ideals of the soul that are just as real as historical events, only in a different sense.[30]

This scholar is careful not to suggest that his interpretation of the miracle implies hostility or rejection. One has to be careful of tone when we utter the word "myth." It is not merely a myth, because it is "archetypal," as he says. As an archetype, that is, a universally recurring motif, it is an ideal trope of the soul. As a recurring image it is "just as real as historical events, only in a different sense." This "different sense" is what we have lost. The virgin birth is real even though it never took place. It is real as an archetype, a motif, a longing of the soul. It is real as mythos, and can be trusted at that level, because it points to something real in our experience: how the soul is unexpectedly inseminated by the divine.

Spiritual Rebirth

The Christmas story remains important to me, but I do not celebrate it in the conventional way. For me it is not a commemoration of a historical event—I don't believe Jesus was born of a virgin, or that he was born in Bethlehem. Nor did it take place on December 25—all of these are inventions of tradition. The idea that Christmas is now a consumerist shopping spree, a festival of buying and selling, of overindulging, eating, and drinking—this aspect repels me. I participate in the ritual because it is what families do, not knowing the real meaning. For the secular world, the idea of happiness conjures up the indulgence of the appetites, a sorry response of a spiritually bankrupt society. It is the only kind of fulfillment that the secular world knows. It knows there is more to life than what we have, but it interprets this "more" in literal ways, as consumerist economies do. Consumerist societies are based on the misrepresentation of spiritual desire, packaged as modernity knows how.

The "more" we long for is rebirth, to be born again, in a new way, to be recreated. The more we long for is to be inseminated by Spirit, to be given a new life, an immortal nature, to connect us to the cosmos and not merely to society, with its tawdry rituals and misunderstandings of myths. The divine insemination is not a once-only event in our lifetime, it has to happen every day, and we have to put a lot of energy into the task of remaking ourselves in the likeness of God. It happens from within, of its own accord, but we have to lend it awareness and understanding.

When I think of Christmas, I think of the birth of the divine child, as a symbol of Jesus' life. To take this literally is to undermine the true meaning of Jesus, which is that he lived and died so we could see our own divine depths. At this level, the divine child born in Bethlehem to a virgin mother on December 25 is entirely "true." It is a mystic symbol of the birth of the soul in us, a soul impregnated with divine pneuma. The soul is not born through intercourse; it is an immaculate conception, something that arises without human intervention. It arises of its own accord, ordained by the spirit that rolls through all things. It happens to us, takes us by surprise, and when I read Luke's story of the annunciation, and see Renaissance paintings of Mary's surprise at the sudden appearance of the angel, I think of our own surprise at the appearance of the spirit in our lives. The deeper we penetrate to the mystery of Jesus, the closer we are brought to ourselves.

The birth of the divine child symbolizes our rebirth. We are born as physical beings, to real parents, and then we are twice-born as spiritual beings, to parents who are in "heaven." The physical parents are not our only parents, which is why we used to have the tradition of "godparents," and why Jesus could not be too concerned about his worldly parents because he had to be focused on the business of his father in heaven.[31] This is the mythic background for why young children, at a certain age, often become inexplicably obsessed with the idea that their parents are not their real parents, but they must be from somewhere else. I had this feeling myself, at about the age of ten, and left home at one point to walk the streets in search of my true parents. My parents were alarmed, my siblings found it funny, but I felt a strong drive to find my true belonging. All this is part of the spiritual quest, the recognition that we are not entirely of this world, but that we have a more distant parentage, a spiritual lineage, an ancestral background.

Jesus was one of the many children in the world who felt strongly that his parents were not the answer to his existence. There was something "more," and that is why he preached the necessity for rebirth: "unless a man is born from above, he cannot see the kingdom of God."[32] In some translations "born from above" is replaced with "born again." He also said: "unless you become like children you will not see the kingdom of heaven." Spiritual rebirth, which grants us the capacity to "see" spiritual reality, is connected to the birth of the divine child in us. It is the inner child, the soul, that awakens miraculously and begins to bear witness to the spiritual realm. Our normal self, the ego, does not see spirit and may even regard it as madness or delusion, because such seeing is not "natural." A secret life unfolds in us as we see a spiritual landscape and behold its splendor.

It is little wonder that ancient cultures saw this awakening of the soul as a visitation from another world, just as Jesus was thought to have come "down" from "heaven." These are metaphors, and have no reference to anything external. But the experience of the soul is so extraordinary that traditions have felt it comes from another world, announced by angels, carried by doves, ordained by a personal God. The birth of the soul is *like* a visitation from another world, but it isn't. It is the spiritual life of this world pushing forward, releasing itself like a plant pushing up from the soil in spring. The seed of the soul has been present all along, but at the right time it comes into view, and we feel that it has come from elsewhere.

How could we deny this and say none of it is true? How could we deny the miraculous events that occur constantly in our lives? When we understand that this is what tradition is about, this is what the Christmas festival is about, with its child, silent night, glowing star, and wise men, we can participate in the event with a clear conscience. All the imagery, all the Christmas trimmings are about celebrating the birth of the soul, which is at the same time a rebirth for the person in whom it takes place. Mary plays a crucial role in this drama. It is only the feminine in us, whether we are male or female, that can give birth to the soul. Only our receiving nature can let God in to impregnate our lives with hope, vitality, and direction. Only the feminine can receive the holy and produce our new or reborn selves.

God comes to birth in my soul, and not only in the soul of Jesus. This is what the myth announces. Heretics, poets, artists, and prophets have always known this. The medieval mystic Meister Eckhart, who was condemned for his "heretical" views, remains one of the strongest voices

The Myth of the Virgin Birth

on the theme of God's continuing incarnation in us. He argued that the point of creation is for God to be born and reborn in the human soul:

> God must give birth to himself in us fully and at all times. He has no choice in the matter; this is simply his nature. If we do not receive the spiritual benefits of this birth, then that is because we are not content to allow God to act in us.[33]

This is the meaning of Christmas, about which a great deal has been written. We need to recover this dimension, as Christmas degenerates into a consumerist festival. We continue the incarnation, and allow it to continue, by allowing God to be born in us. If God is not born in the soul, says Eckhart, it is because

> we obstruct God with our false notions of self and the determination to cling to the nothingness which is the true reality of our own creaturely being.[34]

We are nothing without God, and it is little wonder that tradition emphasizes our wretchedness, because without God in our souls we are lost. The difference between orthodoxy and mysticism is that the former says that only by admitting Christ into our lives can we overcome our sinfulness; mysticism says there is already a Christ-like element in our hearts, and we need to turn to it for redemption. The historical Jesus came to remind us of our Christ-like nature, our original blessing, which is scriptural, but got lost in the obsessive interest in original sin.

If we "imitate" Christ as an external figure, and don't accept that we have a spiritual obligation to free our interiority from the ego, the process of continuing incarnation cannot take place. I wonder if the decline of orthodoxy serves a deeper purpose, which is to release us from the spell of imitation and force us to encounter the Christ within. That is the theme of Drewermann's book *Discovering the God Child Within: A Spiritual Psychology of the Infancy of Jesus*. This is the theme that runs through all mystical writings, and indeed the essence of mysticism is to find *within* what orthodoxy preaches can only be found without. Religion can act as a barrier to spiritual experience, whereas mystical reflection on the virgin birth can provide impetus to the mystery of the divinely generated spirit.

Institutional Literalism

It is extraordinary to see religious leaders insist on the historicity of the immaculate conception as the foundation of faith. In my country,

Tim Costello, a leader of the Baptist communion, has stated in various interviews and lectures that he sees the virgin birth as a historical fact. I find it hard to fathom that he takes this view, but many continue to confuse faith with belief, which is the ongoing and widespread misrepresentation of faith. The former archbishop of Canterbury, Rowan Williams, regarded as a progressive force in religion, is nevertheless stuck in a literal mode. He agrees with scholars that "stories of miraculous birth were a common storytelling device in ancient times, as a way of explaining the life of an important person."[35] He agrees that "resurrection is not a resuscitation [of the crucified body]."[36] But he describes himself as "disappointingly conservative, I am afraid, on both of those [miracles] at the end of the day." He wants to "believe" in both of them, and for him, this means literal belief.

Williams claims that "there are very significant differences between miraculous birth stories in the non-Christian world and the stories as they occur in the gospels." He claims "there are certainly very marked differences in the resurrection narratives between them and anything else."[37] But what are these marked differences? He provides no evidence but merely makes assertions. For him the stories are true because they are Christian and he is a leader of the church. I find it incredible and exasperating, but corners of the mind remain intransigent, even in highly educated people like Williams and Costello. The problem, as always, comes down to disrespect for myth. Williams has been tempted to disregard the literal, but he wants to hold onto something historical: "Increasingly over the last few years I have come to feel that we ought to be less and less comfortable with a Christology that simply disregards the virgin conception."[38]

But his language gives him away. Who is talking about "disregarding the virgin conception"? Here his prejudice against myth is evident. To view this miracle as myth is not to disregard it. One can see from the way he frames the problem that he is trapped in a theology that has no room for myth or symbol. He wants something to be historically true before it can be fully true. This is what is so frustrating about the churches; they return to this position and do not move from it. This is one reason why the churches cannot move forward, and as such, are going down. The "conservatives" are conserving nothing, but are contributing to the destruction of a tradition.

The Less We Believe the Better

One can always rely on Northrop Frye to put things in plain language. Frye was not only a major literary theorist of the twentieth century but an ordained minister in the Canadian Reformed tradition. He said he was frustrated by high-level dignitaries in his church, who would suddenly announce to the world that they no longer "believed" in the virgin birth. But why, after centuries of reflection on the virgin birth as a symbol did they "believe" in the first place? He writes:

> Some prominent cleric may announce, after much heart-searching and self-harrowing, that he can no longer "believe in" the Virgin Birth. What he thinks he is saying is that he can no longer honestly accept the historicity of the nativity stories in Matthew and Luke. But those stories do not belong to ordinary history at all: they form part of a mythical narrative containing many features that cannot be assimilated to the historian's history. . . . However, if he had been a better educated cleric he would not have raised the point in the [first place].[39]

This is the real point: if we were "better educated" we would not need to make these pronouncements, with the heart-searching and self-harrowing. In another place, Frye wryly comments on the

> occasional announcements of church dignitaries that they can no longer believe in the Virgin Birth, with everyone assuming that the statement is heretical instead of merely illiterate.[40]

Such dignitaries think they are being true to their conscience, but they are embarrassing themselves in public. They accept the charge of heresy leveled at them by their own traditions and fail to realize the issue is one of literacy. It is the *belief* that is heretical, not the realization that the symbol is a myth.

But why is it that the true meaning of scripture is not known to those who devote their entire lives to its study and dissemination? The fact that clerics "believe in" the virgin birth is a testimony to systemic ignorance. It is the institutions, not the clerics who "come out" as nonbelievers, that are heretical. The virgin birth is a symbol of the spirit's ability to generate life from itself. The point of the symbol is to urge us to reflect on the possibilities of spirit. As Jung put it:

> Miracles appeal only to the understanding of those who cannot perceive the meaning.[41]

Religion is not a series of dogmas to be believed, but a collection of poems to be experienced. Hence Frye could declare: "The less we believe the better, and nothing should be believed that has to be believed."[42]

Notes

1. Eugen Drewermann, *Discovering the God Child Within: A Spiritual Psychology of the Infancy of Jesus* (New York: Crossroad, 1994), p. 33.
2. Ibid, p. 19.
3. Drewermann, letter to Archbishop Degenhardt 22 January1992, as found at: http://www.drewermann.info/controversy.shtml.
4. Drewermann, *Discovering the God Child Within*, p. 32.
5. Ibid, p. 25.
6. Henry Corbin, *Creative Imagination in the Sufism of Ibn Arabi*, trans. Ralph Manheim (1958; Princeton, NJ. Princeton University Press, 1969).
7. Henry Corbin, "Mundus Imaginalis, the Imaginary and the Imaginal," in James Hillman, ed,. *Spring 1972* (New York), pp. 1–19.
8. An excellent introduction to the thought of Henry Corbin is found in Tom Cheetham, *The World Turned Inside Out: Henry Corbin and Islamic Mysticism* (New Orleans: Spring Journal Books, 2003).
9. Tom Harpur, *The Pagan Christ: Is Blind Faith Killing Christianity?* (2004; Sydney: Allen & Unwin, 2005), p. 3.
10. Ibid, p. 4.
11. Ibid, p. 6.
12. Genesis 3:12.
13. Marina Warner, *Alone of All Her Sex: The Myth and the Cult of the Virgin Mary*, 2nd ed. (Oxford: Oxford University Press, 2013); Rosemary Radford Ruether, *Womanguides: Readings Toward a Feminist Theology* (Boston: Beacon Press, 1985).
14. Marija Gimbutas, *The Language of the Goddess: Unearthing the Hidden Symbols of Western Civilization* (San Francisco: Harper & Row, 1989).
15. Drewermann, *Discovering the God Child Within*, p. 42.
16. Jean Markale, *Cathedral of the Black Madonna* (Rochester, Vermont: Inner Traditions, 2004).
17. Drewermann, p. 32.
18. J. G. Frazer, *The Golden Bough*, 12 Volumes (1906–15; London: Macmillan, 1976).
19. John Shelby Spong, *Jesus for the Non-Religious* (New York: HarperOne, 2007), p. 31.
20. Spong, pp. 31–32.
21. Joseph Campbell, *The Inner Reaches of Outer Space: Metaphor as Myth and as Religion* (1986; Novato, CA: New World Library, (Novato, CA: New World Library, 2002), p. xxiv; p. 32.
22. Drewermann, *Discovering the God Child Within*, p. 28.
23. Ibid, p. 27.
24. Ibid, p. 50.
25. Luke 1:35.
26. W. B. Yeats, "Leda and the Swan" (1923), in *W. B. Yeats: Selected Poetry*, ed. Timothy Webb (Harmondsworth: Penguin, 1991), p. 149–50.
27. Schalom Ben-Chorin, *Mother Mary* (Munich, 1977), p. 47.
28. Yeats, "Leda and the Swan," p. 150, line 14.
29. St Thomas Aquinas, *Summa Theologiae*, Blackfriars edn (London: Eyre and Spottiswoode, 1964–1981), Ia. l.9 *Responsio*.

30. Schalom Ben-Chorin, *Mother Mary* (Munich, 1977), p. 49.
31. Luke 2:49.
32. *The Holy Bible*, John 3:3.
33. Eckhart, p. xxix.
34. Ibid.
35. Rowan Williams, "Quarrying for God," in Roland Ashby, ed., *A Faith to Live By* (Melbourne: Mosaic Press, 2012), p. 14.
36. Ibid.
37. Ibid.
38. Ibid, p. 15.
39. Frye, op. cit., p. 19.
40. Northrop Frye, *Words With Power* (Ontario: Viking, 1990), p. 193.
41. Jung, *Answer to Job* (1952), *CW* 11, § 554.
42. Northrop Frye, *Northrop Frye's Notebooks and Lectures on the Bible and Other Religious Texts*, ed. Robert D. Denham (Toronto: University of Toronto Press, 2003), p. 232.

6

Waking Up

All your words were one word: Wake up.
— Antonio Machado[1]

The Kingdom

Everything Jesus said and did was about one thing: urging us to wake up to the mystery within our lives. This is a different image of Jesus' ministry to those who see him as a moral preacher, miracle worker, messiah, or redeemer. For me, Jesus was a spiritual master who was able to encourage people to transform their lives. They could transform their lives if they found the courage to touch the world of spirit. Spirit was an "other" world, but not otherworldly; it was, and is, in this world. Nor is spirit exclusive to humans. There is a spiritual interiority in everything, and the Neoplatonists called this the anima mundi, the soul of the world.[2] We have access to this universal interiority through our individual lives, but that does not mean it is entirely "human."

Jesus pointed to a second reality so vast it is entitled to be called a *kingdom*. When he says "My kingdom is not of this world,"[3] he refers to a "world" other than that of common perception. But his proclamation has been misinterpreted. As ever, he is speaking metaphorically about this "other" world. The kingdom is not a literal place or an otherworldly abode, as popular sentiment and dogmatic religion have supposed. Like everything he said, he is speaking in the language of mythos. There is no kingdom that might be observed by the common eye:

> The kingdom of God does not come with your careful observation, nor will people say, "Here it is," or "There it is," because the kingdom of God is within you.[4]

Jesus is explicit about the location of the kingdom: it is within. And yet centuries of Christian preaching have located the kingdom anywhere other than within. It has been imagined in the heavens above, in a life after death, or in an ideal social milieu to come. None of these imaginings of the kingdom seem right to me.

Not only is the kingdom close to our experience but it is near to us in a temporal sense: "The kingdom of heaven is close at hand."[5] The kingdom does not exist in a far-off time or place, is not a distant reality, but is here and now. Jesus keeps insisting that it is close, yet despite this, those around him—and many today—interpret him to mean that the kingdom has not yet come, or that it will be announced by cataclysmic events, or that it is a literal place. Some, failing to observe any signs of God's kingdom in the world today, conclude that "Jesus was obviously wrong."[6] But they are not reading the scriptures correctly, and are mistaking metaphors for objects.

In the original scriptures, the Greek word that becomes "kingdom" is *basileia*, but the translation can be misleading. It can lead to the conclusion that God is a *place* rather than a force or activity in the soul. Scholars have argued that *basileia* should be translated as "reign," to avoid the connotation of place and to convey the sense that God is a power that works in our lives. Jesus came to announce a "reign" or spiritual order based on justice and love. God's power is not a thing but an activity, not a noun but a verb. As an activity, we are less likely to think literally about it. The reign of God has "come near" but is not present until it is accepted within our hearts and minds. Whether it is distant or intimate is entirely our concern, and nothing to do with external events. Heaven is a condition of consciousness, but this does not mean it is "created" by us. It is a condition that we arrive at by adjusting our lives to the spirit.

The theological understanding of Jesus' ministry has been misguided in my view. He did not come into the world to "make" the kingdom for us, or give us eternal life in a supernatural act. This is what I was taught in my religious education, and the view stems from the mistaken belief that he was God. He did not come as a "substitutionary atonement" to bring about a rapprochement between a perfect God and sinful humans. Jesus did not come to put in what God left out, or had taken from us at the Fall. All of this is ideology. Jesus taught how we could awaken ourselves to what God had already invested in our nature. He came to *remind* us that we are made in the image of God and destined to further God's work. Jesus reminded us of the preexisting reality of God's abiding presence. This presence was "always already" there, as Derrida put it, and the idea that Christ *is* this presence is idolatry. His ministry was not supernatural but existential.[7] Jesus did not change the nature of reality, or of God, which is the favored view of the churches. He pointed to what already exists, not only in "Christians" but in all people. Like Socrates, he asked us to wake up to what is already present in our nature, and like Socrates he was persecuted and sentenced to death for his efforts. I will return to the parallel with Socrates later.

Jesus was exhausted by the constant misreading of his kingdom as a place or future event, and he uses many parables to say what the kingdom is "like," since it cannot be conveyed in logical terms. Speaking like a poet, he reflects: "How shall we picture the kingdom of God, or by what parable shall we describe it?"[8] It is like a place but not a place; like a treasure in the field but not a treasure;[9] like a mustard seed;[10] like a merchant looking for pearls;[11] like yeast in bread.[12] But it is none of these. How does one describe something that the mind can barely imagine, let alone touch or witness firsthand? Only metaphors and parables can express the sense of interior reality that he is trying to convey. But metaphors are taken literally by unimaginative minds, and Jesus found this in his time as much as we find it in ours. Caird makes an astute point: "Jesus would scarcely have devoted so many of his parables to explaining what he meant by the kingdom of God if he understood by it exactly what everybody else did."[13]

Psychotherapist and priest John Sanford puts it well when he says:

> The kingdom is not something coming upon man from outside of himself, but is a reality within himself, the very foundation of his personal existence, and something which can be experienced by the individual. The kingdom of God as a spiritual reality within men must be described as a psychological reality insofar as it is experienceable by the individual in the development and unfolding of his personality.[14]

This is the first point to grasp in any attempt to bring Jesus' teaching close to our understanding. I don't know how many sermons and homilies I have sat through that have insisted on placing the kingdom outside of ourselves, in a distant future or place. This is bizarre, when one recalls that Jesus said the kingdom had arrived for those with eyes to see.[15] It gives me delight to realize that the sermons I sat through as a child were boring not because the gospels were boring, but because the boredom stemmed from an ecclesiastical misreading. If ministers and priests had realized that the kingdom is about the eternal present, the lessons would have been far from boring! But that is to expect that the ministers of the church could be spiritual and not dogmatically religious. Indeed spirituality could be defined as the awareness that God is close at hand, closer than our breath, and not a distant reality.

Putting on the New Self

In depth psychological terms, the kingdom is synonymous with the discovery of a new self, a new center of authority in the personality. Thomas Merton calls this the "true self," Jung refers to it as the Self—often capitalized to ensure that we do not confuse it with the ordinary ego. However I think we have to be careful of the Jungian habit of referring to the "other" dimension of personality as "self," whether capitalized or not. By definition, the other life in our life is distinct from what we refer to as "myself," "yourself," or "ourselves." In our age, the dangers of narcissism are always lurking close at hand, and if anyone imagines that his or her "self" is divine and possessed of sacred values, we are in trouble and deluding ourselves. This is where the New Age movement goes wrong, in my view.[16] It takes the idea of spiritual interiority literally and fuses it with the ordinary self or ego, thus producing a narcissistic and non-transformative spirituality. There is an interior life which is within, and part of "ourselves," yet this is also radically other, rightly referred to as the "not I."

As argued in chapter 4, the East has a far better grasp of this interior divinity than the West, as we in the West are not gifted with insight into our deep subjectivity. Even the term "subjectivity" is inappropriate, because we are talking about something *objective* that arises from within the personality. Our inherited dualism, a product of the Intellectual Enlightenment, does not allow us to think in terms of anything "objective" within the "subjective." And yet this is precisely the mystery of our lives: objective life wells up from our depths, if we are open and permeable to it. We can block it, if we choose, and many do. But those who are sensitive and receptive cannot help but notice that a large part of our interiority is not of the same nature or substance as the ego. India refers to this "new self" as Atman, the God Within.

We have no equivalent term in the West, and perhaps we should revert to the ancient term "soul" for this experience of interior sacredness. To my understanding, soul is the term for that part of our nature that lies in wait to be penetrated and activated by spirit. The soul is feminine in nature, whereas the spirit tends to be symbolized in myth and religion as masculine. It is the same for men as for women, and thus we are speaking about masculine and feminine archetypes in all people, not about stereotypes of social behavior. The soul is the middle or "third" thing in human nature, which stands between ego and spirit. The soul is imagined in mythology as a vessel or container, such as the retort in alchemical laboratories, or the grail cup in Christian mysticism. The soul receives the life of spirit into itself, and when this takes place, the human being is never the same. From that moment we belong to God, and are no longer "merely" human, and no longer subject to absolute mortality. We have "crossed over" to the other side. Obviously, I am speaking spiritually and not about the immortality of the bodily nature.

When spirit enters soul we are called back to the primordial source and made aware of something divine in our midst. Our essential nature is transformed, and we are reborn to a different reality. Even this is the wrong language, because it suggests that spirit is otherworldly or apart from this reality. In fact spirit is the essential nature of this world, but for the most part we are blind to it, or we try to shut it out as foreign, different, invasive. It often has to break down our defenses before it can be allowed in. Dreams often announce this in mythological code language: strange and scary figures outside our doors and windows bang on the house to be admitted. The stronger our defenses, the more violently does spirit try to destroy our artificially erected and socially sanctioned barricades. It is the most "natural" thing in the world for us to be penetrated by spirit and changed into the likeness of our maker, but socialization makes this appear "unnatural," crazy, or weird. To this extent the human can be a real block to the incarnation of the divine and when this takes place, the divine must wonder what the "point" of humanity is.

Scripture contains several instances of the divine confronted with this dilemma. When we "fall short," the divine reflects on the purpose of humanity, or secretly plots to overthrow it or abolish humanity in a catastrophe. The point of creation, as Eckhart makes clear, is to allow the divine to be born in our hearts. If we forget this, or lose the wisdom that makes this understanding possible, we have forfeited our right to existence. Our lives are not about us, but about something that comes to birth within us. St Paul speaks persuasively about this transformation of personality. In his letter to the Ephesians, he writes:

> You must put aside your old self, which gets corrupted by following illusory desires. Your mind must be renewed by a spiritual revolution

so that you can put on the new self that has been created in God's way, in the goodness and holiness of the truth.[17]

The "old self" of Paul is what I am calling the ego, or more precisely, the ego before it has encountered the sacred. Paul's "new self" is what I am calling the soul, the supraordinate authority in the personality that transcends ego. The soul is something that has to be "put on," as Paul puts it, and calls for a "spiritual revolution" in the personality. The psychological terminology I employ in this book, as in other works,[18] is already present in the scriptures, but I am highlighting it. I say this because some will claim I am "psychologizing" the scriptures, but the psychological dimension is already present, but has been obfuscated by theological tradition, which seems to be opposed to the mystical.

The kingdom of God is outside the ego's domain and not of its world. It is outside the ego, but not outside our psychological experience. This is the point that much theology and sermonizing has failed to grasp. The kingdom is only "far" from us if we identify with the ego; but if we recognize that we contain more than the ego, and can experience within ourselves another center of authority capable of countermanding the ego, we realize that the kingdom is at hand. The soul, once activated, acts like a force or *dynamis*, and it is hardly surprising that the Hebrews referred to it as a terrifying God capable of wrath and vengeance. If the ego does not want to cooperate with the soul, the soul has the power to overturn it and enforce its own reign. This is what the Judeo-Christian tradition has been announcing for thousands of years, and why Jesus suggests that resisting the kingdom is futile because it is capable of arriving unannounced and turning the ego's world upside down.

The soul institutes a "reign" that is governed by wholeness, and this can capsize the ego, which is wedded to one-sidedness and partial vision. The soul asks the ego to support a wholeness that it can barely comprehend. In this sense, God is not so much a theological abstraction, but a symbol for the unknown life in the psyche and cosmos. God is the force or energy that moves toward actualization and seeks its own ends by incarnating its life as an impulse toward wholeness. The church has made an idol of Christ and refused to see the universal significance of the Incarnation. Christ is a symbol of Incarnation, but not the only expression of it. Jung argued that individuation is the psychological equivalent of incarnation in the experience of the individual. Through the individuation process, the soul unfolds in the personality and displaces the ego, and here we see the process of incarnation in action. Sanford puts the experience of individuation in these terms:

> When we find and realize the kingdom in ourselves, we experience a growing wholeness, an increasing sense of the meaning of our individual personality, a realization of new and creative energies, and an expanding consciousness. This leads us beyond our individual ego-existence to an experience with a transcendent source of life, to a creative life in the social sphere. The kingdom involves the realization of our personalities according to the inner plan established within us by God; hence, the unfolding of a Self which predates and transcends the ego.[19]

I agree, but should add that this presents the "coming of the new self" in a rosy and upbeat light. There is more to transformation than most attempts to popularize Jung's psychology are prepared to announce. As we shall see, it presents challenges for individuals, turns their values upside down and shakes their foundations to the core. The coming of the new self does afford the blessings that Sanford outlines, but brings disturbance and disorientation.

Waking Up to a Higher Authority

St Paul writes:

> Awake, O sleeper, and arise from the dead, and Christ shall give you light.[20]

The experience of the kingdom, the new self, or Christ is an awakening to another authority in the personality that was present but not discerned. The mystery of the new self is that it was already present, but the ego, in its sleep, was unable to register it. The ego cannot "see" it, which I assume is the real meaning of the miracles in which Jesus enables the blind to *see*. The new self "predates and transcends" the ego, and appears to be an intruder on its territory, but from another perspective, the ego is the interloper or latecomer, but has been unable to view things this way.

It is often claimed that the "seeing" of the kingdom is what brings the possibility of eternal life to followers of Jesus. I can only assume this means that when one enters into the reign of the new self, one participates in its life beyond time and space. The ego exists in time, and disappears, we assume, at the point of death. If we die as ego there is perhaps nothing left, no trace or essence remaining. But if we have made landfall in the kingdom, we have an afterlife in the sense that our existence has impacted on the eternal and cannot be fully erased. The new self has roots in archetypal reality, and although it incarnates in this world it has dominion beyond it. The new self is a liminal reality that acts as a bridge between eternity and time and can only be described by paradox and riddles. Jesus himself, as a carrier of the "news" of the new self's incursion, is paradoxical: he is both ego and new self, fully human and fully divine, as claimed in the creeds. Jesus is a human approximation of the divine, the "Son" of the "Father," but Son and Father are personifications of the ego/new self axis.

Jesus has come into the world not only to model a new way of living but to announce to all that they are capable of achieving a state similar to his. He teaches those who have "ears to hear"[21] that they "may be sons of your Father who is in heaven."[22] But to do this they have to "pick up [their] cross and follow me."[23] They have to recognize that to carry the new self is a burden for everyone who attempts to go on the path of awakening. The encounter with the new self is a shattering experience for the ego. Its authority is annihilated by the greater authority of the new self, to which it must surrender. This is why individuation is not a fun time for the ego, even though popular New Age ideologies present the spiritual journey as if it were a doorway into bliss. Jesus is not shy about telling us how difficult this pathway is. We must be "born again" if we want to "see the kingdom of God."[24] This second birth is not easy, but forces us to dislodge ourselves from the ego and take a leap of faith into a new life.

In the normal course of events the new self remains dormant. The individual has to "wake up" to this reality, and in Jesus' teaching the emphasis is on vigilance and readiness.

> "Be on your guard, stay awake, because you never know when the time will come. It is like a man travelling abroad: he has gone from home, and left his servants in charge, each with his own task; and he has told the doorkeeper to stay awake. So stay awake, because you do not know when the master of the house is coming, evening, midnight, cockcrow, dawn; if he comes unexpectedly, he must not find you asleep. And what I say to you I say to all: Stay awake!"[25]

Jesus is trying out various metaphors to say something of a spiritual nature. The "master of the house" is the authority of the new self, which may not be sensed now, but will eventually return "home" to the person and claim its due. If we are caught napping, and unprepared for this homecoming, we will miss the most momentous possibility of our lives. Jesus has been frequently misinterpreted, and said to be prophesying a world-destroying event in the outside world. But he is not talking about any such thing. There is nothing supernatural intended: this is a call to wakefulness, similar to what we find in the Buddhist sutras, with which this passage has much in common.

One has to be "ready" for the incursion of the soul, when the "master of the house" will return to reclaim his authority. One "never knows when the time will come." One cannot plan for this event, or schedule it into one's activities, for the new self or soul is an autonomous force that can never be predicted in advance. It has a spontaneous aspect and the ego can never know when the metanoia will take place. But the more alert one is to this possibility, the more likely it is that when it occurs, one will be prepared and able to cooperate with it. To heed the call to change is to be "saved" and given "eternal life." Salvation, in my view, means being saved from the egocentric life and from perishing with it.

Reversal of the Ego's Values

The new self is a dynamic force directed to a goal or *telos* that overshoots the ego but includes it as an element within itself. It does not seek to destroy the ego but relativizes its claims and undermines its illusion of separateness. The new self seeks a supraordinate wholeness that baffles and confuses the ego, because the ego is unable to see the point of this wholeness. It seeks only to fulfill itself and does not realize that its reason for being is instrumental and ultimately, sacrificial. It denies this tragic destiny and pretends it is master of its fate. The ego's values and attitudes are contradicted and reversed by the new self, especially in the early stages of transformation, when the ego doesn't "get it." Hence Jesus' teaching is baffling and enigmatic to the rational mind, as we can see from a brief selection of beatitudes and instructions from the Sermon on the Mount:

> "Blessed are the poor in spirit, for theirs is the kingdom of heaven. Blessed are those who mourn, for they shall be comforted. Blessed are the meek, for they shall inherit the earth."[26]
>
> "Do not resist one who is evil. But if any one strikes you on the right cheek, turn to him the other also."[27]
>
> "Love your enemies and pray for those who persecute you, so you may be sons of your Father who is in heaven; for he makes his sun rise on the evil and on the good, and sends rain on the just and the unjust."[28]

Jesus argues that we can be so generous to others because God is infinitely generous to us. We should care for others because the Father disinterestedly cares for all. God's love is plentiful, and we should extend this unconditional love to others, even—and especially—to those who do not feel loved. Instead of the ego's needy attitudes, its grasping for security and concern for its narrow circle of interest, the new self urges us to expand our horizons and recognize everyone as family. If the ego is contracted and grasping, the new self is expansive and generous; the ego's movement is centripetal and the new self's is centrifugal. Jesus' teaching dumbfounds us with its irrationality, its appeal to parts of us that are still asleep. Huston Smith puts it bluntly:

> The reason we find Jesus' ethic incredible is that we do not share the premise on which it is based.[29]

He is right and wrong; as egos, we do not share Jesus' ethic; as participants in the bountiful life of the new self, we sense the rightness of Jesus' ethic and aspire to engage in spontaneous giving. Smith's "we" is correct only if we assume he is speaking about us as egos. The premise upon which Jesus' teaching is based is the unconditional love of God, which we can only intuit if we have moved beyond the ego.

Losing and Finding Life

To have the new self we must lose the ego, which requires surrender:

> "Whoever seeks to gain his life will lose it, but whoever loses his life will preserve it."[30]

The life of the ego will need to be "lost," and if this is done with good faith, we will be rewarded with a new life. Once again, however, the loss of the ego is more metaphorical than literal. We cannot lose the ego completely, because then we would become dysfunctional and possibly psychotic. The "loss" of which Jesus speaks is the loss of our *attachment* to the ego, or the loss of its authority in the personality. The ego is required on the Way, because its discipline and service is what enables the new self to become established in the personality. Jesus says:

> "No one can serve two masters; for either he will hate the one and love the other, or he will be devoted to the one and despise the other."[31]

One has to be clear about differentiating between master and servant. The ego sees itself as master, but, as the popular saying goes, "The ego makes a good servant but a lousy master." The idea of dedicated servanthood is fundamental to the gospels. It is by "breaking" the hold that the ego has on us, but not breaking the ego per se, that we pick up the burden of the new self and move toward ego-transcendence.

Jesus offers us a consolation in this difficult task:

> "Come to me, all who labour and are heavy laden, and I will give you rest. Take my yoke upon you, and learn from me; for I am gentle and lowly in heart, and you will find rest for your souls. For my yoke is easy and my burden is light."[32]

What is meant by this is that, although the sacrifice is foreboding, once the plunge is taken, and the ego has offered itself in service, the experience loses some of its fearsome character. The individuating ego is then allowed to experience a different side of the new self: its loving embrace, its gentle, relieving, and renewing aspect. Only the non-individuating ego sees the new self as enemy or opponent, as something to be feared and kept at bay. Throughout the gospels, Jesus seems to take the identity of the new self upon himself, and hence to offer oneself to the new self is to offer oneself to Christ. Through the power of this narrative, the "greatest story ever told," the ego and new self become personified as humanity and Christ. The gospels are unforgiving toward an ego that refuses to take the journey: refusal is personified as Satan or devil, or the followers of these powers. If the ego does not serve God, it serves "evil": "You cannot serve God and mammon."[33]

The Mustard Seed

The mustard seed parable is interesting in that it shows that it may take only small things to awaken the person to the reality of the new self:

> "The kingdom of heaven is like a grain of mustard seed which a man took and sowed in his field. It is the smallest of all seeds, but when it has grown it is the biggest shrub of all and becomes a tree so that the birds of the air come and shelter in its branches."[34]

I like this parable because it is so close to our experience. In the course of any life, a person is often alerted to the reality of the new self by seemingly insignificant events. Perhaps it is something that someone says, or a random image that arises in conversation. Perhaps it is a moment of synchronicity when one feels a connection between one's inner life and the world; insignificant to others and almost not worth telling, but it sets off a spiritual journey that leads to the awakening of the new self.

What kick-starts the Way can be small, but through a process of growth and maturation it becomes a mighty power. We are predisposed to be alerted to the new self, and hence the intuitive faculty of the personality is in a state of readiness to external and internal suggestion. The possibilities of initiation are endless, and it is not necessarily an encounter with clergy or scripture that gets us moving. Here as elsewhere Jesus shows himself to be a master of metaphor, and able to choose the right image to evoke his meaning.

Many are Called, Few Choose

Jesus believes that those who seek entrance into the new self will be allowed to enter:

> "Ask, and it will be given you; seek, and you will find; knock, and it will be opened to you. For every one who asks receives, and he who seeks finds."[35]

But he emphasizes that the ego has to be responsive to the new self; the treasure buried in the field requires active seeking and pursuit. The treasure of the new self is not dumped in our lap, but part of the ego's task is to become alert to the greater reality. The reward for taking the directives of the new self is not the usual reward that would be recognized by the ego. It is not this-worldly reward, but reward in the life of the spirit: "Rejoice and be glad, for your reward is great in heaven."[36] "Heaven" is the other world in this one, the place of spirit, the kingdom of the new self. The reward for taking on these attitudes is spiritual richness, and a sense of harmony with the world. Jesus asks us to respond to a new kind of reward:

> "Do not lay up for yourselves treasures on earth . . . but lay up for yourselves treasure in heaven, where neither moth nor rust consumes and where thieves do not break in and steal. For where your treasure is, there will your heart be also."[37]

In this sense, his ministry is about sensitizing people to a different reality, with different expectations, hopes and trials than one would normally expect in ordinary reality. This is why we have to "dream his ministry onward," give it a new language, and hope that people will become responsive to the unseen.

If the ego does not respond to the promptings of the new self, it will decide that spirituality is futile and turn away. Hence Jesus is able to say:

> "For the gate is narrow and the way is hard, that leads to life, and those who find it are few."[38]

Although everyone is called, few respond. This is Jesus' realism at work, and he is saddened by this prospect, because those who do not respond do not have "life." By "life" he means the new life that is made possible by the transcendence of the ego. Religion makes no sense to the untransformed ego, which is oriented to instinctual goals such as self-preservation, fear of the enemy, revenge, power, and defense. The unawakened ego is irritated by the sayings of Jesus. The ego uses reason to debunk the wisdom of the new self, until such time as the ego intuits a higher reason at work. In sensing a higher reason its awakening has begun, and like a grub that has outlived its pupal stage, it is able to overcome its encapsulation, spread its new-found wings, and take flight. In biology this is called metamorphosis, moving from pupa to *imago* (adulthood), and in human life the changed being is indeed introduced to its "imago" stage, where imagos and metaphors guide its way!

Completion, Not Perfection

Jesus wants to open us to a greater life:

> "I have come that they may have life, and have it to the full."[39]

Given this generous and expansive impulse, it is ironic, to say the least, that Christianity across the ages has tried to contract and narrow life by its piety and moralism. A perfectionist ethic has controlled Christianity, and for its scriptural basis, it generally refers to this commandment from the Sermon on the Mount:

> "You must therefore be perfect just as your heavenly Father is perfect."[40]

Like much else in this religion, there may be a gap between what Jesus said and what Christianity believes he said. The typical reading of the statement is quite possibly mistaken. The problem involves a mistranslation of the key word. In the original, the word translated into English as "perfect" is the Greek *teleios*, which means to "mature," to be "brought to completion," or "arrive at an end state." It derives from the root *telos*, meaning goal or end. This word, occurring at least nineteen times in the New Testament, is universally (mis)translated as *perfect*.[41]

When we read Jesus' commandment as translated, most of us decide that religion is not for us. We feel the commandment imposes an impossible obligation on our lives, one we cannot live up to. We cannot be perfect, and the demand to be such is persecutory. Some try to perform according to the dictate, but the majority are content to abandon religion if it sets the bar too high. Besides, the new directive from psychotherapy is that we aim for wholeness, not perfection. It asks us to come to terms with our shadow side, not bury it as we try to reach up to heaven. In this sense, many feel that Christianity has lost its conviction, and is no longer relevant to a psychologically sophisticated age that is suspicious of an exalted ethic predicated on the repression of our instincts. Indeed, in the consulting room and clinical practice, "perfection" has become a dirty word.

In *Civilisation and Its Discontents*, Freud claimed that perfection is a fantasy that brings misery to civilizations and individuals. He referred to perfectionism as part of the "universal neurosis" of religion, and of course he was right. Perfection may be an ego-ideal, and something the infantile ego finds attractive, with its compulsion to "be good" or "perfect" for father, mother, superego, or Heavenly Father. But being good is not the kind of life-ethic that enables us to realize the God within, or approach the new self. I have been fascinated by the amount of commentary that Jesus' commandment has attracted from various quarters. Preachers use it to terrify their congregations and hound them into conformity. Theologians point to it as the key to Christianity, whereas critical thinkers are keen to show that the commandment must not be read literally, that is, at face value.

Jung was one of the first of the modern scholars to question the translation of *teleios*. In *Aion* he argues that the term means *completeness*, and this is a far cry from the "perfection" of the evangelists. He supplies a wealth of material from antiquity to support his claim, from theologians, philosophers, and gnostics. He concludes:

> The problem of how to translate "teleios" becomes crucial. The word ... amounts to much the same thing as "spiritual," which is not connected with any conception of a definite degree of perfection. When it applies to a man ... "teleios" can at most mean "whole" or "complete."[42]

The word "spiritual" in this context refers to the Greek *pneumatikos*, a word used by St Paul in his letters, referring to a person who has been reborn in the spirit. These words point to the same thing: not to morality, but to *being*, or more precisely to a being who has been changed, or turned toward the "end state." We are born as egos but reborn to a new state which demands an overcoming of egotism and a life oriented to wholeness.

The Greek words in the original are as follows:

> "You must be *teleloi* [masculine plural] as your heavenly Father is *teleios* [masculine singular]."

Jesus' words should be read in this sense: "You must allow yourself to arrive at an end state; or be brought to completion." As with the word *metanoia*, which we will turn to presently, *teleios* is an exhortation to turn away from egocentricity toward wholeness. It has nothing to do with "perfection" in the commonly used sense. It invites us to enter a new understanding of ourselves, in which immediate issues are set aside so we can be concerned with what transcends the ego.

Before the world throws out Christianity, based on distaste for the perfectionist and life-denying ethic, we should consider the original intention of the commandment. As David Miller put it:

> One little word—*teleios*—seems to have controlled man's destiny.[43]

He means that this word has caused widespread confusion and has been the basis for much that has been destructive in Christianity, including piety, perfectionism, moralism, hypocrisy, intolerance, inquisitions, witch hunts, torture, murder, and genocide of those deemed "imperfect" by socially constructed standards. We should have been aware long before this of the error of translation. Moreover the same gospel that attributes the "perfectionist" commandment to Jesus informs us that "no one is good but God."[44] This should have alerted us to the mistranslation. But perhaps more importantly is the statement that follows this commandment:

> "Beware of practising your piety before men in order to be seen by them; for then you will have no reward from your Father who is in heaven."[45]

If one strives toward the end state for aggrandizement or status, and if one indulges in showy moralism, one's efforts are in vain and lead to hypocrisy. Jesus was astute at every turn, realizing that everything he said could be taken by the ego and used to reinforce its present condition. This is why some of what he says appears contradictory, because he has to qualify everything to prevent us from making an egocentric system out of his spiritual practice. He tries to trick us out of our mental state, and this trickster element is part of his role as magus.

Another use of *teleios* is found in the letters of Paul. In Colossians, Paul announces the presence of the indwelling Christ in all men. He speaks of "the glory of this mystery, which is Christ in you," and continues:

> "Christ we proclaim, warning every man and teaching every man in all wisdom, that we may present every man mature [*teleios*] in Christ. For this I toil, striving with all the energy which he mightily inspires within me."[46]

It is interesting that the translators use "mature" instead of "perfect" in this instance. But again we see Paul emphasizing the psychological dimension of the Christian message. Christ is "in you," and one can only mature in this recognition by allowing Christ, as the new self, to overtake the ego and replace its authority. This "letting go" into the new self is what is meant by faith. It is by surrendering to the "glory of this mystery" that we overcome the anxiety and insecurity of the ego. Only by letting go into the new self do we have an opportunity to enter eternal life, by which is meant life beyond the ego and its time-space realm. Paul makes no mention of perfection, but insists that people must allow themselves to grow into this new dispensation.

For centuries pietists and churchmen have interpreted *teleios* as a call to the "good," to living a life full of shoulds, oughts, and musts. The early Methodists, Wesley and Fletcher, appear to have been influential in reading Matthew 5:48 in a moralistic sense. Miller argues that "the Wesleyans and their ilk won the popular religious imagination of the West." He points out, however, that the doctors of the church did not make the same "popular" mistake. Clement of Alexandria argued that Jesus was not asking us to be good by our striving, but that "maturity" or "completion" could only come about as a divine gift rather than as a human accomplishment. Similarly, Karl Barth insisted that the commandment in Matthew "is eschatological rather than moral in its intention." It refers to the end state of the human experiment and has an evolutionary thrust.

Literalism, aided by mistranslation, is the source of the destruction of much that is good in Jesus' teaching. This has had widespread ramifications, which David Miller puts this way:

> A literal understanding of the text from Matthew is at the center of an Occidental way of seeing life.[47]

John Sanford, like others, is urged to correct the misunderstanding of this commandment:

> If we understand the Greek word [*teleios*] correctly, we see that Jesus is urging us to be brought to the end state for which we were created and which is brought about through the unfolding of the inner self.[48]

The correct use of a term can change the content of religion and steer a new path to a better future. Those who have appropriated Christianity for so long should be shocked out of their complacency, their assurance that they "know" what it is about. New meanings are waiting to be released from a religion that many have written off. But as I have shown, the original meanings are being made known to a wider circle beyond the few who have understood them.

Transformation, Not Repentance

I want to return to the theme of waking up to the kingdom. Jesus begins his ministry with the message: "Change,[49] for the kingdom of heaven is close at hand."[50] In the original Greek text, the word *metanoia* is used for "change," and is translated into English as "repentance." *Metanoia* means, literally, to "change one's mind," or more correctly, to "change one's consciousness." All through my childhood I believed, based on the preaching of clergy, that Jesus was demanding moral rectitude in calling for "repentance." This may have suited the mindset of my religious teachers, but they were missing the point of his teaching. Jesus is not calling for moral righteousness but for spiritual transformation. He wants people to turn their lives around and focus on the sacred. He assumes there is another center of authority in the personality, which we are not seeing.

His call is designed to activate the other authority, and he expects to achieve this by rituals such as baptism, Eucharist, fasting, and prayer. These spiritual exercises are designed to suspend the authority of the ego and release the soul. He is not calling for better behavior but for initiation. This is hardly unique to Jesus' ministry. Thousands of years before Christ, ancient civilizations established that the "natural" state of humanity is to be caught in the ego. People had to be shaken out of this state, this torpor or unaliveness, by rigorous and even violent ceremonies devised by the tribe. As Eliade put it, the task of religion was to cut across the ego-bound state and change the person:

> In archaic societies, one does not become a complete man until one has passed beyond, and in some sense abolished, "natural" humanity.[51]

The abolition of the natural man is not conceived by ancient traditions as a moral experience, as if by "being good" one is turning to God.

Ancient traditions are calling for structural change, which could be interpreted as living from a deeper level, not from personal needs.

In Australian Aboriginal ceremonies, the male initiate is given a sacred stone or *churinga*, to symbolize the "second body" or new life from which he must live. At the climax of the ceremony, the elder holds out the stone and says:

> Here is your body, here is your second self.[52]

The first priority in these ceremonies is to change the structure of personality, and it is expected that the rest will follow. The initiate will emerge reborn, be given a new name, and expected to live for the community as a whole, including the dead and ancestral spirits. Unless we "die" to our original nature and emerge from this crisis in a renewed state, no spiritual change can occur. The call to psycho-spiritual death is not unique to Christianity, as Eliade makes clear:

> When brought to birth, man is not yet completed; he must be born a second time, spiritually.... The man of the archaic societies does not consider himself "finished" as he finds himself "given" on the natural level of existence. To become a man in the proper sense he must die to this first natural life and be reborn to a higher life, which is at once religious and cultural.[53]

This dimension is lost in modern society, which no longer understands the role or importance of rites of passage. The aim of initiation is to expose the novice to a reality that he or she may not have seen before. This is why, in the Gospel of Thomas, Jesus proclaims:

> I will give you what no eye has seen, what no ear has heard, what no hand has touched, what has not risen in the human heart.[54]

In initiation, something is revealed to the ego that has not been imagined before. *Metanoia* can also mean "to turn around," to face what has not yet been seen, what has not been considered.

The moralistic interpretation of *metanoia* is an aberration in the history of religion. What Jesus is calling for is a transformation of the person, an induction into the spirit. He is saying: "See things from the perspective of the soul, and respect its need for spirit." His call is not for good behavior, but rebirth. Where Christianity went wrong was in reading rebirth as an act of the ego: it called on the ego to transcend itself. This is not possible, which is why Christianity has not lived up to the promise of Jesus. The primary task of religion is not to appeal to the ego to do what it cannot do, but to activate the second self, by rituals, exercises, and psychological transformation. Modern religion is not spiritual enough if it believes that change can come about by preaching to and commanding the ego. The challenge is to lead people into an experience of spirit, and allow it to change the person from within.

Jesus, Socrates, and Waking Up

To close this reflection, I would suggest parallels between the ministry of Jesus and the teachings of Socrates. On the face of it, they appear to have little in common. Jesus is commending people to enter the kingdom of God, and Socrates appears to be engaged in a purely intellectual exercise as a philosopher of mind. But speaking in his defense before the court of Athens, Socrates made it clear that he was not operating at a purely intellectual level, but responding to a deeper calling that he referred to as the "daimonic voice" or "internal oracle."[55] Socrates was on trial for corrupting the people of Greece, and especially the youth, by making them question their cherished beliefs. Socrates said the gods had singled him out as a divine emissary to irritate people, awaken them from their sleep, and bring them into an immediate relationship with the soul. This was sensed by the civic council as a subversion of the rule of law, and Socrates was viewed as an enemy of state. It was deemed that he was trying to unravel the moral and religious threads that bound the state together, and for this reason he was to be tried and killed.

Socrates is often depicted as an atheist, but that is not quite true. He was only an atheist if viewed through the narrow lens of a literalistic religion. He did not "believe" in the physicality of the gods as beings on top of Mount Olympus. He tired at the literal understanding of the gods as external beings, which he thought was a religion for fools. He was not destroying religion per se, but trying to find a higher meaning for religion than superstition and idolatry. His "crime" was in drawing attention to the metaphorical nature of the gods. If viewed literally, these gods were false, mere idols of a lazy mind, but if viewed metaphorically, they had much more validity. Socrates was questioning the projection of sacred powers into anthropomorphic gods and goddesses, and not debunking the powers. The superstitious minds of Athens could not understand his point, which was that gods are metaphors for the sacred potentialities in the human soul.

In this regard, my own deliteralizing project has much in common with his. In one of his discourses, Plato has Socrates say:

> There are gods in a sense higher than that in which any of my accusers believe in them.[56]

It is odd how the same patterns run through history: religions start as legitimate responses to the presence of sacred powers; these religions degenerate into systems of idolatry; thinking persons are forced to debunk the idolatry and draw people back to the unknowable mystery; such persons are persecuted and hounded by those who fail to understand; the persecutors imagine they are defending faith, whereas they are upholding a system of illusion. The religion of state in Socrates' time was based on a literal and decadent interpretation of the Olympian gods, and this system felt threatened by an intelligent mind that saw through the charade. The philosopher Karl Jaspers puts the situation clearly when he writes:

> The symbolic language of myth will always be degraded into a language of the tangible. Every epoch has the critical task of correcting such perversions.[57]

Like Jesus, Socrates did not produce writings, because his teaching was delivered orally and in public. All we have to grasp his character are the words of his followers, notably Plato and Xenophon. It is hard to garner a historical account of Socrates, just as it is with Jesus, because everything written about him is filtered through the projections and images of others. Socrates argued that each man thought he knew a great deal and was wise, but we know little and are not wise at all. Plato refers to Socrates as the "gadfly" of the state, the link being that as the gadfly stings a horse into action, so Socrates stung the Athenians. He targeted the leading lights of Athens, including statesmen, poets, and artisans, undermined their philosophies and ridiculed their views. He told them they were wasting their time by concerning themselves with careers, families, and political responsibilities, and instead they should be worried about the "welfare of their souls."

Like Jesus five hundred years after him, Socrates humiliated the prominent leaders of his time, making them look foolish and turning them against him. Like Jesus, he was accused of heresy and sentenced to death, and like Jesus he resigned himself to the decision of the state because he believed the right time (*kairos*) had come for him to die. Moreover he sensed that death was not the end, but the freeing of the soul from the body. Little is known of the spirituality and beliefs of Socrates, because secular philosophers in our time tend to emphasize his famous "Socratic method" and downplay his religion. But Socrates had strong religious beliefs, even if, as with Jesus, they departed radically from those of the authorities of his time. The Socratic method was twofold, and while the first stage is well known, our universities tend to keep the second stage under wraps, because it is religious.

The first stage of Socrates' method of teaching is what could be called deconstructive. He would engage in dialectical debate with leaders and socialites, in the hope of overturning their views and exposing their cherished opinions as mere vanities. He felt that most of our views were illusory, particularly our anthropomorphic images of the gods. These had to be broken and smashed, so that people could see beyond them to what the images pointed. He tried to force people to admit that their beliefs were not based on reason, but were conventional or arrived at by prejudice. This is the known Socrates, the atheistic or debunking philosopher taught in academic departments around the world. The second stage of the Socratic method is spiritual.[58] The point of his deconstructive strategy was to overturn the acquired layers of mind and expose his conversation partners to the hidden resources of the mind, resources that are shut off from us by conditioning and upbringing. This was what he called true knowing, and it was not merely rational, but revelatory, oracular, and ancestral.

His second strategy, which justified the first, was transformational. Socrates felt that humans live as though in a sleep, never aware of the wisdom that lies latent within them. He attempted to show people the emptiness of their thinking, so as to release what he called the "internal oracle." He tried to smash the revered images of wood and stone so that the spiritual energies in the soul would be released. The deconstructive "sting" would, he hoped, stir these depths to activity, and people would become possessed of an understanding that was not merely human but divine. As Karl Popper said of Socrates, his method was "the art of intellectual intuition . . . of unveiling the Great Mystery behind the common man's everyday world of appearances."[59] The similarity with Jesus is striking, but the next element is different, based as it is on the idea of reincarnation. When our conventions were overturned, we would "forget" what we know, and "remember" the wisdom of the soul, which Socrates believed was a heritage of humanity, locked in the mind like an ancestral core. This "well of remembrance" was lost in our ego-state, since we defend against it with our conventionality.

Socrates believed that the immortality of the soul is expressed in various incarnations at different points in history. The soul migrates from one incarnation to another, a view that is found in most Eastern, especially Indian, religions. People often say this philosophy is exclusively Eastern, but it was present in the religious views of ancient Greece. It may be hard for us to believe in the concept of a reincarnating soul, but if we transpose this view into depth psychology we can see that Socrates was trying to evoke the depth dimension of the psyche. Just as Jesus pointed to this depth as a "kingdom," Socrates pointed to it as a process of reincarnation. In my view, both are metaphors pointing to the same reality.

In terms of depth psychology, Socrates was engaged in psyche-evoking, a rousing to activity of potentials inherent in the depths of the person. Socrates' method was to goad and disorient the normal self, so that traces of an ancestral self could come alive. Not unlike the methods of deconstruction used in our time by Jacques Derrida and his school, Socrates' intention was to reduce our knowledge to nothing so that something greater could be born.[60] Although the typical response to deconstruction is that it is nihilistic, its aim is not nihilism but the release of a deeper wisdom beyond conventional thought. The first stage looks nihilistic but it is a trickster-like method to bring us to the point where accepted beliefs are no longer convincing. Aristophanes represented Socrates as a village clown, and the trickster is an appropriate lens through which to view his spiritual goading.

But this is what Socrates, Jesus, and deconstruction have in common: habitual conventions are exposed as empty so that a hidden fullness can be constellated, a wellspring which lies beyond normal reach. All three methods trick us into breaking out of our mental cages so that soul and spirit can be released. All three imagine the normal state as one of inertia or sleep, and the point of ministry or teaching is to liberate the depths of the person. One difference is that Jesus felt this depth was awoken through compassion and love, and Socrates and Derrida felt it was awoken through reason and thought. There are many ways to awaken the soul, and all have validity if employed correctly. But all three share the same perception that the normal state is one that has to be overcome. It is a sleep from which we must awaken, to behold what Socrates called "the divine faculty of which the internal oracle is the source."[61]

Notes

1. Antonio Machado, "Moral Proverbs and Folk Songs," in *Times Alone: Selected Poems of Antonio Machado*, trans. Robert Bly (Middletown, Conn.: Wesleyan University Press, 1983), p. 24.
2. See my essay "The Return of Soul to the World" in David Tacey, *The Darkening Spirit* (London: Routledge, 2013).
3. John 18: 36.
4. Luke 17:20–21, NIV.
5. Matthew 4:17; 10:7; and many parallels in the gospels.
6. Huston Smith, *The Religions of Man* (New York: Harper & Row, 1958), p. 308.
7. For the existential aspects of Jesus, I have been influenced by my colleague John Carroll, whose book *The Existential Jesus* (Melbourne: Scribe, 2007) constitutes a radical reworking of Jesus' life and work.
8. Mark 4:30.
9. Matthew 13:44.
10. Matthew 13:31–32.
11. Matthew 13:45–46.
12. Matthew 13:33; Luke 13:20–21.
13. G. B. Caird, *The Language and Imagery of the Bible* (London: Duckworth, 1980), p. 12.
14. John Sanford, *The Kingdom Within: A Study of the Inner Meaning of Jesus' Sayings* (New York: J. B. Lippincott Company, 1970), p. 42.
15. Matthew 12:28.
16. See David Tacey, *Jung and the New Age* (London and New York: Routledge, 2001).
17. Ephesians 4:22–24, JB.
18. David Tacey, *The Spirituality Revolution: The Emergence of Contemporary Spirituality* (Sydney: HarperCollins, 2003; London and New York: Routledge, 2004).
19. Sanford, *The Kingdom Within*, p. 42.
20. Ephesians 5:14.
21. Matthew 13:9.
22. Matthew 5:44.
23. Matthew 16:24.
24. John 3:3.
25. Mark 13:33–37.
26. Matthew 5:3–5.
27. Matthew 5:39.
28. Matthew 5:44.
29. Huston Smith, *The Religions of Man* (New York: Harper & Row, 1958), p. 308.
30. Luke 17:33.
31. Matthew 6:24.
32. Matthew 11:28–30.
33. Matthew 6:24.
34. Matthew 13:31–32; also in Mark 4:30–32 and Luke 13:18–19.
35. Matthew 7:7–8.

36. Matthew 5:12.
37. Matthew 6:20–21.
38. Matthew 7:14.
39. John 10:10.
40. Matthew 5:48, JB
41. In addition to Matthew 5:48, there are numerous other places where this translation occurs: Matthew 19:21; Romans 12:2; 1 Corinthians 2:6; I Corinthians 13:10, to mention only a few instances.
42. Jung, *Aion*, § 333
43. David Miller, *Christs: Meditations on Archetypal Images in Christian Theology* (New York: The Seabury Press, 1981), p. 7.
44. Matthew 19:17.
45. Matthew 6:1.
46. Colossians 1:28–29, RSV
47. Miller, *Christs*, p. 5.
48. John Sanford. *The Kingdom Within*, p. 48.
49. "Change" is my preferred translation of *metanoia*, as used in this passage of the New Testament.
50. Matthew 4:17.
51. Mircea Eliade, *The Sacred and the Profane* (1957, New York: Harcourt Brace & Company, 1987), p. 187.
52. Cited by Erich Neumann, in his *The Origins and History of Consciousness* (1949), Princeton University Press, 1973, 289.
53. Eliade, *The Sacred and the Profane*, p. 181–187.
54. *The Gospel According to Thomas*, Gilles Quispel, et al., eds. (New York: Harper & Row, 1959), Saying 70, p. 41.
55. A useful introduction to Socrates and his teachings can be found in Christopher Bruell, *On the Socratic Education: An Introduction to the Shorter Platonic Dialogues* (Lanham, MD: Rowman & Littlefield, 1999).
56. Socrates, as represented by Plato and cited in Ira Progoff, *The Symbolic and the Real* (New York: McGraw-Hill, 1963), p. 42.
57. Karl Jaspers, "Myth and Religion" (1953), in Joseph Hoffmann, ed. and Norbert Guterman, trans., Karl Jaspers and Rudolf Bultmann, *Myth and Christianity: An Inquiry into the Possibility of Religion Without Myth* (1954, New York: Prometheus Books, 2005), p 32.
58. The spirituality of the Socratic method is argued in Pierre Hadot, *Philosophy as a Way of Life* (Oxford: Blackwells, 1995).
59. Karl Popper, *The Open Society and its Enemies* (London: Routledge & Kegan Paul, 1962), p. 133.
60. See my analysis of the spirituality of Derrida in "Jacques Derrida: The Enchanted Atheist," in *Thesis Eleven: Critical Theory and Historical Sociology* (London: Sage), 110(1) June 2012, pp. 3–16.
61. Ira Progoff, *The Symbolic and the Real* (New York: McGraw Hill, 1963), p. 47.

7

Apocalypse

A first "intentionality" of transcendence: someone is searching for me. A God who causes pain, but a God as a You. And by being found by God, my awakening to myself.
— Emmanuel Levinas[1]

Apocalypse as Psychology

The idea of the apocalypse can be read as a process in which the spiritual self "bursts through" into manifestation. Given that humanity tries to avoid or suppress spirit, and given that spirit is part of our nature and demands expression, a pressure builds up in the soul of humanity that is not unlike a volcanic eruption. This internal crisis is regularly projected upon the face of the world as future catastrophic events, holy wars or God-inspired devastations that are viewed as "redemptive" and inaugurating a new order.

The Book of Revelation operates in this mode, and is one of the most visionary works of literature, as well as one of the most dangerous if read from a fundamentalist point of view. Revelation has given rise to much religious enthusiasm and madness, to sects that have eagerly awaited the end of the world, and to cults that have prophesied the eclipse of humanity and the rise of the faithful to a new life in eternal paradise. The book contains extremely violent and conquistadorial language, but in my view it is a symbolic war between that part of human nature that surrenders to God, and that part that puts up a resistance and attracts God's "wrath." Nevertheless the church has used the authority of this book to launch campaigns against the "enemies of Christ," to wage crusades, wars, and massacres against those who stand in the way of Christian triumphalism. The madness, in my view, comes from reading the text literally, and refusing to understand that it is a poetic narrative pointing to a spiritual process that might have little or nothing to do with external events.

The accepted historical reading of Revelation is that it is written by an evangelist, John of Patmos, around 95 CE and addressed to the "seven churches" that were suffering persecution under Roman colonial rule.[2] The book was designed to bring hope and assurance to the fledgling churches. But that is where history ends and myth begins. The work is teeming with archetypal symbols of the soul in turmoil, and full of cosmic imagery that suggests that a profound but unsettling and perhaps psychologically disturbed vision has erupted from the depths of the unconscious. The story that unfolds has little to do with any of the seven churches, and much to do with the transformation process, as the self makes way for, and does battle with, the revelation of the divine. Even where references are made to Roman imperialism and its hoped-for defeat, the archetypal images eclipse historical considerations. We are therefore at liberty to interpret this book as we would a vision of a prophetic artist or poet.

Coming of the New Self

"The time is near"[3] is the preoccupation and expectation of the apocalyptic vision, a vision found in scripture, the arts, high and popular cultures, and religious traditions. Sometimes the end that is envisaged is a scorched-earth scenario in which life is destroyed in a final conflagration or Armageddon. In this context the word "apocalypse" has taken on the meaning of utter devastation, without rebirth except in heaven or another world. Sometimes the apocalypse is conceived less catastrophically as a time of trial in which antagonistic forces bring the world to near ruin, but an act of divine intervention takes place, in which human agency is displaced and divine authority is assumed. But from a psychological perspective, the idea that the end is near is an ever-present fear of the ego, as it intimates the coming of the higher authority of the spiritual self. The apocalypse of the ego is the emergence of the new self, the archetype of wholeness that forces itself on consciousness. When we read the apocalypse this way, a lot of strange material that might seem incomprehensible becomes meaningful.

The word apocalypse comes from the Greek *apokalypsis* and means "the uncovering of what has been hidden." The root is the verb *kaplypto*, which means "to cover or hide," and the prefix is the preposition *apo*, meaning "away or from." An apocalypse literally means to make visible what had previously been invisible. In my reflections on the apocalypse, I have been influenced by Edward Edinger's *Archetype of Apocalypse*, in which he wrote:

> What does the Apocalypse mean psychologically? My essential answer is: the Apocalypse means the momentous event of the coming of the Self into conscious realization. Of course, it manifests itself and is experienced in quite different ways if occurring in the individual psyche or in the collective life a group; but in either case, it is a momentous event—literally world-shattering. This is what the content of the Apocalypse archetype presents: the shattering of the world as it has been, followed by its reconstitution.[4]

We live in a time in which the old is being shattered and something new wants to be born. It is at this time that the archetypal image of the apocalypse is constellated, because civilization itself, and the idea of what it means to be human, is challenged and transformed.

Although irreverent schoolboys have often sniggered over the last words of the Bible: "Surely I am coming soon" (or in the King James: "Surely I come quickly"),[5] the significance of this proclamation is mostly lost on those who oppose religion as upon those who follow it. Edinger employs the term "Self" to refer to what I am calling the new or second self. As we have seen in previous chapters, the idea of the coming of the spiritual self is always present in culture, and for two thousand years it has wrapped itself around the figure of Jesus, turning him into the Christ. In many ways, the spirit is always "coming," that is, it generates a sense of messianic expectation and can be found in numerous cultural contexts. Jacques Derrida argues that "the messianic is a general structure of experience," and "the messianic dimension does not depend upon any messianism, it follows no determinate revelation, it belongs properly to no Abrahamic religion." It is, he says, inherent in culture:

> Messianicity without messianism ... is the opening to the future or to the coming of the other as the advent of justice.[6]

As a worldly event, the messianic brings justice to the world, and as an intrapsychic event, it brings equanimity to the psyche; that is, it restores a law or order that was lost or eclipsed when the ego was brought into being.

The messianic is carried by the archetype of the new self, and true to form, its arrival is typically deferred. It appears as an event at the horizon of consciousness and at the edge of our knowing. In a sense the coming of the spirit can never be finalized, because we are talking about a potentially infinite reality that can never be realized in time. The fact that it never fully arrives is not cause for skepticism or doubt, but cause for a high degree of humility before a mystery we can barely understand. In the movement of the spirit toward realization, there will always be a surplus of meaning, always remain more to be revealed, as our finite images become saturated with significance.

Destruction and Renewal

In our era the idea of the transformation of the ego has arisen again, because there is a great amount of psychic reality that is pushing up from the unconscious and intent on being expressed. The modern Western ego has become too sure of itself and firmly circumscribed, which has activated a compensatory process in the unconscious. Consequently, as Jung put it, the theme of "destruction and renewal has set its mark on our age," and this "makes itself felt everywhere, politically, socially, and philosophically."[7] Jung continues:

> We are living in what the Greeks called the *kairos*—the right moment—for a "metamorphosis of the gods," of the fundamental principles and symbols. This peculiarity of our time, which is certainly not of our conscious choosing, is the expression of the unconscious man within us who is changing. Coming generations will have to take account of this momentous transformation if humanity is not to destroy itself through the might of its own technology and science.[8]

The unconscious life within us is changing, and it is essential that the ego begins to participate in this transformational process. It has to actively engage in its reconstruction, without which it will remain the passive object of a process over which it has no control. When this occurs, the destructive or de-structuring action of the spirit comes to the fore, since the process of renewal can only take place with the cooperation of the ego. If the ego resists change, it can be destroyed by the process that strove to bring it healing and renewal. Depth psychology has always emphasized the need for a two-way, dialogical movement between ego and new self, and it is imperative that the ego becomes aware of its situation.

Spiritual Event and Pathological Obsession

The ego needs to participate in its self-overcoming, so that a truer and deeper self can emerge. The ego resists this process because it makes it feel uncomfortable. Although the "inner person" is ready for change, the ego clings to its habitual position and frustrates a process that has been archetypally sanctioned. Anthony Stevens refers to this as "the frustration of archetypal intent," and spoke of the dire consequences that result for individuals and society.[9] When the ego fails to understand

Apocalypse

what is happening, this lack of awareness creates the conditions for the literalization and projection of archetypal contents. Then the human sphere is beset by "strange ideas" and "weird notions" that may or may not have any bearing on outside reality. In a sense, the inside landscape replaces the outside, and eventually substitutes for it in paranoia and obsession. Our perceptions become clouded and confused by contents that belong on the inside but have found their way to the outside by default.

In this case obsessive ideas and compulsive thoughts take hold of certain people in the community, especially those who are susceptible to the unconscious and able to be used by it to express its inner life. Hence intuitives and artists at the high end of the spectrum, and neurotics and psychotics at the other, are fed information from the psyche that they have to understand or live out as best they can. The idea of "apocalypse" emerges when the figure inside us has built up so much energy and resentment that it can only explode into life with devastating force. This figure becomes super-charged with a life that has not been able to be expressed. It explodes with a life that could have been creative, but now can only be destructive. I have long been convinced that the main element that separates the artist from the madman is the ability to channel archetypal energies into symbols that contain the psychic contents.[10]

When the preacher on the street, or the televangelist on screen, cries out "the end is nigh," he does not know how right he is. This can be seen as a psychological process gone wrong, a response to the inside that has been projected outside and worn on the t-shirt of the fundamentalist as a slogan. The opportunity of seeing the dynamic as an interior process is subverted by literalism, and the more worldly and political the images become, the further away from the psyche we are led. Those who are suggestible are taken in by prophecies of doom, but those who are adjusted to society and its norms are inclined to dismiss the claims as claptrap. The so-called normal person in the street sees the preacher as crazy. But neither the possessed evangelist nor the secular member of society is able to experience the idea of the apocalypse as a transformative internal idea.

Outside religion, the myth gathers force in the "space" cultures of science fiction, popular fantasy, stargazers, UFO spotters, and alien abductions. Large numbers of people are convinced of the existence of higher intelligence beyond earth and are waiting for this to manifest. Some view the interstellar intervention as a matter of urgency: they hope the aliens arrive soon and wrest power from human hands before we blow ourselves up or destroy the planet and its species in a conflagration. However the outer space discourse is similar to the religious narratives in that it is divided between utopian and dystopian scenarios. Some see the aliens as saviors who are destined to pluck us from our confusion and lift us to a new level of consciousness. Others view the aliens as deadly beings who seek to overwhelm humanity and plunder the earth and its resources.

It is important that more of us attempt to understand the apocalypse at a psychological level, so the power inherent in the idea is not arrested in literalism of the fundamentalist or fictional kind. The apocalyptic goal is none other than the transformation of consciousness, and the shift from egocentrism to a larger identity based on psychic wholeness. As it moves across the threshold into awareness, the archetypal idea would be divested of its obsessive features, and the personality would be able to withstand, and be prepared for, the transformation of personality.

Violation of the Ego's Boundaries

The end is certainly nigh for the conventional ego, whose "world" is indeed going to collapse. A source of higher intelligence is waiting in the wings, choosing its moment before it assaults the ego and wrests power from its hands. This intelligence is "alien" to the ego and perceived as coming from outside the ego's sphere. Like the aliens in popular fiction, the wisdom of the second self is greater than that of the ego, more ancient (and at the same time more advanced and savvy), so it can outwit the ego. The ego feels stalked by this alien life, and may even experience it as tyrannical and malign. In every apocalyptic scenario, the ego experiences the spirit as a violation.

Lucy Huskinson explains the archetypal context of this violence:

> The creativity of the Self . . . [is] a Dionysian violence in which the ego is effectively torn apart in order to be born anew. The "violence" of the Self in this context is therefore not malign, as it is not wholly destructive: it does not seek to eradicate all ego-consciousness, but seeks the ego's continual improvement by disrupting its misguided orientations. Violence therefore describes the destruction necessary to initiate the vital creative process of individuation, and the Self is "violent" because it is experienced as an overwhelming force that violates the self-containment of the ego, and forces the ego, often against its will, into a new identity.[11]

However, violence is guaranteed in this struggle, because despite the ego's need to recognize the supremacy of the second self, it cannot and must not capitulate to it. The ego cannot afford a passive surrender, because the spirit can destabilize it and render it dysfunctional. Not that the spirit *intends* this savagery, but it happens. Huskinson quotes Levinas to make the point:

> Violence consists in welcoming a being to which it [the ego] is inadequate.[12]

Jung insists that the ego must stand its own ground, and "have it out" with the unconscious, which must be wrestled with:

> The god appears at first in hostile form, as an assailant with whom the hero has to wrestle. This is in keeping with the violence of all unconscious dynamism. In this manner the god manifests himself and in this form he must be overcome. The struggle has its parallel in Jacob's wrestling with the angel at the ford Jabbok. The onslaught of instinct then becomes an experience of divinity, provided that man does not succumb to it and follow it blindly, but defends his humanity against the animal nature of the divine power.[13]

Jung emphasizes that the ego has to wrestle the second self, and cannot give over to the stronger figure on first encounter. There is a process of negotiation that needs to take place between conflicting parties, and the "animal nature of the divine power" is a mighty force that must be respected. The ego must stand its ground, which means withstanding the "onslaught of instinct." Our task is to defend our humanity and not capitulate to the hostile god, who may show the ego more respect when the ego shows respect for him.

Jung argues that Christian thought has not prepared the modern person for this battle, because Christianity has emphasized the benevolent face of God. When "the god appears at first in hostile form" we may not recognize it because we have not been prepared for its wrath. Jung advises Christians of the modern West to return to the wisdom of the Old Testament to find countless references to the wrath and might of the primal God, an aspect that Christianity has lost sight of and needs to reappropriate. In this sense, Christianity has lulled the modern West into a false sense of security, and may in part be responsible for the ego's unpreparedness for this encounter. Jung's examples of this fateful encounter with God are always drawn from Jewish scriptures, and his favorite examples are Jacob wrestling with the angel, and Job facing the wrath of Yahweh, even though Job had done nothing to deserve the wrath directed at him.[14]

Readers of the New Testament have to read to the end of the scriptures to find the primal violence of the divine in the Book of Revelation. This book is rarely studied critically by followers of the mainline traditions, and Calvin famously declared he could not make sense of it at all. On the other hand, the fanatical branches of Christianity seem fixated on Revelation, reading it as a prophecy of historical events "soon" to unfold. The fact that each generation across two millennia has interpreted the vision in terms of its own history and future does not seem to bother those who find it relevant to today. But scripture scholars generally agree that beneath the teeming morass of symbolism and abstruse imagery we can discern four major elements or stages of apocalypse: revelation; judgment; destruction and punishment; and renewal by the founding of a new world. I will now briefly review each of these.

New Self as Original Self

In depth psychological terms, "revelation" occurs when the ego recognizes it is not master of its house, but a prior claim is made upon its existence. This may be an unpleasant shock or an ecstatic surprise, or a mixture of both. It often occurs in a shattering moment, where the previously invisible reality of the second self is made visible and the ego recognizes it lives in the presence of something greater. Jung writes of the psychological apocalypse this way:

> When the summit of life is reached, when the bud unfolds and from the lesser the greater emerges, then, as Nietzsche says, "One becomes Two," and the greater figure, which one always was but which remained invisible, appears to the lesser personality with the force of a revelation. He who is truly and hopelessly little will always drag the revelation of the greater down to the level of his littleness, and will never understand that the day of judgement for his littleness has dawned. But the man who is inwardly great will know that the long expected friend of his soul, the immortal one, has now really come to make his life flow into that greater life—a moment of deadliest peril![15]

The idea that the greater emerges from the lesser leads to the paradoxical idea that the ego gives birth to the second self, even though the later is greater than the ego. This opens the further conundrum that the so-called "second self" that we encounter in our maturation is the *original self*, which constitutes the origin of the ego and of human life.[16] A strange paradox, perhaps, but it is reiterated in Revelation in

Apocalypse

its mythic language. The Christ of Revelation says at the beginning and end of this text:

> I am the Alpha and the Omega, the first and the last, the beginning and the end.[17]

For John of Patmos, Christ is the origin of our existence and the goal toward which we strive. In psychological language, the second self is the Omega, and the original self the Alpha. But it is the same self, only encountered at different stages of the journey. It seems fascinating that whether we are employing mythological or psychological language, there is no escaping the reality of paradox: the goal to which we strive is the source of our lives. This raises the image of life as a circular process, only we "arrive where we started" and "know the place for the first time."[18] In the course of our journey, we produce, as it were, this divine life from our suffering. This leads to the mystical idea that God is "born" into life by our experience. In alchemy the symbol of the incarnate God, the philosopher's stone, is called the *filius philosophorum*, the son of the philosophers, since they have helped to bring the stone to realization. In late medieval mysticism, Meister Eckhart wrote that God asks to be "reborn in the human soul."[19] In psychological language:

> The supreme psychological goal has not only a divine archetypal begetting but also an earthly ego begetting.[20]

This dimension of the spiritual journey has long been suppressed by orthodox tradition, because it shows that God needs humanity in order to fulfill himself, and religion has insisted that God is perfect and has no need of us. Only we have need of God. However, the missing side of the equation boosts the status of humanity beyond the sinful creatures that dogma and creed have insisted we are.

I would like to introduce a note about psychopathology into this discussion. At the time of the appearance of the second self, the ego may feel it is being watched or observed by an other. If this is expressed pathologically by an ego unprepared for the encounter, it may manifest as an attack of paranoia, a disorienting experience in which the subject imagines him- or herself as being watched by others, monitored by hidden eyes or under surveillance. Psychiatry has yet to discover the spiritual background of paranoid schizophrenia, because it operates in a materialistic paradigm that pretends not to know about such things.

Once it takes depth psychology seriously, which has yet to happen, it will be open to this perspective.

But if the ego is able to recover strength, the pathology of paranoia can be transformed into the experience of living under the watchful gaze of the Eye of God. This is a motif that emerges repeatedly in *The Great Gatsby*, although Fitzgerald uses it ironically to point to what was once experienced in a God-fearing world, but that is no longer experienced today.[21] The invasiveness of the divine is lost if the ego accepts the reality of an invisible other, in which case the negative aspect of the "evil eye" is transformed into the loving gaze of an Other who watches over and supports the ego in its trials. This is a classic case of a close relationship between spiritual and pathological experience, where the one can be seen as the inversion of the other. A purely secular existence means that society will most likely experience more examples of the negative kind, because positive experiences of religious life are not available.

Judgment

The element of judgment may express itself in a number of ways. The ego feels judged as soon as it becomes aware that it is answerable to a hidden order. It recognizes that its actions are now called to account, as its freedom has been limited by a greater authority. To some extent, the ego may even feel its freedom has been something of an illusion, since it is so circumscribed by forces beyond itself. The very appearance of the second self causes moral panic to strike at the heart of the ego, which may become ashamed of some of its past actions and present opinions.

In particular, the ego is judged by the appearance of the shadow, which emerges at the same time as the figure of wholeness. The shadow emerges as a moral challenge to the ego, urging it to become aware that it has to be more responsible for elements that it had previously denied. The ego has to learn to face the shadow, and accept the darker aspect of its nature, which is not something it wants to do. As Jung explains: "the individual is faced with the necessity of recognizing and accepting what is different and strange as a part of his own life, as a kind of 'also-I.'"[22] Such acceptance calls for a broadening of horizons, and a moral vision that explodes the narrow range of the ego, which thinks that what it believes is always right. The "Day of Judgment" falls upon the ego as soon as the watchful eye of the second self begins to dialogue with it, and assess its position vis-à-vis the perspective of wholeness.

Moreover not only do we meet the ego's shadow at this fateful moment. We may also come into contact with the shadow of God, which can be shattering for the ego, and especially for its ideals and images of God and highest objects. The shadow of God is the collective aspect of the shadow, its archetypal character, expressed mythologically as the devil or Satan, and often by what Jung calls the "animal nature of the divine power." The moment of judgment is two way and by no means an experience confined to the ego. In this encounter, the God is forced to expose its own dark side, and its animal nature is on display for the ego to behold.

This deeper aspect of the encounter is never taken into account by literalists, who only see a one-way judgment coming from a perfect God to imperfect humanity. But in Jung's reworking of the myth of Revelation, God himself stands on trial, revealing his shadow side to a terrified and often barely functioning mortal being. For me, Jung's two-way reinterpretation of the judgment strikes a note of truth, and helps us understand that in the process of incarnation and coming-to-be God faces the challenge and indignity of having to recognize his imperfections. It is not only man and woman who become conscious of their shadow; incarnation means the divine becomes conscious of its darkness, as it sees its reflection in humanity. This, I take it, is what Jung means when he says:

> It is not man who is transformed into a god, but the god who undergoes transformation in and through man.[23]

Incarnation is humbling and humiliating for God, because in the individuated human being the creator glimpses its own face for the first time.

Destruction and Punishment

The stage of punishment is evident in the turmoil the ego experiences as it is challenged by the second self. Anxiety is a key symptom of this encounter. The ego is made anxious by the presence of the other, and by the implied or direct judgment coming from the other. The ego can feel enfeebled by the sense of its smallness and the awareness that it could be destroyed. But the second self does not wish to destroy the ego, despite what the ego tells itself in its anxiety, its fear of annihilation and loss of confidence. Huskinson argues that "destruction" has to be re-contextualized as a subjective experience of the ego:

> In the experience of the ego in its encounter with the Self... the ego is exposed to the creative forces of the Self that seek to destroy the

inferior ego-orientation with its tendency to prejudice in order to create a more affluent and well-balanced ego-orientation.[24]

She writes: "the Self... is an affective experience that can bring destruction and transformation to all that was hitherto considered secure and fundamental to ego-consciousness."[25] Edinger follows the same line of thought:

> The Apocalypse bodes catastrophe only for the stubbornly rationalistic, secular ego that refused to grant the existence of a greater psychic authority than itself. Since it cannot bend, it has to break. Thus "end-of-the-world" dreams, and fantasies involving invasion from outer space, and nuclear bombs, do not necessarily presage psychic catastrophe for the dream but may, if properly understood, present the opportunity for an enlargement of personality.[26]

Although Jung emphasizes that the apocalyptic encounter is "a moment of deadliest peril," there is an underlying optimism that the second self does not seek to crush the ego. In this sense, depth psychology presents a picture of the apocalypse that is both utopian and dystopian. But in the final analysis, Jung errs on the side of utopian scenarios, while pointing out that the dream of individuation can turn into a nightmare at any point along the way. Jung has a decisive *faith* that the second self is not malign, and if we learn to trust and to work with it, a positive outcome can be anticipated with some degree of confidence.

The text of Revelation makes it clear that only an ego that refuses to participate in the divine will be crushed. The image repeatedly used in this text seems to be borrowed from the gospel narratives:[27]

> If you will not awake, I will come like a thief, and you will not know at what hour I will come upon you.[28]

It is the "unawakened" person who will have to face the wrath of the divine. This figure is prepared to perform what to the ego are "criminal" acts, to achieve its goal of incarnation. If Revelation becomes increasingly violent in its imagery, it is because the author of the text fears that humanity will be unable to "awaken" to the divine, and thus be subject to the punishment of the second self. Or it could be, and this is only a conjecture on my behalf, that the author of Revelation is himself unable to open to the divine, and the wrath meted out to "humanity" in its "hour of trial" is a global projection of his inability to cooperate with the spiritual forces at work in his nature.

Having read this book several times, I feel there is a disproportionate amount of evil in its representation of God, and Christ often appears as a crazed warrior who seeks "war against [his enemies] with the sword of my mouth."[29] It is hard to reconcile this image of God and Christ with the Christian notion that these beings are benign. Perhaps some of the Old Testament wrath has reappeared, or perhaps, more likely, the author is beset by a deep-seated resistance to his own spiritual nature. His inadequacies before the divine could result in the divine face becoming malign. He may be unable to perform what he commands others to enact: a giving over to God in which the divine is allowed to transform us into its likeness. I have often felt there is more pathology than prophecy in Revelation, and although it is presumptuous to pronounce on its author, the Bible has been sullied by the exaggerated emphasis on destruction. Needless to say, the presence of evil, malice and revenge has attracted the pathological elements of many of its advocates across the ages.

God as Interruption

The Book of Revelation is so difficult that many right-minded believers leave it well alone. Its archaic, mythological character is almost impenetrable, and I have required commentaries to help me to understand it.[30] As indicated, we can get the same message, in more palatable form, from depth psychologists and commentators who are sensitive to the holy war or "jihad" between ego and second self. We can also get the message from the Jewish philosopher, Emmanuel Levinas, whose work employs the same imagery that we find in the New Testament. Levinas does not speak about a war between ego and original self, but he uses the terms "Same" (ego) and "Other" (God). In his "God and Philosophy," he argues that the Other makes a claim on the Same, disturbing the Same and awakening it to a sense of moral and spiritual responsibility:

> Responsibility for the other is precisely what goes beyond the legal and obliges beyond contracts; it comes to me from what is prior to my freedom, from a non-present, an immemorial.[31]

For Levinas ethical responsibility for others is founded on spiritual responsibility for the Other. The core of ethics is spirituality, and without the spiritual the ethical situation of human and social behavior will rapidly deteriorate.

Levinas speaks of the "awakening of the Same—drowsy in his identity—by the Other."[32] The Other shocks and disturbs the subjectivity of the Same, calling it forward to ethical responsibility and choice, which is at the same time an awakening to a reality higher than itself. This connectivity with the Other is achieved through love, encouraged by the conscience, and its loss is attended by shame and guilt.

According to Levinas, our awakening to a larger reality is resisted because it is painful. It is easier to fall asleep within the soft cocoon of the Same, where the ego is, as he says, "drowsy in its identity." I often think of this phrase when I see the sprawl of suburbia in our cities, each family cocooned in a paradise of its own making, hoping for as little interruption as possible to what is perceived as normality. Levinas speaks of the "trauma of awakening"[33] and implores his readers to awaken to the trauma of suffering, which, as a Jewish writer, is exemplified above all in the Holocaust. Using a different set of terms, Levinas speaks of "the More which devastates and awakens the Less."[34] The human person, he argues,

> is disturbed in the core of its formal or categorical *sameness* by the *other*, which tears away at whatever forms a nucleus, a substance of the same, identity, a rest, a presence, a sleep.[35]

The Other is abrasive, as its role is to deconstruct the ego, expose it to critical enquiry, and disrupt its complacencies. This squares with Jung: the role of the unconscious is to deconstruct the conscious and challenge it to move toward fuller realization. Levinas does not employ Jungian terms, but he is talking about the same thing, which is the transformation from an ego-centered identity to a larger identity capable of containing contradiction. As a contemporary philosopher, Levinas is shy of using religious terminology to describe this awakening, but he uses it anyway:

> To use an obsolete language, it is the spirituality of the soul that awakens with the Other.[36]

Levinas implores us to build a spiritual self, so we can restore our relationship to the divine and recover our humanity. He argues that when we restore this pact or covenant the abrasive impact of the Other is reduced. When we turn to the divine with openness to its mystery, it shows a different face to us: it becomes creative and constructive. Jung has the same view, but in psychological language: he says that taking the psyche seriously, acknowledging its reality, "pays the unconscious a tribute that more or less guarantees its cooperation."[37] Jung would argue that the defective element in the psyche is not the Self but the ego.[38] The ego becomes defective because it fails to read the signals of the Self, and subjects itself to the disasters that attend such failures. The idea of a defective Self, or an inherently malign spirit, is ruled out by Jung as unlikely. This is why I have concerns about the author of Revelation. Blake is a trustworthy guide, and he said, "Eternity is in love with the productions of time."[39] For John of Patmos, eternity bares its teeth at time, and this seems hard to believe.

For Levinas, the More which *devastates* and *awakens* the Less continues to bring a degree of discomfort and pain to the ego, but makes possible our experience of love and joy: "Love is possible only through the idea of the Infinite—through the Infinite put in me."[40] He is talking about a new "me," not the old bundle of wishes and desires that constitute the ego, but a new self that awakens to a new reality and greets this reality as liberation and homecoming.

The recognition of the Other in the Same is to be contrasted with the infantile and reductive attempt by the ego to assimilate the Other to itself. This is what happens in some cases of psychosis: the person glimpses the divine, and identifies him- or herself with it. He imagines that he is Christ, or he is God, which is so toxic that it brings on psychological imbalance. Jung calls this "inflation," while the Greeks referred to it as "hubris," a serious and common mental disease. It may be because of this predilection in the human psyche that the churches decided to ban the idea of the interior experience of the divine, although this may be attributing too much intentional wisdom to them. I think their literalism could not get beyond the idolization of Christ and that is the more likely reason for their refusal to open up the interior pathway to God. If the churches cannot do this, the philosophy of Levinas and the psychology of Jung must be our guides.

Rapture

In the popular versions of the apocalypse, religious fanatics place a lot of emphasis on the *rapture*. Following the words of Revelation, they expect to be lifted up to heaven during the "time of trial."[41] Believers anticipate that they are the chosen who will be removed from harm and deposited safely in heaven while the conflagration rages on earth. In the fundamentalist literature, and in the cultic websites in the United States, there are images of abandoned cars on the freeways, as the "just" ones are lifted from their seats and "beamed up" to heaven.

Edinger does not like this aspect of the story, and gives it a negative interpretation: "Such a state of mind is a dehumanizing inflation that seeks permanent release from egohood and materiality."[42] He says those who expect "to meet the Lord in the air"[43] are suffering from delusions of being the elect, special, and chosen by Yahweh. I am less sure about this, because the idea of being chosen, elect, is not constructed as a pathological feature in the scriptures, but is seen as a consequence of possessing faith in God. It might sound inflated to us, but in terms of scripture this provides the ever-present hope of a just and salvific future.

We cannot always transpose our modern views to the scriptures. I would prefer to look upon the rapture symbolically, as part of the mythos of this story. As opposing worldly forces turn against each other and bring on the final catastrophe, the spirit constellates a transcendent rapture as an urgent response to the activation of tension in the soul. The rapture is for me a symbol of "standing above" the conflagration of opposites, and an attempt to view the conflict from a heightened standpoint. This would give new meaning to the idea of being elevated and beamed into heaven. In a sense, when a transcendent calm is awarded us, it feels like a glimpse of heaven to the person who has been torn apart by the war of ego and spirit.

The fact that the rapture is instigated by God, and not by man, suggests to me that the spirit has activated this image of respite, so the ego is given the confidence to believe it can continue the battle with an anticipation of release. But I understand Edinger's point of view when I survey the popular literature and the ratty websites in this field, which express high levels of pathology. In the popular imagination, the salvation experience is supernatural and miraculous, and seems to express the deluded hope of an ego that wants to regard itself as special. But I would argue that the myth is not pathological, and the image of the rapture can be experienced as a creation of the spirit rather than a delusion of the ego.

Founding a New Order

The final stage of the drama is the establishment of a new world order and the sovereignty of deity:

> Then I saw a new heaven and a new earth; for the first heaven and the first earth had passed away, and the sea was no more. And I saw the holy city, new Jerusalem, coming down out of heaven from God, prepared as a bride adorned for her husband; and I heard a great voice from the throne saying, "Behold, the dwelling of God is with Men. He will dwell with them, and they shall be his people."[44]

This comes as a relief for the reader. The note of harmony and unity is brief—there are only two short chapters of this beatific vision—whereas

Apocalypse

there are twenty chapters of war, strife, plague, disease, and mayhem. But the last two chapters of Revelation point to the restoration of the bond between humanity and God, after waves of blood, pain, and catastrophe. John's Revelation is not ecologically friendly, as the "cleansing" that takes place involves the destruction of the world:

> The first angel blew his trumpet, and there followed hail and fire, mixed with blood, which fell on the earth; and a third of the earth was burnt up, and a third of the trees were burnt up, and all green grass was burnt up.[45]

Again we cannot get carried away by this mythology; the author is trying to show that the world "as we know it," has to be sacrificed for the new reign of the divine. But there are "strong Christians" today who take these words literally, and imagine that God's creation has to be "burnt up" so the divine will return to earth. The metaphorical dimension is sorely needed when it comes to the ecological dimensions of this writing, which should be read as the destruction of the ego's world and its substitution by the spirit.

The New Jerusalem is the holy city, the place that is established once the human will gives over authority to the divine. Blake makes much use of the symbol of the New Jerusalem in his poetry: it is the image of spiritual triumph, and the crowning glory of human aspiration. Paradoxically, the fulfillment of human desire can only be realized once the human has abolished its opposition to the Other. In the process of transformation, humility has to be found, otherwise the new situation can be abolished and everything turns to mayhem. The human who basks in the glory of the New Jerusalem must be mindful of the precariousness of this condition. The ego is not abolished, but is subjugated by the greater authority: "Nevertheless not my but thy will be done."[46] The paradise of the New Jerusalem can only be achieved if "life" as we have understood it has been sacrificed, which accords with the saying of Jesus: "Whoever seeks to gain his life will lose it, but whoever loses his life will preserve it."[47] In many ways the Revelation of John of Patmos is in accord with the sentiments of the gospels, but the unrelenting bleakness of the path to paradise is an introduced feature.

One of the interesting features of the New Jerusalem, from our point of view, is that it contains no churches or temples:

> And I saw no temple in the city, for its temple is the Lord God the Almighty and the Lamb.[48]

With many churches and sacred buildings closing down in Western societies, and being sold to retailers and developers, the first impression this creates is of a godless society that has no room for the sacred. But it could be that the old religious order is disintegrating, not because civilization is going to the dogs, but <u>because the sacred is being expressed in the secular</u>. One cannot be too sanguine about this, because secular society is overrunning the old religious order, and getting rid of its liturgies and shrines. This is a regression to some extent, but at the same time it could point to the founding <u>of a new world order in which the dualism between sacred and secular has been abolished</u>. After all, if we are experiencing an "apocalypse now," and if Levinas, Jung, and Edinger are pointing to a psychological understanding of the revelation of the sacred, the old shrines that saw sacredness in an externalized system need to collapse. Part of the apocalypse is the disintegration of the old dualism between sacred and profane.

Notes

1. Emmanuel Levinas, *Of God Who Comes to Mind*, trans. Bettina Bergo (Stanford, CA: Stanford University Press, 1998), p. 130.
2. The churches have traditionally claimed that Revelation was written by the apostle John, author of the gospel of John. However, scripture scholars have cast doubt on this in recent decades, and it looks unlikely that the author of Revelation, referred to as John of Patmos, was the gospel writer.
3. Revelation 1:3; and repeated throughout the text.
4. Edward Edinger, *Archetype of Apocalypse: A Jungian Study of the Book of Revelation* (Chicago: Open Court, 1999), p. 5.
5. Revelation 22:20.
6. Jacques Derrida, "Faith and Knowledge: The Two Sources of "Religion" at the Limits of Reason Alone" (1998), in Gil Anidjar, ed., *Acts of Religion* (London: Routledge, 2002), p. 56.
7. Jung, "The Undiscovered Self: Present and Future" (1957), *CW* 10, § 585.
8. Ibid.
9. Anthony Stevens, *Archetype: A Natural History of the Self* (London: Routledge & Kegan, 1982), pp. 110–39.
10. This is the theme of my book *Gods and Diseases* (Sydney: HarperCollins, 2011; London: Routledge, 2013).
11. Lucy Huskinson, "The Self as Violent Other," *The Journal of Analytical Psychology*, 47:3, 2002, p. 438.
12. Huskinson, p. 445.
13. Jung, *Symbols of Transformation* (1912/1952), *CW* 5, § 524.
14. See Jung, *Answer to Job* (1952), *CW* 11.
15. Jung, "Concerning Rebirth" (1940/1950), *CW* 9, 1, § 217.
16. Original self is a term borrowed from Thomas Moore, *The Original Self* (New York: HarperCollins, 2001).
17. Revelation 22:13; also Rev 1:8 and 21:6.

18. T. S. Eliot, "Little Gidding" (1942), *Collected Poems 1909–1962* (London: Faber, 1965), p. 222.
19. Meister Eckhart, "German Sermons" (1292), in Oliver Davies, ed., *Selected Writings* (London: Penguin, 1994), p. 142.
20. Edinger, p. 20
21. F. Scott Fitzgerald, *The Great Gatsby* (1925; New York: Penguin, 2008), p. 26.
22. Jung, "The Stages of Life" (1930/1931), *CW* 8: 764
23. Jung, *Symbols of Transformation*, § 524.
24. Huskinson, p. 438.
25. Huskinson, p. 437.
26. Edinger, p. 13.
27. Luke 12:39
28. Revelation 3:3.
29. Revelation 2:16.
30. Apart from Jung and Edinger, I have found illumination from Gilles Quispel, *The Secret Book of Revelation* (London: Collins, 1979).
31. Emmanuel Levinas, "God and Philosophy" (1975), in Sean Hand, ed., (New York: Basil Blackwell, 1989), p. 180.
32. Levinas, "God and Philosophy," p. 209.
33. Ibid, 175.
34. Ibid, 175.
35. Ibid, 170.
36. Ibid, 172.
37. Jung, *Aion* (1951), *CW* 9, 2, § 40.
38. This argument is put by Marie-Louise von Franz in, *The Problem of the Puer Aeternus: The Adult Struggle with the Paradise of Childhood* (Zurich: Spring, 1970), p. 181.
39. William Blake, "The Marriage of Heaven and Hell" (1793), *Blake: Complete Writings*, ed. Geoffrey Keynes (Oxford: Oxford University Press, 1976), p. 151.
40. Levinas, "God and Philosophy," p. 177
41. Revelation 3:10.
42. Edinger, p. 39
43. 1 Thessalonians 4:17.
44. Revelation 21:1–3.
45. Revelation 8:7.
46. Matthew 26:39; Mark 14:36.
47. Luke 17:33.
48. Revelation 21:22.

8

Satan and Literalism

Symbolism is not the apprehension of another world, but the transfiguration of this world.
— Norman O. Brown[1]

We have seen in previous chapters that Jesus attempted to deliteralize his disciples' understanding of spiritual elements, such as the kingdom of heaven, God, and his own status. Such things are not merely static nouns that we can dispense with when we "stop believing" in religion. As nouns they can be set aside by disbelieving modernity, but the names point to realities that have to be reckoned with, whether we believe or not. The problem of literalism, and attempts to subvert it, are present in the scriptures. My deliteralizing project develops an interpretive movement already in the texts themselves, and I am emphasizing this direction for the reader, who may have decided that the abstract nouns—Satan, God, Angel—are meaningless. If we change the nouns of religion into the verbs of spirituality, we have gone a long way to redeeming the religious enterprise for modern times.

I would like to turn to two more contexts in which a nonliteral approach is demanded of us. First, the rebirth narrative in John, in which Jesus meets Nicodemus; and second, the temptation narrative in Matthew, in which Jesus encounters Satan.

Nicodemus and the Rebirth Story

The theme of Jesus' discourse with Nicodemus is that rebirth can only be understood by a metaphorical sensibility. Scripture scholars are not convinced that this "meeting" with Nicodemus happened as described in John. Instead they refer to this as a "teaching story" or parable whose aim is not historical accuracy but spiritual vision. Here we find Jesus, a metaphorical thinker, trying to explain the idea of rebirth to Nicodemus, a literal thinker. It stands as one of the Bible's most definitive statements of the need for metaphorical thinking in our understanding of spiritual transformation. It also stands as one of the greatest poetic scenes of the holy book, and a fitting context for Jesus to reveal his poetic nature in arguing a case for metaphor.

Nicodemus, a Pharisee, comes to Jesus by night, to learn from him the mystery of rebirth. He comes in the night because Jesus is viewed as a radical who disturbs the establishment, and the rabbi does not want to be chastised by his peers for consulting with a reprehensible figure. Some believe the story reflects John's anti-Semitism at the time of writing. I can't agree with this, as John was himself a Jew. Rather, he is opposing the old Jewish political and religious order. Nicodemus is described as a "leading Jew," and John is scoring points at his expense, making Christianity appear superior to Judaism in its possession of the secret of rebirth. John portrays the Pharisee as a fool for not understanding the basics of religious transformation. Nicodemus opens the dialogue by approaching Jesus: "Rabbi, we know you are a teacher who comes from God," and John's structural irony suggests that Nicodemus' authority comes not from God but from human institutions.

Jesus responds to Nicodemus' call for instruction by saying:

> I tell you most solemnly, unless a man is born from above, he cannot see the kingdom of God.[2]

Nicodemus replies, sounding like a student overawed by a master's wisdom:

> How can a grown man be born? Can he go back into his mother's womb, and be born again?[3]

Jesus responds, echoing his previous words:

> I tell you most solemnly, unless a man is born through water and the spirit, he cannot enter the kingdom of God: what is born of the flesh is flesh; what is born of the Spirit is spirit.[4]

Jesus is saying: as a man is, so he thinks. If we remain earthbound, and confined to our fleshly nature, we think literally about these things and get nowhere. If we want to aspire to the spirit, we have to break with earthbound, literal thinking, and begin to think metaphorically. If we think literally about rebirth, we end up confusing it with incest, "going back into the mother's womb." Such thinking is a perverse distortion of spiritual teaching. This is what literal thinking does, it perverts the spiritual message.

Satan and Literalism

Metaphorical thinking, Jesus seems to imply, comes from the spirit as a gift to us. Such thinking is "born of the Spirit," and hence generates a new approach to reality. The "kingdom of God," which is so hard to grasp by secular understanding as to be incomprehensible today, might be reconceived as a deeper realm to which we have access not through intellect, but through intuition, poetry and insight.

Jesus does not let Nicodemus off lightly. He admonishes the priest for his literal-mindedness:

> Do not be surprised when I say: You must be born from above. The wind blows wherever it pleases; you hear its sound, but you cannot tell where it comes from or where it is going. That is how it is with all who are born of the Spirit.[5]

This is a beautiful and haunting passage; one of the great passages of world literature. It is even more wonderful in the King James Version:

> Marvel not that I said unto thee, Ye must be born again. The wind bloweth where it listeth, and thou hearest the sound thereof, but canst not tell whence it cometh, and whither it goeth: so is every one that is born of the Spirit.

It has to be said that the older English translations are often better than the modern. They are more evocative, and achieve a condition closer to the original poetry of the text. They are not abstract instructions or exhortations, but the power of these words takes us into the realm to which they point. We feel the "wind" or "spirit" (Greek: *pneuma*), and hear it, but can only marvel at where it comes from and where it is going. The words place us in the realm of mystery and enigma, which is the condition of religion. The spirit is a transcendent reality and we ought not pin it down with the intellect, because it "bloweth where it listeth." Two thousand years before Keats defined the state of mind in which a poet writes poems as "negative capability," that is, a suspension of reason to enable another perception of the world to appear, we have Jesus the poet describing the same nonlinear condition as the one in which the sacred can be apprehended. The older translation stays in the mind, but the newer ones miss some of this mythopoeic power.

Jesus' reply to Nicodemus achieves the state of poetry, and is the reply of wisdom to the stupid but all too common logic of Nicodemus. Jesus is a poet by virtue of the fact that he knows truth and dwells in it. Nicodemus, however, cannot shift from his logic to Jesus' wisdom.

153

Beyond Literal Belief

He turns to Jesus after hearing his poetry, and asks: "How can that be possible?"[6] Whereupon Jesus is forced to admonish the rabbi:

"You, a teacher in Israel, and you do not know these things!"

or in the King James Version:

"Art thou a master of Israel, and knowest not these things?"[7]

Once again there is the suggestion that the priests of Judaism are divorced from the experience of spirit. The rabbis might know the letter of the law but not the spirit of the law. This is an indication that institutions corrupt the teachings of religion, whether the institutions be Jewish, Christian, or whatever. Does my own criticism of the Christian churches suggest I am anti-Christian? I don't think so, as there is such a thing as constructive criticism: criticizing with a view to reforming what has been smothered by tradition and hardened by convention.[8] John's criticism is mild compared with the more radical critique of Jewish leaders found in the gospel of Mark. The main point is not about race or creed, but about spirit being known not by institutional learning, but by imagination and poetry. It is poetry and metaphor that allows us to see the kingdom. Only metaphor and symbol can "carry us over" to spiritual thinking.

Incest Fantasies and Sexual Abuse

Although Jesus does not say "Get thee behind me Satan" to Nicodemus, the latter's thinking puts him in the devil's party. Throughout the gospels it is the devil who thinks literally about things of the spirit, turning them into common objects or abominations of egotistical desire. Today we remain caught at the pre-symbolic level, and are not "twice-born" or able to interpret the needs of the spirit. When the incest image arises for us, as it does for Nicodemus, who goes "by night" with his urgent question for Jesus, it expresses a need for transformation. But if there is no symbolic comprehension it can be acted-out in a literal way. Some perpetrators of incest and sexual abuse are unconsciously seeking an experience of rebirth as they go about their erotic molestations. Incest is a flexible term, and does not only refer to Nicodemus contemplating a sexual return to the mother. By "incest" we refer to all kinds of illegal and inappropriate sexual activities between family members, or between those entrusted with a parental role and their charges.

I find it significant that we are in the midst of an epidemic of clerical sexual abuse today. As police investigations and parliamentary commissions are conducted worldwide, we are made aware of the extent and long-standing nature of crimes of this sort. We have seen that "rebirth" is a pressing and urgent religious need, and if churches lack ways and means to bring this transformation about, the desire for rebirth can fall to a lower level and find a kind of pseudo or pathological outlet in criminal activities. There is so much infantilism and unconsciousness about sexuality in religious traditions that the sexual urge readily falls prey to misdirected spiritual impulses of this kind.

Like Nicodemus, many clergy are religious but not spiritual: they understand the letter but not the spirit of the law. They don't know how to redirect the libido from primitive urges to the higher life of the spirit. There is as yet very little understanding of the relationship between aberrant forms of sexual behavior and the unlived life of the spirit. Perhaps as well as focusing on the findings of a criminal court of law, the perpetrators of these crimes need to listen carefully to the words of Jesus on the possibility of spiritual rebirth. They are finding an ersatz solution to their spiritual desire in criminality, but what they need to be shown is that there is so much more than their current desires would lead them to believe.

The devil's approach to rebirth is a tawdry path, which does not deliver the sought-for prize of transformation. Instead of achieving rebirth, when the impulse is taken literally it lands such men in courts of law, police stations, jails and detention centers. Spiritual rebirth is so much more than the devil in our desires could ever imagine. Sexual addictions are regarded by depth psychology as unconscious and perverse attempts to seek rebirth of the personality. The psycho-spiritual approach to this problem has been explored by Robert Stein in *Incest and Human Love*.[9] Speaking of the perpetrators of crimes of sexual abuse, he writes:

> Healing does not lie in attempting to overcome these "perverse" desires, but in being able to experience fully the incestuous desires emotionally and imaginally.[10]

The desires are indeed "perverse," but the quotation marks suggest there is something more in the desires than we can see at first. Common sense recoils from the incestuous desires and pulls away in distaste. As such, the sacred element in the crime is not noticed, much less taken seriously. But common sense is not enough to help us understand the things of the spirit. We need insight and uncommon sense to break open the sacred inside the profane. As Jesus says to Nicodemus: "what is born of the flesh is flesh; what is born of the Spirit is spirit."[11] If you use the natural mind you will be stuck in the literal, but if you use the poetic or symbolic mind, you will find your way to the spirit.

This is why the art of metaphorical thinking is important for our spiritual and sexual health. It not only frees us from misreadings of ancient texts, but it frees us from criminal acts, such as incest and child sexual abuse. When we lose vision, there is a high price to pay. In proverbs we are told "Where there is no vision, the people perish."[12] In the Revised Standard Version this becomes: "Where there is no vision, the people cast off restraint."[13] We could reframe this as: "Where there is no metaphorical awareness, the people act out primary impulses." There are health and legal implications to thinking metaphorically about needs of the spirit.

As Freud put it, when the incest taboo breaks down, civilization is in crisis and quickly degenerates. But Freud did not take the further step that Jung took: when we interpret the desire for incest symbolically we find a new entrance into spiritual life. Jung found Jesus' discourse with Nicodemus moving. In his work on incest fantasies in his clients, *Symbols of Transformation*, he commented on the gospel passage as follows:

> Jesus' challenge to Nicodemus [is this]: Do not think carnally, or you will be flesh, but think symbolically, and then you will be spirit. It is evident that this compulsion towards the symbolical is a great educative force, for Nicodemus would remain stuck in banalities if he did not succeed in raising himself above his concretism. . . . The reason why Jesus' words have such suggestive power is that they express the symbolical truths which are rooted in the very structure of the human psyche. The empirical truth never frees a man from his bondage to the senses; it only shows him that he was always so and cannot be otherwise. The symbolical truth, on the other hand, which puts water in place of the mother and spirit or fire in place of the father, frees the libido from the channel of the incest tendency, offers it a new gradient, and canalises it into a spiritual form.[14]

Today there is no Christ-figure to instruct the Nicodemus in all of us. Culturally we possess no wisdom by which the incest tendency can be "canalized into a spiritual form," as Jung put it. Psychologists, therapists, and community workers can warn offenders to stop committing sexual crimes or risk severe punishment and social reprimand. But they cannot suggest how the offending act can be transformed into a symbolic experience or spiritual revelation.

Such widespread pathologies reflect the social cost of abandoning what Jung called the "symbolic life."[15] We think we have outgrown the need for symbol, ritual, and liturgy, in which we enact rites of renewal and rebirth. The modern person links such activities with the superstitious peoples of the past, who conceived of other worlds or different realities. For many of us, there is no "other world," no "kingdom of God." But whether we *believe* in the kingdom or not is beside the point. The fact is that this "kingdom" is a reality and not an object of belief. We have to adjust ourselves to spiritual reality, and if we fail to make this adjustment, we will go mad or be driven to criminal behavior.

Whether we believe or not, the "other" dimension is present and real. If we make no room for it, its forces act on us negatively, compelling us to dehumanizing behavior. The force that could bring transformation, brings violence and degeneration. Our society, ostensibly governed by reason, is torn apart from within by the savage gods. In this context, Jung wrote:

> It is as necessary today as it ever was to lead the libido away from the cult of rationalism and realism—not, indeed, because these things have gained the upper hand (quite the contrary), but because the guardians and custodians of symbolical truth, namely the religions, have been robbed of their efficacy by science. Even intelligent people no longer understand the value and purpose of symbolical truth, and the spokesmen of religion have failed to deliver an apologetic suited to the spirit of the age.[16]

The soul seeks transformation, with or without the aid of clergy as the "guardians and custodians of symbolical truth." But without religious outlet, the psyche will resort to pathologies to express its deep-seated impulses. We can only heal these epidemics by returning to the spiritual perspective. Without this perspective we are, in mythological terms, caught up in the diabolical thinking of Satan.

Satan as the Personification of Literalism

"All this I will give you," he said,
"if you will bow down and worship me."[17]

Early in his ministry Jesus is tempted by the devil, and although this is usually regarded as a temptation to power and wealth, it is, above all, a temptation to literal thinking. Jesus refuses literal thinking and the "worldliness" that such thinking entails. It is telling that church teaching rarely emphasizes the problem of literalism in these passages, because it is steeped in literal thinking itself. The relevant passages are found in Matthew 4, where Jesus is "led by the Spirit into the wilderness to be tempted by the devil."[18] The fact that this encounter with the devil was orchestrated by the Spirit is significant, for it is through this encounter that Jesus comes to develop his own metaphorical conception of the kingdom.

Jesus fasted in the desert for forty days and nights and was hungry. In this context the devil appears and tempts him, first by asking him to use his power to turn stones into bread, and secondly by asking him to throw himself down from the pinnacle of a temple, allowing him to be supported by angels. Thirdly, the devil takes him to a mountaintop from which the regions of the world can be seen and offers them to him. "If you are the Son of God," says the devil, "tell these stones to turn into loaves." But Jesus replied:

> "Man does not live on bread alone but on every word that comes from the mouth of God."[19]

The strategy is to shift human need from the physical to the spiritual plane. It makes us think immediately of the fourth petition of Jesus' prayer, which is usually rendered in English, "give us this day our daily bread."[20] However, in the original Greek, the meaning is different. The adjective translated as "daily" is, in Greek, ἐπιούσιος, or epiousios, revised to *supersubstantialis* in the Latin Vulgate, referring not to earthly bread but spiritual food.[21] The word is more correctly translated as food (as in manna) for tomorrow, not food for today. The prayer is a call to be nourished spiritually by "every word that comes from the mouth of God." It is appalling that the English translation would delete the spiritual dimension and substitute for it a literal one, as if to appeal to the "dumbing down" of religion for widespread appeal. In the wilderness scene it is the devil who asks for common bread to satiate physical needs, and Jesus who resists this to focus on the bread for tomorrow. Therefore, if in the "Lord's Prayer" we ask for the common bread of the day, we are of the devil's party. This is one example of the distortion of the gospel for populist needs.

Then the devil takes Jesus to the parapet of the temple and commands him to throw himself down from its great height. The devil quotes scripture: "He will put you in his angels' charge, and they will support you on their hands in case you hurt your foot against a stone."[22]

Jesus rebukes the devil by quoting a different passage of scripture: "You must not put the Lord your God to the test."[23] Then comes the final temptation:

> Next, taking him to a very high mountain, the devil showed him all the kingdoms of the world and their splendour. "I will give you all these" he said "if you fall at my feet and worship me." Then Jesus replied, "Be off, Satan! For scripture says:
> You must worship the Lord your God, and serve him alone."
> Then the devil left him, and angels appeared and looked after him.[24]

I have been influenced by Wolfgang Giegerich's analysis of this passage. In the essay "God Must Not Die!," Giegerich points out that the devil in this sequence of temptations "is not absolutely evil":

> He does not represent the dark side. He does not want to seduce Christ to commit a crime, to gratify evil lusts. Instead he merely represents the natural, concretistic perspective versus a non-literal one.[25]

In psychological terms, we might say the devil is not pure evil, but represents the ego and its desires. Those desires are hunger, the desire for spectacle and certainty, and the desire to rule and find power in a worldly sense. In particular, what this scene dramatizes is not a fight with a supernatural demon "out there," but Jesus' struggle with his own egotism, his desire for worldly conquest. This is a psychodrama, an imagined stage performance, for teaching purposes, in which Jesus confronts his power impulse or what Jung would call his "shadow."

Because Jesus' spirit lives in the divine light, his ego falls into his shadow and greets him as a demon. It sometimes happens that if the ego is not allowed to live, it finds semi-autonomous expression in the world, and appears as a kind of *doppelgänger* who tries to trick and deceive the individual. But this scene is pure myth; it never happened as fact, but it did happen, in a sense, in psychological terms. It represents Jesus' necessary encounter with his egotistical desires. He cannot live a full life without taking the ego into account, without it confronting him as a "problem." As we have seen, this series of events is willed by God, or orchestrated by the spirit. Jesus has to decide which side he is on; is he with the ego and its urges, or the spirit and its transpersonal desires?

All three temptations are important, but undoubtedly the most important is the last one, in which he is tempted to have power over "all the kingdoms of the world." This seems to be a pivotal temptation, since it serves to inspire in Jesus a sense that he can be a masterful participant in a "kingdom" of a different kind. When he is brought before Pilate in trial, Pilate asks him if he is the king of the Jews, and asks if he has a kingdom. Jesus replies:

> "My kingdom is not of this world; if my kingdom were of this world, my men would have fought to prevent my being surrendered to the Jews. But my kingdom is not of this kind."
>
> "So you are a king then?" said Pilate. "It is you who say it," answered Jesus. "Yes, I am a king, I was born for this, I came into the world for this: to bear witness to the truth; and all who are on the side of truth listen to my voice."[26]

What Jesus has done is transform the devil's call for power into a power of a different kind. "Yes, I am a king" he admits. He does have power; he has integrated the devil's call at a higher level.

The Sublimation of Base Instincts

What this passage shows is that spiritual life is not generated by extinguishing the devilish impulses, as Christian morality has long argued, but by transforming them into impulses of a different order. As Giegerich puts it:

> Rather than rejecting "kingdom" altogether and opting for something totally different, Jesus pushes off from and sublates, sublimates, distils, evaporates the concept of "kingdom."

Giegerich continues:

> So what we witness here in this scene is the first-time conquest or birth of this new objective soul dimension, the dimension of spirit as logical negativity, through the process of negating the natural desire or the naturalistic understanding of the desire. Jesus, we might say, sees through the superficiality of the literal (political) kingdom. He gets a clearer, deeper self-understanding about his actual desire. He for the first time becomes aware that he is indeed striving for "kingdom," but also comes to realize that he would only fool himself if he gave in to this wish for "kingdom" in the external sense of literal, political power as offered by the devil, and that that sense of kingdom would not at all give him what his soul in truth needs.[27]

This is an important point because it shows that Jesus gains his power not through repressing base urges, but through channeling them to a higher level. He does not crush the devil's desire, but overcomes "the naturalistic understanding of the desire."

The way of transcendence is not a moralistic condemnation of the ego and its desires, but a turning-around of these urges to serve different ends. All through the scriptures we are told that we should undergo *metanoia* or transformation to be able to enter the realm of God. But as I have explained, in the English version this is changed to "repentance." This is a poor representation of the gospels, which has played into the hands of a moralistic attitude that believes religion is synonymous with suppression. Jesus does not ask for repentance but for metanoia. Jesus gives the devil his due, or rather, it is the devil who plants in Jesus the seed of his own aspiration for spiritual kingship. The devil is *himself* at a lower level; himself before metanoia has taken place.

If we look closely at the three temptations, we see that Jesus applies his spiritual method to all of them. In response to the temptation to seek only physical food, he says, "Man does not live on bread alone." In response to the temptation to perform miracles that would make him fascinating to the masses, he says, "Blessed are they who have not seen, and yet have believed."[28] In relation to the temptation to rulership he says, "My kingdom is not of this world." The devil's offers look attractive, but are illusory. They satisfy short-term needs, but not the needs of the soul. They are rejected because they do not satisfy the inner self, which is only satiated by a deeper kind of nourishment. They are "wrong" because their promises are hollow and short-lived. The point I am making is that spirituality is not about suppressing desire but transforming it. The "seed" of the desire is in fact good, not evil. It kick-starts the spiritual process, which is a matter of taking that seed and "growing" it into a developed reality. Each of the devil's temptations is taken to heart and developed at another level. As Giegerich puts it:

> Jesus overcomes the worldly naturalism of the meaning of the words used [by the devil] and opens up a new dimension and inner depth of meaning of the same words that did not exist before.[29]

Herein we glimpse the gap between Christ and Christianity. Christ is not condemning devilish impulses in the ego, but showing those impulses that the rewards for which they crave are tawdry and hollow. The gospel Christ is just as interested in rewards as the devil, but Jesus wants the best rewards and the greatest riches. He reveals the devil to be mean-spirited and limited. The "pleasure principle" is switched up, not down, and it is then directed to nonliteral goals. Spirituality is not the blocking of desire but its fulfillment. The gospel Christ is close to the "antinomian" thinking of William Blake, who wrote:

> Those who restrain desire do so because theirs is weak enough to be restrained; and the restrainer or reason usurps its place and governs the unwilling. And being restrained, it by degrees becomes passive, till it is only a shadow of desire.[30]

Elsewhere in this poem, Blake says, "Evil is the active springing from Energy."[31] Evil is not the opposite of Good, but Good at a lower level. It is the Good without the advantage of nonliteral thinking. When the untransformed self feels empty, it thinks of filling up with food and drink. When the untransformed self thinks of spirituality, it thinks of miracles and wonders performed for entertainment. When the untransformed self thinks of rebirth, it thinks of transgressive and incestuous sexuality. When the untransformed self thinks of power, it thinks of politics and takeovers. But if reality is expanded, and things unseen are brought into the equation, the desires of the lower self find a more rewarding outlet. Evil in this sense is the good that has not yet reached its potential. The unholy is the holy without vision. This is why God orchestrated these temptations, to show Jesus that the path he had to travel was a pathway to the nonliteral and metaphorical.

Conventional morality is stifling and anti-life, as Nietzsche charged, because it fails to see the value of the so-called evil or shadow side of life. Its moralism jumps on this side and shuts it down. But this side contains the energy needed for transformation. Evil is the primary force that needs to be respected. If it is reviled or condemned, we have no libido to bring the spiritualization of humanity to fulfillment. Christianity has misunderstood the temptations of Jesus, and once again, literalism has played a part in blocking the understanding of these temptations. By assuming the devil to be an external or cosmic force, and not Jesus himself in another form, we misread the spiritual psychodrama represented in the gospels. Overlooking the psychological dimension has frozen religion into a moralistic system that does not serve life and nor does it serve development.

Jung says this about the encounter with the devil:

> We say that the devil tempted Christ, but we could just as well say that an unconscious desire for power confronted him in the form of the devil. The devil wants to tempt Jesus to proclaim himself master

of the world. Jesus wants not to succumb to the temptation; then, thanks to the function that results from every conflict, a symbol appears: it is the idea of the Kingdom of Heaven, a spiritual kingdom rather than a material one. Two things are united in this symbol, the spiritual attitude of Christ with the devilish desire for power. Thus the encounter of Christ with the devil is a classic example of the transcendent function.[32]

The "transcendent function" is expressed when two incommensurables collide, producing at first a stalemate or conflict, and then a resolution in which the conflict is shifted to a higher level. In this case, Jesus' ego and spirit want different things, but the resolution of the conflict is the idea of the kingdom of heaven. He can be a "king" in another world, which is another world in this one. He can become a master of the art of bringing eternity into time, God into humanity. This is his birthright, as he tells Pilate: "I was born for this, I came into the world for this."

According to this reading, the devil goes away, not because he has been banished or expunged, as fundamentalists like to imagine, but because the devil is no longer needed. He no longer needs to be part of the psychic economy, as his desires have been outgrown. He no longer functions as a personification of desire, since desire has been shown a greater splendor, a bigger glory. One gives the devil his due by trumping him and aiming for something more. As I have said, this is the opposite of tradition's insistence that we "get to heaven" by overruling instincts. Instead Christ shows how we transcend the conflict by offering our libido a higher gradient. He is a wily and shrewd therapist, not a life-denying moralist.

Giegerich is again persuasive:

> One might even surmise that the devil's spelling out his offers was indispensable for Jesus to clearly become aware of and define the totally other dimension of spirit that was to be his own specialty. Without getting the literal option clearly spelled out he could not have clearly pushed off to the figurative sense of kingdom that was his own goal. So the devil, rather than being his shadow in the usual sense of the word, was his psychopomp. He helped Jesus to find himself, to find into his own.[33]

The devil spelled out the literal option, and seeing the literal on offer—"all of this could be yours"—Jesus is able to say, in a sense, "It's not good enough, thanks all the same. I want more." Jesus wants more than the devil could imagine. He takes desire up a notch. This aspect of his life and ministry is misunderstood by the tradition that uses his name. Blake understood Jesus in this light, but most clergy have no notion of this libidinal Jesus. Their dualism prevents them from seeing him in this light. Dualism is reinforced and set in stone by literal thinking, and only metaphorical thinking can help us understand the fluid nature of the forces of good and evil, and their interplay in the formation of Jesus' character.

Notes

1. Norman O. Brown *Love's Body* (New York: Random House, 1966), p. 220.
2. John 3:3.
3. John 3: 5.
4. John 3: 5–6.
5. John 3: 7–8.
6. John 3: 9.
7. John 3: 10.
8. Prophetic criticism is described in Walter Brueggemann, *The Prophetic Imagination* (Minneapolis, MN: Fortress Press, 1978).
9. Robert Stein, *Incest and Human Love* (Baltimore: Penguin Books, 1974).
10. Robert Stein, "On Incest and Child Abuse," in *Spring 1987* (Dallas, Texas), p. 64.
11. John 3: 5–6.
12. Proverbs 29:18, *KJV*.
13. Proverbs 29: 18, *RSV*.
14. Jung, *Symbols of Transformation* (1912/1952), *CW* 5, § 226.
15. Jung, "The Symbolic Life" (1939), *CW* 18.
16. Jung, *Symbols of Transformation*, § 226.
17. Matthew 4:9, *NIV*.
18. *JB* Matthew 4:1.
19. Matthew 4:3–4.
20. Matthew 6:11; and Luke 11:3.
21. This word is apparently not found elsewhere in the classical Greek literature.
22. Psalm 91:11–12.
23. Deuteronomy 6:16.
24. Matthew 4:8–11.
25. Wolfgang Giegerich, "God Must Not Die!," in Greg Mogenson, ed., *God Must Not Die! (Or Must He?): Jung and Christianity* (New Orleans: Spring Journal, 2010), p. 17.
26. John 18: 36–37.
27. Giegerich, p. 19.
28. John 20:29.
29. Giegerich, p. 18.
30. William Blake, "The Marriage of Heaven and Hell" (1793), in ed., Geoffrey Keynes, *Blake: Complete Writings* (London: Oxford University Press, 1976), pp. 151–152.
31. Blake, ibid., p. 151.

32. Jung, letter to A. Zarine, 3 May 1939, in ed., Gerhard Adler, *C. G. Jung Letters*, Volume 1 1906–1950 (London: Routledge & Kegan Paul, 1973), pp. 267–268.
33. Giegerich, p. 20.

9

Resurrection: Ascending to Where?

Someone may ask, "How are dead people raised, and what sort of body do they have when they come back?" They are stupid questions.
— *St Paul*[1]

The Resurrection Conundrum

The resurrection, more than the virgin birth, is the cornerstone of Christian teaching. Theologians have said if there is no resurrection there is no faith. Or should that be: no belief? And why does it always have to be *physical* resurrection? Can't a spiritual resurrection be real enough to inspire faith? I agree with radical theologian Rudolf Bultmann, who said: "If the resurrection were a historical fact, faith would become superfluous."[2] If followers of religion have true faith, they should not require proofs of a historical or physical kind. Faith is precisely that which requires no evidence. This strikes me as a central contradiction at the heart of this religion: it urges faith, but requires proof, and as such, does not understand what faith is. St Paul wrote: "If Christ is not raised from the dead, your faith is vain."[3] But Paul did not insist on a physical resurrection, which he dismissed as a "stupid" idea, as in the quotation above.

I am prepared to believe in a spiritual resurrection, for which one would require no support apart from intuition or faith. But a physical resurrection, as proclaimed by doctrine or creed, is not only unlikely but preposterous. The question is: why did the church go down this path? There are "sightings" of the resurrected Jesus in the gospels, but these can be read as teaching or allegorical stories. Scripture scholars tell us that the Johannine scene in which the "Doubting Thomas" is confronted by the risen Christ, and invited to inspect Jesus' crucifixion wounds with his hands, has no basis in fact, is not corroborated by other gospel accounts, and is a fabrication of the early church.[4] The sightings of the risen Christ <u>are spiritual metaphors, in which the hopeful philosophy is put that the spirit never dies</u>, but goes on living after death. We can cope with this today, can't we? But I gather this was not enough to found a religion in the past.

As I have explored in chapters 4 and 5, Jesus had become fused with the archetype of spirit. It follows, then, that Jesus could never die, and the basis of the tradition is that he goes on living. His "afterlife," or resurrected body, is symbolic of the continued life of the spirit. Paul refers to his "glorified body," but that does not refer to a physical corpse being brought back to life in some kind of resuscitation. The gospel sightings, probably based on real experiences of personal visions or apparitions, are designed to inspire belief in the soul's immortality. They are not ghost stories about the postmortem appearance of a crucified body. As this chapter will argue, the sightings of a resurrected Jesus can be <u>read as parables and their meaning fully discerned if read symbolically</u>.

It is a tragedy that tradition has insisted that belief in an impossible event is synonymous with faith. This distortion is evident in the gospel redaction to which I have referred. The various church scribes and editors who wrote what we now call "John" have Jesus saying: "put your hand in my side; do not be faithless, but believing." Thomas answered him: "My Lord and my God!"[5] That was supposed to be the last word, but of course it isn't. It is so patently a distortion, or, in a kinder manner, an elaboration of a symbolic process. It may have fooled many in the past, but does not fool us today, given the advanced nature of scripture scholarship and its ability to detect inauthentic intrusions. The tragedy is that religion places faith in the same category as fraud or deception. If anyone doubts the scene of the Doubting Thomas, he or she is said to have no faith, and in the past such doubters were put to death or persecuted by the church. The church has never apologized for these atrocities, and nor has it apologized to the millions who succumbed to its assertions of factuality. Today the pious hyperbole is maintained, and countless numbers do not know the difference between faith and belief.

St Augustine put it starkly when he said: "On no point does the Christian faith encounter more opposition than on the resurrection of the body." Let's be clear about this: no physical body, Jesus' or any other, has gone into liftoff mode and headed skyward. To think this way is sheer fantasy and a denial of the finality of death. And yet in the history of the church, the physical resurrection was the "ultimate miracle that proved that Jesus was God and Christianity the one true religion."[6] To

Resurrection

say that Jesus is God, and can appear physically after death if he wants, is idolatry. The only way that the dire situation can be redeemed is to adopt a symbolic approach to the "body," as indeed St Paul did in his letters. Paul used the word "body" in a variety of ways, but his distinctions were ignored by tradition, which insisted on misreading him to satisfy a longing for the physical immortality of Jesus.

In ancient times, "body" was used in different contexts, and spirit and soul were referred to as the "subtle bodies" of our nature.[7] Tradition exploited this ambiguity to make assertions about the immortal nature of our bodies. I dare say that the early church believed that making these assertions would strengthen its cause and attract people to the fledgling religion of Jesus. Relying on the credulity of uneducated folk, large numbers would flock to the new faith, heartened by the prospect that even death could be avoided by its followers, as long as they "believed." But in our time, this strategy, if such it was, has backfired. Most educated people find the assertions of Christianity repellent and do not want any part of it. So what may have worked hundreds of years ago, and saved a new faith from extinction in a crowded marketplace of religious philosophies, has failed in our time. We are left with the embarrassment of a Christian legacy that tries to argue a case for the impossible.

My view is that we should look back to a time when these absurdities did not exist, so we can recover a true faith, and not a parody of faith thought up by councils. Although death may indeed have no dominion over spirit, it has dominion over the body, as any gravedigger will attest. Some of the creedal statements sought to fly in the face of the reality of death. Take for instance, the creed adopted at the Council of Lyons, which asked Christians to repeat: "We believe in the true resurrection of this flesh that we now possess."[8] There is not much subtlety here! Not only is this incredible, but it is contrary to Paul's letters. Even modifying the Apostles creed, so that instead of professing, "I believe in the resurrection of the flesh" it now reads "body," is not enough, unless we redefine what body means, given its contexts in ancient times. At the very least, we need a new creed that does not make use of these anomalies, a creed that accepts the facts of science rather than contradicts them.

Some apologists of the church attempt to make the contents of belief digestible by playing around with terms. Sandra Schneiders proposes that "Jesus' resurrection is not physical but *is* bodily and his body continues to mediate his relationship with his disciples."[9] She wants to make a distinction between flesh and body, so that "flesh" denotes "Jesus' career as a mortal" and "body" refers to "his glorified life." That way, she says, we can speak confidently about the bodily resurrection: "In his glorification Jesus goes to the Father as a human bodyself."[10] We ought to be wary of this kind of wordplay by those who seek to prop up collapsing dogmas. By changing the language, they seek to close the gap between theological assertion and credibility, but in doing so they refuse to acknowledge that church teaching has been misleading people for centuries. Such apologists wave a linguistic wand and hope that everything will remain intact.

Schneiders shows her true colors when she asserts: "Unless a real, living body can be ascribed to Jesus after his death, any talk of actual personal resurrection, his or ours, belongs in the realm of mythology, that is, of likely stories about otherworldly reality."[11] This is utterly wrong, and yet typical of theological writing. Unless there is a "real living body" it is said to be pure myth—and that term is used, yet again, in the negative sense of counting for nothing, or mere illusion. There is in this tradition an obsession with the body, a revulsion for and hostility to myth and an unwillingness to engage the substantial reality of spirit.

The literalism of the church may have misled people with good intentions, by offering hope in the resurrected spirit of Jesus, and in the common resurrection of all who participate in his spirit. But hope should not require hyperbole and fraud to makes its presence felt. The modern apologists, and there are hundreds of them, cannot pretend that a rupture has not occurred between church teaching and modern understanding. We cannot recapture St Paul's understanding of the body, and continuing to use this term perpetuates long-standing deceit. In their defense, theologians claim they do not want to take on a dualistic vision of spirit and body, but I find this disingenuous. The fetishization of the body of Jesus is something to overcome, and although it keeps many theologians in gainful employment, it is not helping the world to understand spiritual reality. The next step, and the most important one, is to ask whether we can find meaning in a revised and deliteralized concept of resurrection. It is upon such reconstructed meanings that the future of this tradition depends.

Joseph Campbell's Straight Talking

There is a large library of works on the resurrection, which I find daunting, attracting my attention and yet generating distaste at the same time.[12] The fetishization of Jesus' body is appalling in this literature,

Resurrection

and writers spend hundreds of pages trying to determine just what kind of "body" he has at the resurrection. If the bones of Jesus were discovered somewhere in Palestine, it would stop this endless and futile speculation. In this chapter I will be confining myself to the writings of St Paul, Crossan, Jung, and Campbell. Joseph Campbell has the gift of plain speaking and puts the resurrection conundrum in simple terms. If, he says, the meaning of the resurrection is to be found in literal terms, we are forced to reject it, as it does not make sense:

> A metaphor is an image that suggests something else. For example, Jesus ascended to heaven. The denotation would seem to be that somebody ascended to the sky. That's literally what is being said. But if that were really the meaning of the message, then we have to throw it away, because there would have been no such place for Jesus literally to go. We know that Jesus could not have ascended to heaven because there is no physical heaven anywhere in the universe. Even ascending at the speed of light, Jesus would still be in the galaxy. Astronomy and physics have simply eliminated that as a literal, physical impossibility.[13]

A lot of thinking ends here: it is impossible, could never happen, and atheism is the result. Or there is the early theological view expressed by Tertullian: the ascension of the body is impossible, therefore I must believe it.[14] However I would say: this is impossible, therefore it is not a discourse about historical events. The scripture is speaking another language, about things that logic cannot fathom. It is "speaking otherwise," using metaphors to say something that cannot be said. Campbell argues that we ought not concern ourselves with what the resurrection denotes, but focus on what it connotes:

> If you read "Jesus ascended into heaven" in terms of its metaphoric connotation, you see that he has gone inward—not into outer space but into inward space, to the place from which all being comes, into the consciousness that is the source of all things, the kingdom of heaven within. The images are outward, but their reflection is inward. It is a metaphor of returning to the source, alpha and omega, of leaving the fixation on the body behind and going to the body's dynamic source.[15]

After the rejection of physical resurrection, there is the second, more important move of reading the story in terms of its connotation. It is the connotative meaning to which mythos points, and if, as I have been arguing, scriptures were written in the mode of mythos, we are mistaken if we fail to take the connotation into account.

The metaphorical mode uses an image to suggest something else. The image of Jesus ascending into heaven is used to describe something that is indescribable, namely, "returning to the source." That is something we *can* believe in, even though we have no way to describe it, apart from the images we already have. But once we see that the denotative meaning is not to be taken literally, but is a literary device used to describe what is indescribable, then we are on the right level with this story. As we have seen throughout, one cannot read scripture correctly unless one has the literary key, and the key is its second level of meaning, not its first. The point of the first level is to make the second possible. Insofar as the second level is not taken into account, we have not understood the narrative at all.

In response to Campbell's view of the resurrection, his conversation partner, Bill Moyers, puts what one might call the literal or naïve religious protest:

> But aren't you undermining one of the great traditional doctrines of the classic Christian faith—that the burial and the resurrection of Jesus prefigures our own?[16]

Moyers does a good job of playing the role of Campbell's dumb sidekick, making Campbell appear as an intellectual giant beside his hum-drum commentary. Moyers plays the role of the uncomprehending Nicodemus, while Campbell is cast in the role of Jesus, the one who tries to get the less intelligent to understand the role of metaphor. Campbell is urged to reply:

> That would be a mistake in the reading of the symbol. That is reading the words in terms of prose instead of in terms of poetry, reading the metaphor in terms of the denotation instead of the connotation.[17]

The literal notion of the resurrection, and the literal promise of our resurrection, is false. To indulge in this is to tell lies for God, or more correctly, to tell lies for religion. It is a form of fantasy thinking, a denial of our death and Jesus' death.

If the bones of Jesus are discovered in Palestine, it ought not shatter our faith—and if it does, our faith is based on superstition. The resurrection is a spiritual event, and heaven is a spiritual place. If we must think in terms of a "location" of heaven, Campbell's notion of inward space is as good as any. He says Jesus returns to the kingdom within. But even this idea is a metaphor, if one that suits the psychological tenor of the time. We can never escape the metaphorical when talking of the spirit; it forces us into the language of poetry. The best we can do is exchange one set of metaphors for another—replace metaphors of an "outer space" heaven with new metaphors of "inner space." But there is no unmediated representation of these realities. Campbell sums up the resurrection well when he says:

> The Christ in you doesn't die. The Christ in you survives death and resurrects.[18]

This is its true meaning, and, to use Campbell's language, one wonders why religious tradition does not "leave the fixation on the body behind and go to the body's dynamic source." However, I would caution against taking Campbell too literally. The "interior" Christ is as much a metaphor as the dogmatic idea of the risen Jesus sitting on the right hand of God. The problem with metaphors, especially new ones, is that their fascination militates against us seeing them nonliterally. Their attraction beclouds our ability to see beyond them to the mystery to which they point.

Jung: Cutting through Spiritual Materialism

Jung believes that tradition's inability to accept the spiritual nature of the resurrection is a sign of its impoverishment and the materialism of its outlook. Although religion is supposed to represent spirit, Western religion, he claims, is not spiritual, because for it nothing is *true* unless it occurred in historical time and as material fact. Christianity is plagued by a materialistic attitude that prevents it from viewing its own stories in spiritual terms. This is what Jung calls the "Western prejudice," the widespread belief, found in religious and secular traditions, that something is not true unless it happens in physical manifestation.

In an essay on the resurrection written for members of his seminar on *Aion*, Jung wrote, "indubitably resurrection is one of the most—if not the most—important item in the myth or the biography of Christ and in the history of the primitive church." He continues:

> To the primitive Christians as to all primitives, the Resurrection had to be a concrete, materialistic event to be seen by the eyes and touched by the hands, as if the spirit had no existence of its own. Even in modern times people cannot easily grasp the reality of a psychic event, unless it is concrete at the same time. Resurrection as a psychic event is certainly not concrete, it is just a psychic experience. It is funny that the Christians are still so pagan that

> they understand spiritual existence only as a body and as a physical event. I am afraid our Christian churches cannot maintain this shocking anachronism any longer, if they don't want to get into intolerable contradictions.
>
> As a concession to this criticism, certain theologians have explained St Paul's glorified body given back to the dead on the day of judgment as the authentic individual "form," viz., a spiritual idea sufficiently characteristic of the individual that the material body could be skipped. It was the evidence for man's survival after death and the hope to escape eternal damnation that made resurrection in the body the mainstay of Christian faith. We know positively only of the fact that space and time are relative to the psyche.[19]

If Jung accuses the early Christians of being primitive thinkers, Paul was certainly not one of them. Paul's thinking about the resurrection is highly sophisticated, as we will see. I think the primitive thinkers were not the religious writers, but the church councils that moved to set in stone the notion of a physical resurrection. The councils were "fixated on the body" as Campbell puts it, rather than on the dynamic source from which the body draws its life.

Was this fixation on the body some kind of compensation for the fact that Christianity had left the body out of most of its moral equations? Its morality was otherworldly to the point of being body-denying, as Nietzsche charged. Was the physicality of the resurrection the return of the repressed in some form? Why does the physicality of the major story have such persuasive power over so many minds?

If we look closely at the gospels we find there is no physical resurrection or postmortem sightings in Mark, the earliest of the gospels, as his testament ends with the empty tomb.[20] Significantly, and in a blatant gesture of tampering to impose an ideological message, we find that an addendum to Mark's gospel has been added by church authorities. Mark ends his gospel at chapter 16 verse 8, but, unsatisfied by his downbeat ending, 16:9 to 16:20 has been "added" by later authorities, in which triumphal claims of sightings of the resurrected Jesus are announced. For Mark, the postmortem sightings were not relevant or part of the story, but authorities could not resist "improving" on his gospel to impose the view of the councils and stamp the text with the affirmation of a physical resurrection. Such tampering with scripture makes a mockery of the time-honored idea that this is the Word of God.

In the fourth gospel, John's Jesus is already transcendent and Godlike at the beginning of the narrative, and there is no need of a physical resurrection to prove his divinity. If we look closely at the letters of

St Paul, as Jung suggests we do, we do not find support for a physical resurrection, but on the contrary, Paul castigates those who think about the resurrection in literal terms.

Paul's Mysticism

Paul suggests that the resurrection has to be understood symbolically, and rails against those who want to see it as a merely physical event:

> Someone may ask, "How are dead people raised, and what sort of body do they have when they come back?" They are stupid questions. Whatever you sow in the ground has to die before it is given new life and the thing that you sow is not what is going to come.... The thing that is sown is perishable but what is raised is imperishable.... When it is sown it embodies the soul, when it is raised it embodies the spirit.
>
> If the soul has its own embodiment, so does the spirit have its own embodiment ... Or else brothers, put it this way: flesh and blood cannot inherit the kingdom of God, and the perishable cannot inherit what lasts for ever.... When the last trumpet sounds, the dead will be raised, imperishable, and we shall be changed as well, because our present perishable nature must put on imperishability and this mortal nature must put on immortality.[21]

There is nothing here to support the doctrine of a physical resurrection. Paul shows impatience with the idea and does not see it as central to the faith. Questions about a physical resurrection, he says, are "stupid": to reduce the resurrection to a physical event is to lose the true meaning of the risen Christ.

I have quoted from the Jerusalem Bible, but the King James Version gives an even clearer depiction of the distinctions Paul is trying to make:

> All flesh is not the same.... There are celestial bodies, and bodies terrestrial: but the glory of the celestial is one, and the glory of the terrestrial is another.... So also is the resurrection of the dead.... It is sown a natural body; it is raised a spiritual body. There is a natural body and there is a spiritual body.[22]

In this version Paul does not protest about "stupid questions" but says those who ask such questions are "fools."[23] Paul is uncompromising about the fate of the physical body, including the body of Christ: "What you sow does not come to life unless it dies."[24] The body is a "seed," he says, and the seed must die. "What is sown is perishable, what is raised is imperishable."[25] He continues: "It is not the spiritual which is first but the physical, and then the spiritual."[26] How more clear can he make it? He adds: "flesh and blood cannot inherit the kingdom of God."[27] There is no doubt in Paul's mind about the fate of the body: it is, like the first Adam, "of dust," and, "as was the man of dust, so are those who are of the dust."[28] The link is to Genesis: "for dust thou art and unto dust shalt thou return."[29]

The confusion arises when we encounter Paul's use of the word *soma*, Greek for body. Paul uses *soma* to refer to the physical body, the soul, and the spirit, and this is where our complications arise. Some have misread his statements on "celestial bodies" as a reference to the physical. For Paul, the physical is cast aside as a husk, and a spiritual body "put on." But we no longer think of spirit as a "body," but as a presence, or an archetype, and this stands at the heart of the confusion. Paul makes it clear that resurrection does not mean a *resuscitation* of the body. When he refers to a glorified body, he is not referring to the body as we know it, or "as we now possess," to contradict the creed of Lyons.

Paul's glorified body is synonymous with spirit, and a physical resurrection is not on his agenda. When he speaks of the resurrected body he uses the Greek *pneumatikos* (spiritually), and, as Northrop Frye asserts, "whatever else the word means, it means 'metaphorically.'"[30] Christ rose from the dead "metaphorically." It is not metaphorical in the sense that it is make-believe, or did not happen. It is metaphorical in the sense that nothing physical occurred, and no camera could have "recorded" this event. Something took place, but it can only be known, expressed, in metaphors. The images we use are at best lame, at worst, idolatrous. If we expect to be able to see the resurrection with our eyes, Paul would accuse us of being foolish. The Pauline testament is thus at odds with the church's insistence on the physical nature of the resurrection.

It has often been said that St Paul is the main theologian and doctrinal hero of the Christian evangelicals, but his thinking is far more mythic and symbolic than evangelicals would care to admit. Even if Paul's language about different kinds of "bodies" has created confusion, his stance on the spirit is metaphorical and not literal. Paul and Jung are saying the same thing when it comes to the interpretation of miracles. The mystery is that spirit does not experience a common birth and does not suffer a common death. The mystery is that spirit is immortal and everlasting, and after his death Christ rises in spirit and acts as source and inspiration for those who wish to follow in his spirit. This is not a mystery unique to Christ, but a mystery experienced by all of us, all of the time. Jung is not impressed by what Christianity has made of Christ:

> The gospel writers were as eager as St Paul to heap miraculous qualities and spiritual significances upon that almost unknown young rabbi, who after a career lasting perhaps only one year had met with an untimely end. What they made of him we know, but we don't know to what extent this picture has anything to do with the truly historical man, smothered under an avalanche of projections. Whether he was the eternally living Christ and Logos, we don't know. It makes no difference anyhow, since the image of the God-man lives in everybody and has been incarnated (i.e., projected) in the man Jesus, to make itself visible, so that people could realize him as their own *homo*, their self.[31]

Jung accepts that the figure of the savior needs to be projected so that the archetype becomes discernible. The projection of unconscious contents is inevitable, he says. What he criticizes is the extent to which this projection took place, its intensity and obsessive quality, so that the archetype of spirit is no longer accessible to the interiority of the person because it has been externalized. We need to take some of the burden of "Christ" from Jesus and take it on ourselves, so we too can suffer a spiritual passion and transform our lives. I hope I have shown that one can be religious without being a literal thinker, and one can be a Christian and yet refuse the doctrines of the church. Indeed, one can turn the tables on this question and ask: how Christian is the church? Do we have Christianism instead of Christianity? If St Paul is our authority on these matters, the church does not appear to be "Christian" in its reading of the resurrection.

Many of the teachings of the early church lack all the subtleties and distinctions of Paul. For instance, Irenaeus and Justin Martyr in the second century wrote against the idea that only the soul survived. Justin Martyr insisted that Christ promised to raise the body and the soul from the dead:

> Seeing as ... the Saviour in the whole Gospel shows that there is salvation for the flesh, why do we any longer endure those unbelieving and dangerous arguments, and fail to see that we are retrograding when we listen to such an argument as this: that the soul is immortal, but the body mortal, and incapable of being revived? For this we used to hear from Pythagoras and Plato, even before we learned the truth. If then the Saviour said this, and proclaimed salvation to the soul alone, what new thing, beyond what we heard from Pythagoras and Plato and all their band, did He bring us? But now He has come proclaiming the glad tidings of a new and strange hope to men.[32]

It is true that before Christianity, Greek philosophy had proclaimed that the soul was immortal and the body mortal. Some of the church fathers wanted Christianity to stand for the immortality of the body, and this was, in my view, based on a misreading. I stand by Paul, and against the church, on this matter. Ironically, some of the framers of doctrine quote Paul as their authority, in which case they are misreading Paul as well as the gospels. All one can say is that the minds that framed doctrine were not clear-headed, but were inventing a religion of their own.

The Parable of Emmaus

One of the key resurrection stories is the "sighting" of Jesus on the road to Emmaus, at the end of the gospel of Luke.[33] I have always had a special fondness for this story, and yet I have felt that the conventional reading of it is wrong.

In helping me understand the narrative of the Road to Emmaus, I have found the reflections of Crossan to be indispensable. In *The Power of Parable: How Fiction by Jesus Became Fiction about Jesus*, Crossan asks:

> Were the resurrection stories about Jesus intended as parables? Had we been reading parable, presuming history, and misunderstanding both, at least since literalism [had] deformed the Christian imagination?[34]

Crossan says "almost everyone," by which he means scholars of the New Testament, accept that the story of the Jerusalem to Jericho road with its Good Samaritan is "a fictional story with a theological message." "But what about the story of the Jerusalem to Emmaus road with its Incognito Jesus after the resurrection?" Most theologians do not see this as allegorical, but Crossan writes:

> Is the Emmaus story fact or fiction, history or parable? Many would say that the Emmaus story actually happened. But why is that so, when just a few chapters earlier [in Luke] a similar story is considered pure fiction, completely parable?[35]

Crossan argues that a double standard operates in our reading of the New Testament. Most Christians concede that Jesus' stories are fictions told for theological purposes. The stories of the Lost Sheep, the Prodigal Son, the Hidden Treasure, the Valuable Pearl, or the Unmerciful Servant are regarded as parables, that is, metaphors that have been extended

Resurrection

into narratives. But the stories told *about* Jesus, unlike the ones told *by* him, are regarded as factual. Metaphor and story are permitted in one domain, but forbidden in another. Stories are not seen as "real" or "true" enough to carry conviction and inspire faith. The things told about Jesus are claimed to be literally "true," but Jesus was content to allow his stories to be fictional. Jesus was a poet with a great imagination, but his followers are literalists without imagination. We pay for this by a diminished understanding of faith.

Crossan reflects:

> A first clue that the Emmaus road story was meant as parable and not history is that when Jesus joins the couple on the road, they do not recognize him. He is, as it were, traveling incognito. A second clue is that even when he explains in detail how the biblical scriptures pointed to Jesus as the Messiah, they still do not recognize him.[36]

These might seem to Crossan as "clues" to the "fictional" nature of these stories, but conventional wisdom has never seen it that way. The notes to the Bibles in my possession tell a very different story. The editors of *The New International Study Bible* claim that the two disciples, one called Cleopas, the other unnamed,[37] were "kept from recognizing him by special divine intervention." "His body," the editors continue, "was of a different order; it was the glorified body of the resurrection."[38] In *The Jerusalem Bible*, the editors of that work of scholarship write:

> In the apparitions described by Luke and John, the disciples do not at first recognize the Lord: they need a word or sign. This is because the risen body, though the same body that died on the cross, is in a new condition; its outward appearance is therefore changed.[39]

This literalism is breathtaking. The editors are treating these apparitions as eyewitness accounts. Paul insisted that the glorified body is not the same as the earthly body, and yet the editors claim the Emmaus travelers meet "the same body that died on the cross." Theologians ask us to become fools for the church, and we have to become foolish to believe them. That is why I have a poor regard for theologians, and prefer commentators from other disciplines. Theologians insist that to become religious we have to believe in a supernatural world of ghostly apparitions. By misreading allegories as histories they are turning spirituality into spiritualism or magical thinking. On many occasions, theologians have lost my respect because they perpetuate the pious fraud of which Keats spoke.

Theologians are highly educated but apparently incapable of appreciating the literary genre of the Bible. The fact that they might be on the wrong wavelength never seems to occur to them. Indeed, their shared illusion is dignified by being elevated to the level of "faith." As faith, it remains untouchable. They never suspect they might be, as Crossan puts it, "reading parable, presuming history, and misunderstanding both." Defenders of faith resort to speculation about the "condition" of the body after the resurrection, rather than understand that they might be caught in the wrong frame. They prefer Jesus to be seen as a wandering ghost or occult apparition, rather than a spirit in the hearts and minds of human beings.

Crossan argues that "the definitive clue to the story's purpose is in the climax,"[40] and it is to this that we now turn:

> As they came near the village to which they were going, he walked ahead as if he were going on. But they urged him strongly, saying, "Stay with us, because it is almost evening and the day is now nearly over." So he went in to stay with them. When he was at the table with them, he took bread, blessed and broke it, and gave it to them. Then their eyes were opened, and they recognized him; and he vanished from their sight. They said to each other, "Were not our hearts burning within us while he was talking to us on the road, while he was opening the scriptures to us?"[41]

This is a parable or teaching narrative about how we find Jesus, if by "Jesus" we mean spirit. We find Jesus by befriending the stranger on the road, by opening our hearts and minds to the outsider in our midst, to those who are "other" than ourselves. This is the same message as that of the Good Samaritan, which also appears in Luke, and is regarded as parable. Yet the Emmaus story is seen as history. Apparently no believing Christian wants the Road to Emmaus to be "only a metaphor," but this statement, "*only* a metaphor," says less about the story than it does about the poverty of our imagination. Story represents the truth of spirit, which, as Van Gogh remarked, is truer than literal truth.

Emmaus Never Happened, Emmaus Always Happens

Crossan summarizes the metaphorical reading of the narrative: "Emmaus never happened; Emmaus always happens."[42] The first part of this statement is negative for believers, since it collapses their faith into fiction. It brings with it disappointment, deflation, even depression. They want this visitation to be true, but they have a too narrow conception of truth. The protest is that it *must* have happened because

Resurrection

it's God's Word. That in itself begs many questions. We have made the error of assuming that God and his Word are literal objects or events.

The second part of Crossan's formulation brings with it the realization that story captures God's Word more fully than history: "Emmaus always happens." In other words, the mythos of Emmaus is true for all time, and whenever we open ourselves to the possibility of befriending the stranger on the road, we find the living reality of the spirit of Jesus. This maxim of Crossan's is therefore a kind of double whammy: it destroys naïve faith, and yet it builds a mature faith that is not dependent on supernaturalism.

The fact that Jesus "vanished" in an instant ought to remind us that we are in the landscape of story. It is a bit like the witch in *The Wizard of Oz*, who suddenly vanishes in a puff of green smoke beneath a pointy black hat. This is symbolic action, having to do with the play of archetypes in psychological space. Jesus wasn't "there" in the first place, which is why he can vanish in an instant. He was there notionally, or as we might say, in spirit. He was present as a content of awareness, and as such, he can be withdrawn from the scene. Jesus comes in and out of awareness, depending on our receptivity to spirit.

The Emmaus story is structured as a lesson in the art of conducting the Eucharist. This is so blindingly obvious it is astonishing that church people have not discerned this long ago. My view is that it was indeed read as parable in the days of the early church, but that by the time of the first councils and the invention of dogma, the parabolic aspect was lost and it was read literally. Two disciples are hurrying toward Emmaus from Jerusalem after the crucifixion. Why are they on the road, and why are they hurrying? The suggestion is that they are fleeing Jerusalem because they fear that the fate that has befallen their leader might befall them. They are hotfooting it from the scene of devastation. Fear and anxiety propels them to take to the road, and this can be seen as part of their denial of Jesus' fate—they are running away, just as Peter denied his Lord, and Judas betrayed him to authorities.

The pattern of denial and betrayal continues with these lesser-known disciples, Cleopas and his companion, not only in their act of flight but in their denial of the spiritual meaning of Jesus' life. As they are joined on the road by Jesus, they tell the stranger about the external political facts of what has taken place:

> The chief priests and our rulers handed him [Jesus] over to be sentenced to death, and they crucified him; but we had hoped that he was the one who was going to redeem Israel.[43]

They had hoped he was going to redeem Israel, but he did not. This is not a Christ-like attitude, which is that Christ *has* set Israel free by revealing the immediacy of the Kingdom. This is an older, popular, pre-Christian expectation of a strongman Messiah, one who would perform military miracles, liberating Israel from Roman rule and opposing its colonial forces. The disciples clearly don't "get" what the Christian story is about: it is not about political might or military victory, but spiritual liberation. These disciples, then, are not yet "Christian." They have not yet "seen" the Christ.

This is what the parable is about. On the road to Emmaus the disciples do not *see* Jesus—and this has a double meaning: not seeing him in their midst, as a traveler on the Way, and not seeing the import of his ministry. They refer to Jesus as a figure who had "proved he was a great prophet by the things he said and did in the sight of God and of the whole people."[44] His more transformative role has been lost; if it was ever understood by these muddle-headed disciples. They convey the banal, external facts of his passing:

> Some of our friends went to the tomb and found everything exactly as the women had reported, but of him they saw nothing.[45]

Here is another reference to "not seeing"; they "saw nothing." To this, the risen Christ can only say: "Oh, how foolish you are!"[46] These are followers who are terrified and bereft. They had "hoped" for a military conquistador who was sent from heaven, but their hopes were dashed. Their aspirations are worldly; they do not possess *pneuma*, spirit.

This story seems to me to be a swipe at those who profess to follow Jesus. Many claim to follow him but do so blindly and without inspiration. Our ability to see the spirit has to be *awoken*, and in this parable, the awakening takes place in two stages: readings from the scriptures and the breaking of the bread. This whole scenario is a metaphor of the Eucharist, and why the Eucharist is necessary to awaken the spirit of Jesus in his followers. Jesus says in an immoderate voice:

> "You foolish men! So slow to believe the full message of the prophets! Was it not ordained that the Christ should suffer and so enter into his glory?" Then, starting with Moses and going through all the prophets he explained to them the passages throughout the scriptures that were about himself.[47]

This precedes the passage already cited, where the disciples persuade him to stay for supper. After explaining the scriptures he joins them at table, and,

> he took the bread and said the blessing; then he broke it and handed it to them. And then their eyes were opened and they recognised him; and he vanished from their sight.[48]

This is the first Eucharist after his death. It has all the components of an ordinary church service: there is the blindness, stupidity, and fear of the participants, and there is the potential for a breakthrough of the divine that is brought to a realization in the breaking of the bread. Crossan comments:

> The Christian liturgy involves both scripture and Eucharist with the former as prelude and prologue to the latter. So also with the twin components of the Emmaus story. First comes the scripture section, but even with Jesus as its interpreter the result is "burning hearts," that is, hearts ready to do—but to do what? In the Eucharist section we get the answer to that question. It is to treat the stranger as oneself, to invite the stranger into one's home, to have the stranger share one's meal. And it is precisely in such a shared meal that Jesus is recognized as present—then, now, always.[49]

The parable acts as the prototype of awakening. We are walking on the path of life and do not recognize God at our side as we journey along. We have the assistance of scripture, but it alone does not open our eyes. The scriptures are inspired narratives, but do not always transform us. Something more is needed; in order to bring about *metanoia* or rebirth a tradition has to be converted from external message to internal realization.

This is what is achieved in the ritual of the breaking of the bread and the sharing of the host. We have to eat, digest or "take in" the divine, and then we can see. We have to "put on" Christ, as St Paul says,[50] and then our eyes are opened and we awaken from ignorance. Ritual completes what scripture begins but is unable to achieve by itself; hence the Road to Emmaus is Luke's beautifully wrought parable about how to awaken faith.

The Unacknowledged God in Our Midst

The mythic nature of the Emmaus story is more apparent when we realize that the motif of a God appearing in disguise in the midst of a community is a literary trope of classical myth. Centuries before the

Christian story, the Greeks had explored this same literary form. In Euripides' tragedy *The Bacchae*, the god Dionysus comes to Thebes, disguised as a stranger. He is outraged by King Pentheus' refusal to honor him and appears in disguise to ensure that his divinity is acknowledged. The people do not recognize him, and Pentheus attempts to throw Dionysus into prison. The god takes human form as part of a plan to set things right. The author of the gospel of Luke is, in my opinion, drawing on this long-standing literary trope as he tells the Emmaus story. In other words, this is an example of a gospel narrative that is designed to appeal to gentiles who already know the Greek stories. It is designed to appeal to them, to resonate in their imaginations and memories.

Christ appears to the disciples because they are running away from the crucifixion and have dishonored the spiritual meaning of his ministry. They expected a political hero and instead received a defeated solitary mystic. As with Dionysus, Christ appears with a sense of outrage and injustice, shouting at the "foolish men" who are "slow to believe the full message of the prophets." Pentheus is torn to pieces by a frenzied mob of female worshippers, while the two on the road escape with a dressing down, stern words of correction, and burning hearts. But the point of this parable is to declare that the "god" is in our midst, even when we fail to discern it. As the Latin inscription puts it: *Vocatus atque non vocatus deus aderit* (Called or not called, God is present).[51]

The Emmaus story recognizes the weakness of the human condition and mocks our ignorance. But it allows for the possibility of redemption. We were blind, but now we can see. Even when we were blind, our hearts were burning with the presentiment that there was something more that we could not grasp. The burning hearts suggests a passion that is present in *potentia*, even if not realized. The disciples are fleeing from the city and its turbulence, but even as they flee the spirit of Christ will be with them, in their weakest hour, in their moment of desolation. Even as we run from truth, the spirit will be at our side, as support, and also as an ironic and mocking presence, challenging our ignorance as we walk the path.

Once this deeper dimension is understood, the need for a literal reading of the narrative falls away, and we are left with the truth. Instead of puzzling our heads about ghosts, apparitions, and the precise medical condition of a postmortem body, we move to the meaning of this parable as soon as the literal interpretation is overcome. I have read numerous works in which educated theologians reflect endlessly about how Jesus could be "present" after his death. It is mind crushing to think that the best religious educators in the tradition still operate in this mode. But when the literalism of belief is peeled away, the illumination of faith is allowed to appear. Belief and faith are opposites in this sense, and teachings that emphasize belief are obfuscating the radical nature of faith.

Notes

1. 1 Corinthians 15:35.
2. Rudolf Bultmann, "New Testament and Mythology: The Problem of Demythologizing the New Testament Proclamation" (1941), in Schubert M. Ogden, ed., *New Testament and Mythology and Other Basic Writings* (Philadelphia: Fortress Press, 1984), p. 31.
3. I Corinthians 15:14.
4. John 20:24–28.
5. John 20:27–28.
6. Sandra Schneiders, *Jesus Risen in Our Midst* (Collegeville, MN: Liturgical Press, 2013), p. 8.
7. A point made by Patricia Berry, *Echo's Subtle Body* (Dallas: Spring Publications, 1982).
8. Council of Lyons II: DS 854.
9. Schneiders, p. 35.
10. Schneiders, p. 44.
11. Schneiders, pp. 9–10.
12. Schneiders refers to "thousands of books and articles on the resurrection" in the wake of Vatican II (1960s and 70s), and in recent times "more than five hundred bibliographical references" have been cited on the resurrection, *Jesus Risen in Our Midst*, pp. 8–9.
13. Joseph Campbell, *The Power of Myth* (New York: Doubleday, 1991), pp. 67–68.
14. Tertullian's famous saying: *credo quia impossible* is found in his *De Carne Christi*, sec. 5, ll. 24–6.
15. Campbell, p. 68.
16. Ibid.
17. Ibid.
18. Campbell, p. 46.
19. Jung, "On Resurrection" (1954), *CW* 18, § 1574.
20. Mark 16:8.
21. *JB*, 1 Corinthians 15:35–53.
22. *The Holy Bible, Authorized King James Version* (Oxford: Oxford University Press, 1976), 1 Corinthians 15:39–44.
23. *KJV*, 1 Corinthians 15: 36.
24. *The Holy Bible, The Revised Standard Version* (New York: Collins, 1952), 1 Corinthians, 15:36.
25. *RSV*, I Corinthians, 15:42.
26. *RSV*, 1 Corinthians, 15:46.
27. *RSV*, 1 Corinthians, 15:50.
28. *RSV*, I Corinthians 15:48.
29. *KJV*, Genesis 3:19.

30. Northrop Frye, *Northrop Frye's Notebooks and Lectures on the Bible and Other Religious Texts*, ed. Robert D. Denham (Toronto: University of Toronto Press, 2003), p. 435.
31. Jung, "On Resurrection," § 1570.
32. Justin Martyr, "Fragments of the Lost Work on the Resurrection" (2nd century), in Alexander Roberts, James Donaldson and A. Cleveland Coxe, eds., *Apostolic Fathers, Justin Martyr, Irenaeus; Ante-Nicene Fathers*, Vol. 1 (Chicago: Christian Literature Company, 1885; Reprint, Peabody, Mass.: Hendrickson, 1994).
33. Luke 24:13–33.
34. John Dominic Crossan, *The Power of Parable: How Fiction by Jesus Became Fiction about Jesus* (New York: HarperOne, 2012), p. 3.
35. Ibid.
36. Crossan, p. 4.
37. Luke 24:18.
38. *The New International Study Bible*, notes to Luke 24:16 and 24:36.
39. *The Jerusalem Bible*, note to Luke 24:16.
40. Crossan, p. 4.
41. Luke 24:28–32.
42. Crossan, p. 5.
43. Luke 24:20–21.
44. Luke 24:20.
45. Luke 24:24.
46. Luke 24:25.
47. Luke 24:25–26.
48. Luke 24:30–31.
49. Crossan, p. 4.
50. Romans 13:14.
51. This was the answer given by the Delphic Oracle to the Lacedemonians when they were planning a war against Athens. This was also the inscription Jung carved above the door to his house in Zurich.

10

Psyche and Symbol

An archetypal content expresses itself, first and foremost, in metaphors.
— Jung[1]

Dreaming the Myth Onward

Before Armstrong, Frye, Crossan, or Campbell made their discoveries about the metaphorical dimension of religion, Jung had arrived at the problem from the psychological side. Jung was not a "progressive" who wanted to throw out symbols because no one could understand them. Nor was he a conservative who relished the "sacrosanct unintelligibility"[2] of religious statements. He had some aspects in common with both groups, but belonged to neither. Like progressives, he was frustrated by the way in which tradition had turned metaphors into history. But unlike progressives he had the patience to work through the stories, interpreting them anew for a modern world. Like conservatives, he respected what had been handed down by tradition and found meaning in the creeds and dogmas of the West. But unlike them he interpreted them symbolically and never accepted the face value of religious statements.

Jung is a major figure in the project of deliteralizing religion and returning it to its base in myth. He brings a vast and comprehensive knowledge to bear on the subject and introduces a psychological depth not found in other commentators. Jung's message is that we have discounted myth and need to develop a new appreciation of its revelatory power. The truth-bearing capacity of metaphor is where we locate the values of the soul. He argued that the well-being of the soul depends on our ability to turn from our obsession with external facts and find respect for the nonliteral. Jung took risks with truth and tried to relate religious statements to the modern psyche. He felt truth must never remain static but had to be updated. He put the situation paradoxically: "Eternal truth needs a human language that alters with the spirit of the times."³ Jung was prophetic to the extent that he saw the spirit of tradition languishing in its literalized forms, and it needed to be liberated from its theological imprisonment and made available to all.

The Jewish idea of *midrash* is the one that comes to mind when trying to convey what Jung was doing. Midrash is the art of reinterpreting truth for new and rising generations that are at odds with conventional expressions of truth. Successive generations are in danger of losing touch with their heritage, and midrash was the term for reinterpreting the legacy so it remains relevant and contemporary. Jung was not Jewish, but he was a midrashic scholar in grand style, devoting decades of research to the task of digging up the buried treasure in traditions that modernity had rejected. As a young man he wanted to become an archaeologist and, in a sense, he fulfilled that dream in another field, becoming an excavator of the soul. He claimed that myths were too valuable to allow to die or be disposed of. We must "dream the myth onwards and give it a modern dress."⁴ Myth must be taken up in a redemptive spirit and interpreted in new ways. Unlike Bultmann, whose demythologizing led to the abandonment of the symbolic, Jung believed that demythologising should give way to remythologizing. Remythologizing is not just pretending that old myths can live again in the old way. That is part and parcel of the fundamentalist project. Remythologizing is allowing myths to live again by taking them out of their deadening theological contexts and linking them to psychological meanings.

Reworking the Past

For Jung the symbols are permanent, and we should not expect to get rid of them. But the way they are interpreted is constantly changing. The theological monopoly on religious symbols has to be broken, so we might experience them in new ways. All aspects of faith need to be removed from their prescientific dress and translated into terms that can be understood today. This involves, above all, drawing attention to the need for a metaphorical reading of scripture and dogma. The modern mind has to be introduced to a new way of reading, a new "hermeneutics," based on mythos. If this modality has been lost by scientific advancement, we should make an effort to recover it. Jung was not convinced that this re-education would come from within religious traditions, since they are mired in the bog of literalism. He believed it would be the momentous contribution of depth psychology and psychoanalysis.

In 1910 Jung had written with excitement to Freud that the true task of psychoanalysis was not to explore the unconscious in a materialist frame, but engage in the revival of religion by locating the mystery in the souls of human beings.

> I imagine a far finer and more comprehensive task for psychoanalysis than alliance with an ethical fraternity. I think we must give it time to infiltrate into people from many centres, to revivify among intellectuals a feeling for symbol and myth, ever so gently to transform Christ back into the soothsaying god of the vine, which he was, and in this way absorb those ecstatic instinctual forces of Christianity for the one purpose of making the cult and the sacred myth what they once were—a drunken feast of joy where man regained the ethos and holiness of an animal.[5]

Paul Bishop sees this as Jung's desire to "transform Christ into Dionysus,"[6] and it can be misread in this way by those who are unfamiliar with the gospel of John, Jung's favorite gospel. His reference is not to the Greek god of revelry but to the ecstatic-gnostic image of Jesus as the wine-producing god of the vine: "I am the vine and you are the branches...."[7] Jung goes on to tell Freud that there is an untapped resource in religion, which he felt was a key to unleashing the passions which psychoanalysis, in turn, sought to release in the modern person. Jung bemoans the fact that religion had, for inexplicable reasons, turned from its ecstatic impulses toward an all-too-prevalent moralism, and for this reason religion had become a "Misery Institute." He felt that "infinite rapture and wantonness lie dormant in our religion, waiting to be led back to their true destination."[8]

But the sober Freud was in no mood to play a redemptive role in the return of religion. Freud was undoubtedly offended by Jung's reference to "our religion," since Freud was a Jew, albeit a secular one, and in his naïve enthusiasm Jung appears to have forgotten this. Even if he were religious, which he was not, Freud would not have shared Jung's passion for the redemption of Jesus. Freud was firmly of the persuasion that God was dead, and we were all better off as a result.[9] Nor was Jung's enthusiasm for reviving religion shared by others in the psychoanalytic circle, which served to alienate him from his fellow investigators and precipitate his excommunication in 1913.

Jung's interest in religion made him appear unacceptably conservative to his colleagues, and although his interest in "spirituality" is of interest in our time, in his own day it was seen as eccentric and counter-progressive. Above all, it was seen as unscientific to harbor enthusiasms for discredited systems of belief. Jung was attacked from both sides: the sciences saw him as too religious, and the religious saw him as not religious enough, since they claimed he was "reducing" revelation to "mere" psychology. The charge of psychologism was often made against Jung, but it was misguided, in my view.

Jung had no intention of reducing religion to academic psychology with its rational explanations. His interest was in linking religion to a "depth" psychology that took the unconscious into account. The unconscious for Jung was not merely a Freudian rubbish dump for impulses that had been suppressed. It was a dimension of mind that was surrounded on all sides by mystery, and Jung was so impressed by the spiritual potentials of the *psyche* that he often avoided this clinical term to speak of the *soul*. The term "soul" had long been discredited by science and philosophy, but Jung took it upon himself to bring it back into scientific discourse, a burden that was almost too great to bear, since he drew to himself the criticism that science had already dished out to the "religious" ideas of soul and spirit. He was almost a martyr to his cause and his reputation is only now beginning to improve, since the values that attacked him are now themselves under attack in a postmodern and post-secular world.[10]

Jung felt Christianity was a wonderful myth, sorely in need of revision and extension. He believed myths have to be adapted to cultural circumstances, so they remain relevant. Without this adaptation myth would languish and with it the spirit of the people whose lives have been shaped by it. In "Late Thoughts," Jung turned to reflections on Christianity and its critical condition:

> [Humanity] sickens from the lack of a myth commensurate with the situation. The Christian nations have come to a sorry pass; their Christianity slumbers and has neglected to develop its myth further in the course of the centuries. Those who gave expression to the dark stirrings of growth in mythic ideas were refused a hearing. . . . People . . . do not realise that a myth is dead if it no longer lives and grows. Our myth has become mute, and gives no answers. The fault lies not in it as it is set down in the Scriptures, but solely in us, who have not developed it further, who, rather, have suppressed any such attempts. The original version of the myth offers ample points of departure and possibilities of development.[11]

Psyche and Symbol

The myth as evident in the scriptures is not at fault; rather, the West is at fault for refusing to develop the myth further. Jung felt that the myth was crying out for the further development of the archetype of the feminine and the role of evil or what he called the "shadow."[12] In some respects these themes were taken up by alchemy, esotericism, artists, and writers. But the official holders of the myth, the churches, were interested only in "suppressing" attempts to develop the myth further, and now the Christian West is suffering the cost of this suppression. The myth is dying for want of development.

It is dying because the holders of the myth did not realize it was myth. They saw it as theology and dogma. They turned it into logos, and deprived the narrative of its mythical ground. The literalization of the narrative was central to this process. It was uprooted from its ground, and ever since it has been languishing. Church traditions did not realize it was what Jung called a *mythologem*, that is, a myth that needs to be extended and developed over time. He compared the mythologem to a vital organ of the body, and just as the organ withers and dies if not exercised, the same occurs with myth. It is ironic that those who claim to "preserve" Christianity in its present form, who oppose creative adaptation or new interpretation that might link it with a new era, are its executioners. They are killing the myth with rationality. The best thing that could be done for religion is to take it away from theologians who want to mummify it and hand it over to poets, visionaries, and philosophers who might breath new life into it.

In this regard, Jung's views are corroborated by the findings of the philosopher Vittorio Macchioro, who argued that transforming religion into its original mythos was the best thing that could be done for its well-being:

> The only way to deliver Christianity from its [current] imposition is to transform theology into mythology, that is, to cease to consider it from a religious viewpoint as a sort of knowledge and to view it in the light of the history of religion as a complex of symbols by means of which man realizes his faith.[13]

I am uncertain of the extent to which Macchioro may have been aware of Jung's work. But it is close to his own, as is clear when he writes about the "great danger" and the "hope" of converting theology into mythology:

> From this reduction of theology to mythology rises what seems to some a great danger, others a great hope, the hope for a possible reintegration of Christianity. The history of Christianity has been a long

> process of disintegration. From the Apostolic Age down it has shown a dispersive tendency, a tendency to divide, dissolve into churches, sects and heresies. This centrifugal tendency is remarkable in a religion which had its center in a person and ought therefore to present the greatest unity. The whole sad history of Christian disintegration takes its rise from the theory of the cognitive function of theology.
>
> But with the reduction of theology to mythology the reintegration of Christianity becomes possible. The dogma-concept may be replaced by the dogma-symbol, which permits harmony in difference. Hence the great importance of every inquiry into the mythological origins of theology.[14]

What he is saying in philosophical language is what Jung is saying in psychological terms. The "mistaking" of mythology for theology has led to a misunderstanding of its nature and function. Theology has frozen a living thing into concepts, whereas the myth wants to live at a narrative and noncognitive level. When myths are mistaken as facts, and symbols as dogmas, the mythos hardens, fragments, and shuts down. Myths and symbols thrive on different perspectives, reinterpretations, and performances. They invite theatrical or dramatic representations, and this variety is healthy for the organs of mythos. But if the myth is dried out and preserved as a cognitive system, the outcome is disintegration, schism and sectarian hatreds among its adherents, each claiming to hold the truth. The unity of the mythos is lost and this can only be recovered if theology is transformed back into mythology. When religion is changed from a collection of concepts to a narrative of symbols, the result is the recovered health of the mythos.

The Therapeutic Function of Myth

Jung saw religions as therapeutic systems that help regulate and control the mental life of the community. When they break down the psyche is attacked by nonrational forces that are unable to be controlled. Psychic forces previously held in symbolic containers are "let loose" upon unsuspecting humanity. Such forces, no longer honored by the culture or individuals, turn against the human ego that refuses to honor them. In ancient Greek times, this would have been understood as the vengeance of the defiled Olympian gods. In the Hebrew Bible it would be interpreted as the wrath of an angered Yahweh. We cannot mythologize it that way anymore, but we can view it in terms of the compensatory functioning of the unconscious: when ignored it rises up in protest. In our time there is no living mythos or religion to placate these forces, and just because we have stopped believing in religion does not mean they suddenly go away.

We live in a secular age that knows nothing about gods or God and is embarrassed by such archaic and "irrelevant" discourse. We have lost wisdom and occupy ourselves with knowledge and information. We are unprepared for the assault of psychic forces, and our consciousness has no way of understanding what is happening. Hence ours is an age of anxiety, because the deepest parts of the self are not being satisfied. Jung famously said "the gods have become diseases,"[15] by which he meant that archetypal forces express themselves negatively in a culture that ignores them. Jung is decisive on this matter: we either cultivate faith consciously or disintegrate under the sway of unruly forces. Christianity is at a loss to understand his argument, since it has an idealized understanding of God. How could a God of love turn against us in this fashion? The Jewish idea that Yahweh can turn against his people has been expunged, making the Christian West even less likely to read the situation correctly. I have written a book on this topic and will leave it for now.[16]

Spirit requires mythos, and a culture without a mythos has no way of regulating the forces that hold sway in the unconscious. The task of religion is to "link us back" to the mythic domain and placate the forces beyond rationality:

> What is the use of a religion without a *mythos*, since religion means, if anything at all, precisely that function which links us back to the eternal myth?[17]

Religion, he reminds us, derives from the Latin *religio*, to "link back." "This original form of *religio* ('linking back') is the essence, the working basis of all religious life even today, and always will be, whatever future form this life may take."[18] What religion links back to is the sacred, the holy, and that which is beyond awareness:

> Religion is a vital link with psychic processes independent of and beyond consciousness, in the dark hinterland of the psyche.[19]

We can only know this reality indirectly, through metaphor and symbol. It is not that metaphors obscure or distort the real, but they bring out its deeper dimension. As Jung put it: "The archetype does not proceed from physical facts, but describes how the psyche experiences the physical fact."[20] This is why metaphor is indispensable; it describes how the soul experiences a fact. This is the perspective we have lost, which is why metaphors are said to hide truth, and historical facts reveal it.

We have confused the nature of the real by trusting too much in logos. It is an overdose of logos that has made us unreceptive to the sacred and its symbolic language. Religion and myth perform the vital function of reconnecting consciousness to its source, to a life independent of itself:

> If this link-up does not take place, a kind of rootless consciousness comes into being no longer oriented to the past, a consciousness which succumbs helplessly to all manner of suggestions and, in practice, is susceptible to psychic epidemics.[21]

To lose our myths is to lose our well-being. Without them, we become rudderless, lacking purpose and direction. We become strangers to ourselves, and suffer from alienation. If governments understood how much our health depended on the cultivation of a symbolic life, they might put more emphasis on exploring the connections between mind and body, psyche and society, attitude and well-being.

Myth as Psychic Truth

People often say myth is "nothing but" illusion, or "merely" a product of the mind. As Jung put it: "Where, exactly, does this immense prejudice come from?"[22] If we say that a myth or miracle is "nothing but" a symbol, this means we do not comprehend its meaning. The "nothing but" indicates our ignorance before a mystery that has not been discerned. Mythos is so undervalued that many see it as synonymous with deception or make-believe. It is, however, the basis of all religions, but in the West it was removed from this basis around the third and fourth centuries. At this time authorities tried to bolster the new faith, depriving it of its mythic qualities and changing it into history. Jung writes:

> It has been assumed, perhaps as the result of a growing impatience with the difficult factual material, that Christ was nothing but a myth, in this case no more than a fiction. But myth is not a fiction: it consists of facts that are continually repeated and can be observed over and over again.[23]

This can be confusing because Jung is talking about *psychic*, not physical, facts. For him psychic facts are real, and it is the psychic reality of the Christ story that interests him, and that has inspired many throughout the ages. By restoring religion to its realm of *mythos*, Jung felt it could be restored to integrity and given new importance. For us this means relating religion to psyche, which is our modern "myth" for the place where mystery resides. Ironically, Jung wanted to promote religion by demoting it, that is, by taking it down from its supernatural heights and linking it to processes of the psyche.

This would give religion back its practical and empirical basis, by making it relevant to processes taking place in every psyche. By restoring *mythos*, Jung would restore our capacity to *see* the images of eternal reality. He wanted psychology to serve as the handmaiden of a revived religion. Indeed, psychology is the site where science and religion meet. Depth psychology based on the unconscious becomes the locus for the recovery of wisdom in a scientific age. The virgin birth and physical resurrection, Jung believed, were not historical facts, but spiritual truths, to be reflected on for their metaphorical richness as events of the psyche. They are not events that occurred once, but mythic events that happen all the time. Hence he describes myths as psychic facts that are "continually repeated."

This was not welcome news for organized religion, which is far more interested in what happened two thousand years ago, than in what happens in the psyche today. It has staked its claim on history and finds Jung's mythos to be abhorrent. Religion could therefore not open up to what Jung was offering: a scientific approach to the spirit. After two thousand years claiming the miracles and wonders were literally true, the church could not turn around and say: okay, we see your point, and will explore your argument. Naturally it had to hit back, to attack Jung and destroy his reputation. All one has to do is look up "Jung and Christianity" on the Internet to see attempts to ridicule and undermine his credibility. The Catholic Church launched a new attack on Jung a few years ago,[24] and one can see that it feels nervous about his arguments, otherwise it would not spend so much energy trying to discount him.

The church cannot accept his mythos view of religion, because it shares the modern world's devaluation of psyche. The psyche is not respected, it is seen as "just" the psyche, and things belonging to it are "merely" psychological. The church could not afford to have its ancient God-inspired truth reduced to something "only" psychological. It shares the Western prejudice of not understanding what the psyche is. It is soul, the carrier of *pneuma*, the divine imprint within the human. Such a claim seems implausible and unduly "mystical" to a church that is steeped in the doctrine of original sin. To accept

Jung's argument it would have to revise its idea that the human being is not directly related to spirit and cannot be trusted to bring such a connection into reality. Precisely because humanity is "fallen," religion claims humanity requires a bridge to the sacred, and that bridge is the worship of Christ and reverence for the clerical tradition that follows in his steps. This has caused religion to externalize the spiritual life and take away the internal dynamic of the soul that might make this *religio* possible. The church argues that the clergy are closer to God than the laity, and it serves the task of bridging the gulf that separates humanity from God.

The church as an institution will find it impossible to accept Jung's claims about the spiritual potentials of the human being. It will remain resistant to his demotion of literal truth that seeks a promotion of its symbolic forms. But while the institution might be unable to move, the tradition might think otherwise. Tradition and convention are not the same thing. Tradition still harbors the originating spiritual impulse, while convention is a product of social artifice. Only institutionalized convention is steeped in ideology and prejudice. The spirit that informs tradition might find the courage to agree that the message of scripture is symbolic and not literal. Tradition might be able to extricate itself from the supernatural worldview, and admit its concept of God is antiquated and in need of revision. The institution of the church, however, will continue to be outraged by Jung and reject most of what he stands for. The church will continue to declare that Jung's message is heresy.

Mystery Without Literalism

For new readers, the best place to discover what Jung has to say about scripture is his five-page introduction to *Answer to Job*.[25] Perhaps the title of this piece, "Lectori Benevolo," or "To the Kind Reader," is a form of propitiatory magic or wishful thinking, because Jung is aware that many of his readers will be far from kind. He opens his introduction to *Job* by admitting that he runs the risk of being "torn to pieces by the two parties who are in mortal conflict about [religion]."[26] He is referring to believers and nonbelievers. The first take the statements of scripture literally, the second assume they are illusory. The conflict between them "is due to the strange supposition that a thing is true only if it presents itself as a physical fact." He explains:

> Some people believe it to be physically true that Christ was born as the son of a virgin, while others deny this as a physical impossibility.

> Everyone can see that there is no logical solution to this conflict and that one would do better not to get involved in such sterile disputes. Both are right and both are wrong. Yet they could easily reach agreement if only they dropped the word "physical." "Physical" is not the only criterion of truth: there are also *psychic* truths which can neither be explained nor proved nor contested in any physical way.... Beliefs of this kind are psychic facts which cannot be contested and need no proof.[27]

He goes on to present his clearest case about the nature of religious truth:

> Religious statements are of this type. They refer without exception to things that cannot be established as physical facts. If they did not do this, they would inevitably fall into the category of the natural sciences. Taken as referring to anything physical, they make no sense whatever, and science would dismiss them as non-experienceable. They would be mere miracles, which are sufficiently exposed to doubt as it is, and yet they could not demonstrate the reality of the spirit or *meaning* that underlies them, because meaning is something that always demonstrates itself and is experienced on its own merits.[28]

Our concept of truth is defective if we believe that only physical facts are true. Jung is aware that the typical believer is unable to comprehend this point of view, since the institutions have conditioned followers to believe that something is "true" only if it happened as fact. Jung becomes impatient with institutions, and wonders whether they are generating more ignorance than awareness. If they are not enabling people to enter into the spirit of a critical spirituality, but merely into a credulous or blind faith, Jung doubts that such traditions deserve to continue in the future. He is unsentimental about this possibility, and seals the fate of such traditions by indicating that they are fraudulent. Ironically, in a breathtaking reversal of received opinion, religions are true if they declare their mythic nature, and false if they pose as history or fact.

Jung wants to slough off the infantile traits of Christianity, yet he wants to preserve what is noble in it. He says a literal understanding of the miracles is not needed to get the message of the gospels. That message comes through in the moral and spiritual values that are apparent in Christ's ministry. We don't need supernatural "acts" to demonstrate his worth:

> The spirit and meaning of Christ are present and perceptible to us even without the aid of miracles. Miracles appeal only to the understanding of those who cannot perceive the meaning. They are mere

substitutes for the not understood reality of the spirit. This is not to say that the living presence of the spirit is not occasionally accompanied by marvellous physical happenings. I only wish to emphasize that these happenings can neither replace nor bring about an understanding of the spirit, which is the one essential thing.[29]

Regardless of whether miracles are true or not, they cannot "bring about an understanding of the spirit." The mere existence of miracles does nothing to change the consciousness of the reader of scripture; it does nothing to bring the believer into a relationship with spirit. It satisfies the primitive human desire for a sign, but that, according to scripture, is unholy and unreliable. In Matthew we are told that "It is an evil and unfaithful generation that asks for a sign!,"[30] and thus the gospels confirm Jung's argument that miracles do not bring a person into a relationship with spirit. Only faith can do that, or what today we might call "intuition." Miracles excite the need in us for supernatural displays, the same kind of delight that we gain when, for instance, looking at acts performed by a stage magician. But none of this concerns the spirit, but merely that part of us that seeks the spectacular.

Jung is at pains to convince his readers that psychic facts cannot be dispensed with lightly. He knows his argument has to contend with the age-old prejudice about what constitutes "reality," and that is why he keeps trying to approach the reality of the psyche from different angles:

> The fact that religious statements frequently conflict with the observed physical phenomena proves that in contrast to physical perception the spirit is autonomous, and that psychic experience is to a certain extent independent of physical data. The psyche is an autonomous factor, and religious statements are psychic confessions which in the last resort are based on unconscious, i.e., on transcendental, processes. These processes are not accessible to physical perception but demonstrate their existence through the confessions of the psyche. The resultant statements are filtered through the medium of human consciousness: that is to say, they are given visible forms which in their turn are subject to manifold influences from within and without.[31]

The psyche, like spirit, is a "transcendental" factor, and as such there are no ways of accessing the psychic process apart from symbolic images. The metaphors of the psyche are not invented arbitrarily by gospel writers or poets, but are impressed on their consciousness by the creative imagination. As Jung says later:

> Ideas of this kind are never invented, but enter the field of inner perception as finished products, for instance in dreams. They are

spontaneous phenomena which are not subject to our will, and we are therefore justified in ascribing to them a certain autonomy. They are to be regarded not only as objects but as subjects with laws of their own.[32]

Here Jung seems to be exaggerating to make a point. I don't think religious ideas enter the minds of writers as "finished products" from a cosmic source. Surely such ideas are suggested to writers by tradition, training, and cultural factors. I doubt that these ideas come to writers "finished," as if they were taking divine dictation. But I can't see Jung's argument damaged by suggesting, for instance, that apostles and scribes are inspired by seed-ideas, and such materials have to be shaped by the mind before they find expression. To be "inspired by God," or to write the "word of God," need not mean that one is divested of one's volition and freewill.

Respect to a God Unknown

Jung raises an argument about the unknowable nature of God. He points to one of his central preoccupations: whether our expressions of the sacred have any bearing on the sacred itself:

> [W]henever we speak of religious contents we move in a world of images that point to something ineffable. We do not know how clear or unclear these images, metaphors, and concepts are in respect of their transcendental object. If, for instance, we say "God," we give expression to an image or verbal concept which has undergone many changes in the course of time. We are, however, unable to say with any degree of certainty—unless it be by faith—whether these changes affect only the images and concepts, or the Unspeakable itself. After all, we can imagine God as an eternally flowing current of vital energy that endlessly changes shape just as easily as we can imagine him as an eternally unmoved, unchangeable essence.[33]

All statements about God are provisional. Despite what religions think about their revelations, such revelations are not absolute, and Jung introduces a note of relativity into all discussions of religion. This is what makes many people nervous. He is saying that the so-called Word of God is not definite, beyond challenge, or eternally valid, but it is simply the "best possible expression of something as yet unknown." The consolation for religious is that it is our "best" chance at knowing God, but Jung believes it is not our only chance, and nor is it beyond reproach. He is a relativist when it comes to such phenomena; no single revelation is binding but all have some significance. Jung's relativity does not, however, extend to uncertainty about the existence of God:

> There is no doubt that there is something behind these images that transcends consciousness and operates in such a way that the statements do not vary limitlessly and chaotically, but clearly all relate to a few basic principles or archetypes.[34]

This is an important point, lost on his critics. He is a relativist only in terms of our knowing, not in terms of the objects that our knowing points to. In this way Jung demonstrates his indebtedness to Kant, who was the first to make distinctions between what we can know and the realities we strive to understand.

Jung is aware that he is asking a lot of believers to think in terms of a difference between religious statements and the objects to which they point. He says, "the naïve-minded person has never separated [religious symbols] from their unknowable metaphysical background."[35] Such people "instantly equate the image with the transcendental x to which it points."[36] Nietzsche referred to this as "word magic," but the technical term is hypostatization, treating something conceptual as if it were real. Religious traditions encourage such thinking, because it shores up their status and strengthens their following. In my experience, however, it only alienates people, especially those who understand that the relation of signifier to signified is arbitrary. As Jung puts it, a religious image "does not posit" the transcendental object to which it points.[37]

The Assumption of Mary

In "Answer to Job" Jung gives an example of his symbolic approach when applied to a dogmatic assertion. The bodily assumption of the Virgin Mary, or *Assumptio Mariae*, was proclaimed as dogma by Pope Pius XII in 1950. Jung was excited by this dogma, as it seemed to him that a developmental process was underway. The masculine religion of Christianity was changing into something more complete, and moving toward a more androgynous position. Hitherto Christianity was in danger of being "nothing but a *man's religion*, which allows no metaphysical representation of woman."[38] The dominance of the Father and Son, he felt, was being compensated by the rise of the feminine:

> The feminine, like the masculine, demands an equally personal representation. The dogmatizing of the Assumption does not, however,

according to the dogmatic view, mean that Mary has attained the status of a goddess, although, as mistress of heaven and mediatrix, she is functioning on a par with Christ, the king and mediator. At any rate her position satisfies the need of the archetype. The new dogma expresses a renewed hope for the fulfilment of that yearning for peace which stirs deep down in the soul, and for a resolution of the threatening tension between the opposites.[39]

Jung spoke of the dogma as an expression of "divine intervention arising in the collective unconscious,"[40] to compensate the masculinity of religion. He argued that only Catholic sacramentalism and mystical spirituality could allow Christianity to summon the imagination to connect with the spirit of the time. He applauds Catholicism for having the courage to believe that, "with the assistance of the Holy Ghost, the dogma can progressively develop and unfold."[41] He is delighted that the Catholic Church is able to respond to the "popular movement" in which "the visions of Mary have been increasing in number over the last few decades."[42] He wrote:

> The motive and content of the popular movement which contributed to the Pope's decision solemnly to declare the new dogma consist not in the birth of a new god, but in the continuing incarnation of God which began with Christ.[43]

Contrary to Protestant commentators in his day, Jung argued that the dogma of the Assumption was validated by the desire of the spirit to express itself more fulsomely in a new time. Protestant theologians, as well as "English archbishops," were scandalized by the Vatican's superciliousness and arrogance.[44] It seemed to them that the Vatican was being self-interested and conceited, bowing to public pressure to include a feminine dimension of the divine. To Protestants, the Vatican was inventing a dogma out of thin air, without scriptural foundation or precedent.

Although Protestant by birth, Jung attacked Protestantism, arguing it had lost touch with the spirit that makes continuing revelation possible. The aging and cantankerous Jung flew into a rage, pronouncing:

> The failure to understand that God has eternally wanted to become man, and for that purpose continually incarnates through the Holy Ghost in the temporal sphere, is an alarming symptom and can only mean that the Protestant standpoint has lost ground by not understanding the signs of the times and by ignoring the continued operation of the Holy Ghost. It is obviously out of touch with the

tremendous archetypal happenings in the psyche of the individual and the masses, and with the symbols which are intended to compensate the truly apocalyptic world situation today.[45]

This vigorous defense of the Catholic position, however, overlooks a crucial fact. At risk of appearing to offer a bad pun, Jung and Rome are working from different "assumptions." The Vatican views the Assumption literally, and Jung does not. Rome's dogma is about a physical miracle, and its constitution states that the Virgin Mary "having completed the course of her earthly life, was assumed body and soul into heavenly glory."[46] Jung does not believe in a physical assumption, any more than any other Protestant of his time. His mind was modern and not prone to superstition. Rome would find his support cynical, undermining, or sacrilegious. To this extent, Jung's championing of the Catholic cause can appear disingenuous.

Despite trying to bury it, his conscience cannot allow him to overlook this problem. There is an important footnote, which reads:

> The papal rejection of psychological symbolism may be explained by the fact that the Pope is primarily concerned with the reality of metaphysical happenings. Owing to the undervaluation of the psyche that everywhere prevails, every attempt at adequate psychological understanding is immediately suspected of psychologism. It is understandable that dogma must be protected from this danger. If, in physics, one seeks to explain the nature of light, nobody expects that as a result there will be no light. But in the case of psychology everybody believes that what it explains is explained away. However, I cannot expect that my particular deviationist point of view could be known in any competent quarter.[47]

Why is this relegated to a footnote when it should be incorporated into his argument? The answer is that Jung is so carried away by his reading of the Papal Bull that he does not want to detract from it by pointing to its literalism. In the footnote is the sobering voice of reason, which is trying to understand the Assumption in symbolic terms. Jung himself is part of the Protestant community that he harangues and berates, although in his essay he wants to side with the Catholic cause, since it shows evidence of dreaming the myth onward. But he is unable to support Catholic literalism and cannot protect the dogma from the enquiry and doubt of rational thought.

Jung is caught in the knot of his complex nature: his soul wants to be Catholic, but his mind remains Protestant and cannot believe what has been pronounced in such a superstitious manner. Later his passion for Rome subsides, and he becomes cool headed about the dogma and its assertion of a physically impossible fact:

> It does not matter at all that a physically impossible fact is asserted, because all religious assertions are physical impossibilities. If they were not so, they would, as I said earlier, necessarily be treated in the text books of natural science. But religious statements without exception have to do with the reality of the *psyche* and not with the reality of *physis*.[48]

This heralds the return of the Jung we know: an astute and fierce critic of Christian literalism. His thinking about the reality of the psyche represents an attempt to hold the tension between Catholic substance and Protestant principle. He wants the nourishment of soul *and* the honesty of critical thinking, and for him these are brought together in the symbol, something that is spiritually but not literally true. The living symbol represents the synthesis that can unite our hunger for myth and our desire for scientific understanding.

But Jung's thinking, which insists on the psychic but not physical reality of religious assertions, cannot be supported by Protestantism or Catholicism. To that extent his outlook remains "a deviationist point of view," not able to be incorporated into either mainstream tradition. The "reality" of the symbol is the key to a future religious awareness, but due to the "undervaluation of the psyche that everywhere prevails" Christianity is unable to follow Jung's lead. For all their espoused differences, Catholic and Protestant theologies are expressions of the same Western psyche that has undervalued the symbol, leading the former to hypostatize the symbol as fact, and the latter to freeze the sacred in a historical revelation that has no "mystical" presence. Catholicism degenerates into mumbo-jumbo and sacrosanct unintelligibility, and Protestantism into secular humanism and social work. Jung's suggestion that dogmas are "psychologically true" is cold comfort to traditions that have emphasized historical and concrete thinking.

Elevation of the Symbolic

To Jung, the major ideas of religion were part of an archaic system that had to be reinterpreted for a new consciousness. They represented childhood or infantile ways of imagining God. Not only was the image of God out of date, but the entire story of Christian faith was mythological and had to be translated into a new language—even if, as he said, the new language would be another set of metaphors. The virgin birth, the resurrection, the second coming were symbols of the life of the spirit. The time had arrived, he believed, for us to take on the enormous task of reinterpreting all religious truths. He wrote in 1952, after the proclamation of the Assumption of Mary:

> This is a favourable opportunity for [modern man] to ask himself, for a change, what is the meaning not only of the new dogma [the *Assumptio Mariae*] but of all more or less dogmatic assertions over and above their literal concretism. . . . He should bend to the great task of reinterpreting all the Christian traditions. If it is a question of truths which are anchored deep in the soul—and no one with the slightest insight can doubt this fact—then the solution of this task must be possible.[49]

He was performing a deconstructive task similar to that found in postmodern philosophy, decades ahead of schedule. The religious symbols did not point to historical events or metaphysical objects in outer space. They pointed to a different kind of reality, to events in the soul. He was constantly trying to define, and redefine, the meaning of the symbol.

Equally, he reflected on the reality to which the symbols point. In "Psychology and Literature" he said "the true symbol is an expression for something real but unknown."[50] "What most people overlook or seem unable to understand," he said, "is that I regard the psyche as real." "They seem to believe only in physical facts."[51] "Most people" in the West seemed to have, or suffer from, a constricted view of reality. The symbol can be psychologically and spiritually real, pointing to events that take place constantly in the soul.

> By a "symbol" . . . I do not mean an allegory pointing to something all too familiar, but the expression of something profoundly alive in the soul.[52]

The assumption is that events "alive in the soul" are taking place all the time. Jung tried to get religious people to understand his view of symbolism. But it is difficult, if not impossible, to convince a religious tradition that has been based on assumptions of "historical fact" that its core elements may not have happened as fact. The gospel writers were poets amplifying the meaning of events by supplying images that brought out the deeper dimension of what took place. These images are not illusions, but truths that reveal the depth dimension of events.

The error is not in the images themselves, not in the scriptures, but in how we interpret them.

We might see similar category errors in our response to dreams. A person or figure in a dream does not necessarily refer to the person we know in external social reality. It refers to a psychic or internal reality of the mind, and to view the dream as a message or fact about someone in real life is to misconstrue the dream's meaning. For Jung, Christianity has been operating in a childish mode for centuries, and it need not continue in this mode, since it now has the knowledge at its disposal to introduce a new understanding of truth.

The symbol is not just a booby prize for those who have been disenchanted. The symbol is the royal road to the sacred. It is "the best possible description of a relatively unknown fact,"[53] "an expression for something that cannot be characterized in any other or better way."[54] Moreover "whether a thing is a symbol or not depends on the attitude of the observing consciousness."[55] So here is a conundrum: unless we express reverence for the images, they do not transport us to the places to which they point. This is why the loss of literalism can be disastrous for some: when the spell is broken, there is nothing left. Images can only function as icons if we give them value, if our imaginations allow them to resonate. Many a believer feels let down, deflated, and inclined to go into reverse, claiming that he or she has been duped. Therefore, we have to work with diligence on educating the imagination and on restoring sacredness to the images.

Notes

1. Jung, "The Psychology of the Child Archetype" (1940), *CW* 9, 1, § 267.
2. Jung, "A Psychological Approach to the Dogma of the Trinity" (1942/1948), *CW* 11, § 170.
3. Jung, "The Psychology of the Transference" (1946), *CW* 16, § 396.
4. Jung, "The Psychology of the Child Archetype" (1940), *CW* 9, 1, § 271.
5. Jung, Letter to Freud, 1910, *The Freud/Jung Letters*, ed. William McGuire (London: Hogarth Press, 1974), p. 294.
6. Paul Bishop, *Analytical Psychology and German Classical Aesthetics: Goethe, Schiller, and Jung*, Vol. 1, *The Development of the Personality* (London: Routledge, 2008), p. 40.
7. John 15:5.
8. Jung, Letter to Freud, p. 294.
9. Sigmund Freud, *The Future of an Illusion* (1927), in Anna Freud, Alix Strachey and Alan Tyson, eds., James Strachey, trans., *The Standard Edition of the Complete Psychological Works of Sigmund Freud* (London: Hogarth Press, 1953–1975), Vol. 21.

10. The contemporary relevance of Jung's thought is further discussed in my section, "Jung's psychology and the future," in "General Introduction" of Tacey, ed., *The Jung Reader* (London: Routledge, 2012), p. 14ff.
11. Jung, *Memories, Dreams, Reflections* (1963; London: HarperCollins, 1995), p. 364.
12. I have written a book on these developments; see Tacey, *The Darkening Spirit: Jung, Spirituality, Religion* (London: Routledge, 2013).
13. Vittorio Macchioro, *From Orpheus to Paul: A History of Orphism* (New York: Holt, 1930; reprinted New York: Lightning Source Incorporated, 2003), p. 218.
14. Ibid.
15. Jung, "Commentary on "The Secret of the Golden Flower"" (1929), *CW* 13, § 54.
16. David Tacey, *Gods and Diseases* (Sydney: HarperCollins, 2011; London: Routledge, 2012).
17. Jung, "Answer to Job" (1952), *CW* 11, § 647.
18. Jung, "The Psychology of the Child Archetype" (1940), *CW* 9, Part 1, § 271.
19. Jung, ibid., § 261.
20. Jung, ibid., § 260.
21. Jung, ibid., § 267.
22. Jung, "Symbols and the Interpretation of Dreams" (1961), *CW* 18, § 606.
23. Jung, "Answer to Job," § 648.
24. Pontifical Council for Culture and Pontifical Council for Interreligious Dialogue 2003: *Jesus Christ: The Bearer of the Water of Life: A Christian Reflection on the "New Age."* Vatican, Rome. Located at: http://www.vatican.va/roman_curia/pontifical_councils/interelg/documents/rc_pc_interelg_doc_20030203_new-age_en.html.
25. This can be found as chapter 10 in Tacey, ed., *The Jung Reader* (London: Routledge, 2012), pp. 253–256.
26. Jung, "Lectori Benevolo," "Answer to Job," *CW* 11, § 553.
27. Jung, ibid., § 553.
28. Jung, ibid., § 554.
29. Jung, ibid., § 554.
30. *Jerusalem Bible* (Garden City, New York: Doubleday, 1966), Matthew 16:4.
31. Jung, "Lectori Benevolo," § 555.
32. Jung, ibid., § 557.
33. Jung, ibid., § 555.
34. Jung, ibid., § 555.
35. Jung, ibid., § 558.
36. Jung, ibid., § 558.
37. Jung, ibid., § 558.
38. Jung, "Answer to Job," § 753.
39. Jung, ibid, § 754.
40. Jung, ibid, § 754.
41. Jung, ibid, § 655.
42. Jung, ibid, § 748.
43. Jung, ibid, § 749.

44. Paul E. Duggan, *The Assumption Dogma: Some Reactions and Ecumenical Implications in the Thought of English-Speaking Theologians* (Cleveland, Ohio: Emerson Press, 1989).
45. Jung, "Answer to Job," § 749.
46. Pius XII, in his Apostolic Constitution, "Munificentissimus Deus: Defining the Dogma of the Assumption," par. 44, Vatican, November 1, 1950. Located at: http://www.vatican.va/holy_father/pius_xii/apost_constitutions/documents/hf_p-xii_apc_19501101_munificentissimus-deus_en.html.
47. Jung, "Answer to Job," § 749, footnote 2.
48. Jung, ibid, § 752.
49. Jung, ibid, § 754.
50. Jung, "Psychology and Literature" (1930/1950), *CW* 15, § 148.
51. Jung, "Answer to Job," § 751.
52. Jung, "Psychology and Literature," § 159.
53. Jung, "Definitions" (1921), *Psychological Types*, *CW* 6, § 814.
54. Jung, ibid., § 816.
55. Jung, ibid., § 818.

11

After Belief

The crisis consists precisely in the fact that the old is dead and the new has yet to be born; in this interregnum arise a great many morbid symptoms.
— Antonio Gramsci[1]

After Literalism

Once the literal approach to religion is undermined, what then? If our culture insists that only historical events have validity, and only what can be empirically verified has truth, we are in dire straits. If nothing is sacred, nothing matters, and we move toward nihilism and brutality. We catch a snapshot of our predicament by looking at the upheavals of the twentieth century. By the turn of the twentieth century, religion was in serious decline, as the truth of Christianity began to be questioned. The tradition known as the "Christ-myth theory" had its origins in the eighteenth century, but by the early 1900s it escalated in significance. This theory argued that because scripture was mythical, none of it could be taken seriously. As Christopher Hitchens put it in our time:

> Either the gospels are in some sense literal truth, or the whole thing is essentially a fraud and perhaps an immoral one at that. Well, it can be stated with certainty, and on their own evidence, that the gospels are most certainly not literal truth. This means that many of the "sayings" and teachings of Jesus are hearsay upon hearsay upon hearsay, which helps explain their garbled and contradictory nature.[2]

Hitchens is the most recent voice in the so-called "mythicist" tradition, which discredits sacred writings on the basis that they are not literally true.

In 1909 the German philosopher Arthur Drews popularized the ideas of Bruno Bauer, whose book *A Critique of the Evangelical History of the Synoptics* had argued that religion was mythical and unreliable.[3] Claims were made that Drews was anti-Semitic and trying to discredit the life of Jesus for the sake of Aryanism. The supporters of Drews caused a sensation by plastering Berlin's billboards with posters asking, "Did Jesus Christ Ever Live?" This served to weaken Christianity in Germany at a vulnerable time. As Germany approached war, and as religious belief was undermined by rationality, Germany found itself dispensing with the age-old faith and taking on <u>nationalism as a pseudo-religion.</u> Ironically, although Christianity was weakened by accusations of its mythical nature, an even more ancient form of myth began to surface in Wotanism and Nordic cosmology. These German-based mythologies provided fuel for the nationalistic sentiments that gave rise to National Socialism. It was as if one form of myth was rejected, only to be replaced by another far more virulent.[4]

Meanwhile, in Russia, Lenin was quick to seize upon the ideas of Drews' *Die Christusmythe* to support his own state-sponsored atheism.[5] The arguments of Drews were included in school and university textbooks in the Soviet Union from 1920 onward. Lenin supported the "Christ-myth theory" and promoted contact between Communists and Christ-myth theorists. He saw myth theory as a bulwark against "religious obscurantism," and mythicism became a platform upon which he promoted his "scientific atheism."[6] The Christ-myth theory, together with Nietzsche's pronouncements on the death of God, provided the cultural leverage and moral weakening that led to the proliferation of extremist nationalisms and ideologies that devastated the twentieth century. It seems that humanity cannot live without a mythos, and when one is torn down, others rush in that are by no means better than the ones they replace. We are going to continue to pay a high price for any corrosive rationalism that discredits religion and its moral values.

Naturally, these toxic exploitations of myth theory served to strengthen the church's resolve against myth. In 1907 the Catholic Church issued a decree, signed by Pope Pius X, entitled "A Lamentable Departure Indeed," that condemned mythicists and relativists who were claimed to be undermining the foundations of the church.[7] This decree, with its "Syllabus Condemning the Errors of the Modernists," was followed by the encyclical "Feeding the Lord's Flock," which characterized modern biblical criticism and myth theory as "the synthesis of all heresies."[8] "The number of the enemies of the cross of Christ has in these last days increased exceedingly, who are striving, by arts, entirely new and full of subtlety, to destroy the vital energy of the church, and, if they can, to overthrow Christ's kingdom itself." With myth theory feeding into atheism and tyranny, few in the churches, except Rudolf Bultmann, were able to accept the presence of myth, although even Bultmann tried other ways to get rid of it, as we shall see. In the main, Protestant and Catholic churches clung to historical positivism, as the new scholarship and philosophical enquiry eroded the old dispensation in which the literal reading of scripture could be taken for granted.

Modernity stood between two undesirables: a moribund religious orthodoxy that continued to assert the historicity of its beliefs, and political ideologies that were plunging the world into moral chaos because they had glimpsed the mythical nature of religion. Will a middle path ever be found? We have yet to see what might arise once Western civilization grasps the mythical and learns to respect it.

The churches were reactive in the early modern era and continue to be reactive today. Western knowledge had determined that myth was illusion, and instead of challenging this assumption and arguing for truth in myth, religion took fright and made rearguard claims about its historicity. It was an expedient move, but it merely delayed the day of judgment, which has arrived. Schopenhauer was one of the first to understand this conundrum. In the 1850s he wrote:

> The bad thing about all religions is that, instead of being able to confess their allegorical nature, they have to conceal it.

Accordingly, "we have the great mischief of a continual fraud." However, this philosopher could see that the fraud would eventually run out:

> Nay, what is worse, the day arrives when [doctrines] are no longer strictly true, and then there is an end of them; so that, in that respect, it would be better to admit their allegorical nature at once. But the difficulty is to teach the multitude that something can be both true and untrue at the same time.[9]

While it would have been better to admit the allegorical nature of scripture at the outset, we are now faced with the enormous task of "teaching the multitude that something can be both true and untrue at the same time." That is, we have to teach people, young and old, that there are different kinds of truth, and historical fact is only one kind. Can I go before devout believers and tell them that the Virgin Birth or Physical Resurrection never happened as claimed, but that they contain another kind of truth? Can this be taught to the multitude at this stage, after hundreds of years of being told that myth is false and the gospels true because they are historically accurate?

Faith Without Belief

Matthew Arnold thought long and hard about this problem in the 1870s. In a sense, the question he posed back then has still not been answered:

> To pass from a Christianity relying on its miracles to a Christianity relying on its natural truth is a great change. It can only be brought about by those whose attachment to Christianity is such that they cannot part with it, and yet cannot but deal with it sincerely.[10]

It is this "pass" as Arnold calls it, this rite of passage from illusion to truth, that has still to be negotiated. I am not sanguine about how we are going to manage it. Religion is on shakier ground than has been acknowledged, and the spike in fundamentalism is a defensive reaction. Scholars have often announced that the miracles are metaphors, but this has not always inspired in them increased respect for their sacredness. Too many people decide religion is metaphorical and lose all sense of its importance. The metaphors are dead and no longer touch them. They are as remote and dormant as ancient artifacts, because unillumined by the light of faith. In the past, the "shock" of a miraculous event was supposed to jump-start faith in believers. It was regarded as a conversion to read scripture and announce: "Yes, I'm a believer!" The church regarded this as a triumph, and told people to continue in this mode throughout their lives and leave their minds at the door as they entered the house of worship. Thinking was discouraged, as it brought doubts.

But today most educated people can see the miracles and wonders are metaphors, but how can these metaphors speak to them of spiritual reality? The fact is that we require faith to be moved by these images: a kind of catch-22 situation. Since the shock factor of heralding them as true has been lost, how are people to sense the truth of these images? Only the eyes of faith can see mystery in the metaphors. On numerous occasions I have been made aware that believers have no idea what is meant by myth. They assume that to talk of myth in religion is to debunk it. Unbelievers feel smug about their unbelief, in the sense that: "I knew all along this wasn't true." Believers feel devastated that their faith is exposed as groundless: "how could the church have pretended that this was historical? I feel outraged by the fraud."

Scripture scholar Kevin Treston puts our crisis this way:

> Christianity urgently needs to recover an appreciation of the world of *mythos* if it is going to communicate the gospel effectively. The prospects are bleak if it operates out of a literalist mode within a scientific cultural environment. Unless people appreciate the levels of *mythos* and logos in religious language, they can too readily dismiss Christian beliefs as a whole series of fables.[11]

If the church meets with catastrophe at this point in history, it has only itself to blame. By preaching the message that myth is bad and history good, it has poisoned the water that may kill it off.

The problem with Western religion is that it has not been spiritual enough. It has confused faith with belief in impossible events and has been living on borrowed credibility for a long time. It is not as if great minds have not warned of this predicament. We can no longer deny the scholarship that has been assembled over the last two hundred years. We cannot ignore the voices that argue that the gospel writers were writing in the mode of *mythos*, and had never intended their stories to be taken literally. We cannot continue to promote a false view of scripture because we are afraid to face truth. We cannot keep telling lies for God, in the belief that our lies are keeping religion alive. In the present we are caught between a religious historicism we can no longer embrace and a metaphorical approach that might lead to the collapse of religion. But truth is always the best option, even if truth is not understood at first, and may be opposed by believers and religious leaders who are still locked in a defensive mode.

Vision and Uncommon Sense

How to make symbols come alive in a culture in which they have died? How to promote the idea that symbols have much to say, even though we may see them as arbitrary or "made up"? I have used the following quote before, but it bears a second hearing:

> Whenever we suppose to take [the scriptures] "literally" we misunderstand them. And whenever we try to read them "symbolically," we risk deflating the seriousness of their claims on us and flattening their validity into something arbitrary and aesthetic.[12]

It is a risk, Drewermann says, but a risk we have to take. In this chapter I will briefly explore a tradition known as progressive religious thought, and here we see what Drewermann and others fear: symbols are deflated, flattened, meaningless. If the rational mind, acting without vision or imagination, decides that religious facts are symbols, the result is catastrophic. At times I think it is almost better for people to remain in naïve literalism than embrace a new "enlightened" view of religion that leads to nihilism.

As Drewermann points out: "religious myth is not something that can be grasped intellectually."[13] The imagination has to supply or "fill in" what the rational mind is unable to provide, which is respect for symbols as vehicles of truth. Logos cannot achieve a spirituality on our behalf. Only mythos can perceive religious symbols in the correct way. Logos is outwardly focused and orientates us to fact and world. Logos is wonderful when applied to science, technology, politics and any field requiring reason. But it is disastrous when applied to religion, philosophy, poetry or myth because the essence of these endeavors requires an imaginative response. Without imagination, the "spirit" of these endeavors dies and they no longer speak to the soul.

The spiritual aliveness of symbols is dependent on the consciousness of the observer. The symbols can be alive for one person, and dead for another. But the symbols are the same in either case. To most people, symbols are puzzling and bothersome. Most believe them literally, or not at all. Either way, they are mistaken. William Blake said we have to acquire insight, vision, or imagination to see eternity in a grain of sand. In popular parlance, we need to develop a third eye to perceive symbols correctly, to allow them to speak to us. By "third eye" I mean the eye of insight, and in this the West is lacking, because all of its emphasis has been upon the two eyes that stare outwardly at the world. To understand religion we need uncommon sense, and that is the problem we face. We cannot see the spirit unless we have been "transformed" to another way of seeing. Unless we have allowed mythos to function as a different capacity of mind, there is no going over to the other side.

It is almost as if half our brain is dead. We are a left-brained culture, attuned to experiencing things through rationality, but to attune ourselves to religion we have to reactivate the right brain, which we are told governs music, poetry, creativity, and art. Religion is an art, not a science, and it is an art we have lost the ability to appreciate. The Holy Trinity seems bizarre to common sense, but the activation of mythos is necessary for us to perceive God, Christ, and Spirit. To understand such things is "like" becoming a child, "like" being reborn, insofar as we have allowed a lost part of ourselves to live again. When this capacity is not activated, we live in a flat world without depth or verticality. Thus the religious problem cannot be solved by the intellect alone, and educating the intellect may be important for acquiring knowledge, but when it comes to religion it has no real impact. The soul or heart needs educating, and that is something our education system has not yet begun to ponder.

Bultmann's Progressive Thinking

Progressive religious thought can lead to a perpetuation of our disenchanted reality if we are unable to muster the support of the mythos side of the brain. If progressive religion is rational rather than poetic, if it fails to understand that we require a second innocence to respond to metaphors, it is furthering the cause of desacralization. I will provide a summary of this crisis, beginning with the chief exponent of progressive religious thought, the German modernist Rudolf Bultmann.

Bultmann (1884–1976) advocated an approach to scripture called "demythologization." He invented the progressive approach to religion, which saw through the "facts" of scripture to the symbols he thought they were. Bultmann was a minister who was not only embarrassed but outraged by the fact that myth was misrepresented as fact by his tradition. Needless to say, he received a great deal of criticism for his stance, and although the churches viewed his work as near blasphemy, he drew support from the philosophical community, or that part of it that was concerned with religion. Bultmann recognized that the churches lived in a "bubble" of irreality, and scholars outside the bubble had long recognized that the main body of religious narrative was myth.

His work appears at first glance to be in harmony with mine: exposing the mythic nature of what passes for history and reworking the content so as to place faith on an imaginative footing. When I give talks on metaphor in scripture, audiences assume I am an advocate of Bultmann's "demythologizing"—a term he branded as his own. But such is not the case. Bultmann points to the possibility that as we peel away the literal much else will be cast out as worthless. I refer to Bultmann not as an example of what we must do, but an example of the caution needed at this time, which is a dangerous interregnum.

Bultmann argued that the mythic view of religion was not his discovery, but went back to German philosophers before him. He referred to the discoveries of Hegel, Schelling, Feuerbach, Schopenhauer, and Nietzsche, and blasted church leaders for ignoring the findings of these great thinkers. He argued that the churches demonstrated a head-in-the-sand approach, a view that if they ignored the critique of literalism, the problem would disappear and everything return to normal. Bultmann laments the backward stance of the churches:

> If for the last twenty years we have been called back from criticism to simple acceptance of New Testament proclamation, theology and the church have run the risk of uncritically repristinating [repeating] New Testament mythology, thereby making the proclamation unintelligible for the present. The critical work of earlier generations cannot be simply thrown away but must be positively appropriated.[14]

If the critique of the mythological content of religion does not occur, he says "sooner or later... the church [may not] exist at all."[15] Modern people will not be fooled. They will walk away and lead a secular life rather than have religion at the cost of deception. Bultmann calls on churches to offer a faith that can stand up to criticism and not hide from this challenge.

Saving the Myths

I agree with the first part of Bultmann's project. His call for recognition of the presence of myth and his demand that the churches face this crisis are important in my view. But I disagree with his second part. He wants to get rid of myth and find some new way to understand religion. He says:

> Insofar as religion is mythological talk it is incredible to men and women today because for them the mythical world picture is a thing of the past.[16]

Religion cannot be dismissed as "mythological talk." It is the revelation of the sacred through carefully crafted mythological narratives. I don't want to get rid of the myths; I want to understand them, by using the insights of depth psychology. These stories have hidden meanings and cultural subtexts that go back thousands of years, and can be found in non-Judaic-Christian cultures as well. Bultmann's tone is abrasive. In *Jesus Christ and Mythology* he tries to reassure us that he is not rejecting scripture wholesale:

> To demythologize is to reject not Scripture or the Christian message as a whole, but the world-view of Scripture, which is the world-view of a past epoch, which all too often is retained in Christian dogmatics and in the preaching of the Church. To demythologize is to deny that the message of Scripture and of the Church is bound to an ancient world-view which is obsolete.[17]

But in everything he writes about the "obsolete" language of myth, Bultmann makes an error, which George Caird of Oxford refers to as "an enormous and unargued assumption." Bultmann assumes "that biblical man took the picture language of the Bible as flat statement of fact."[18] In other words, he thinks ancient people were as silly as modern people in that they received biblical language literally. Bultmann projects our mistake into the past and arrives at an erroneous view of ancient times. Like Armstrong and Crossan after him, Caird claims that the reverse is true: we are dull enough to read picture language literally, while ancient people saw the connotation, not the denotation of images. Our failure to understand myth does not mean it is obsolete. It means we need re-educating so that we might understand it and give it the respect it deserves. It is the language that the spirit has always used to announce its revelations, and it is the language spirit will continue to use.

Instead of theologians getting impatient and wanting to throw out myth, why don't they consult classicists, philosophers, and depth psychologists, and find out what it means? There is not enough humility in theology, no sense that theologians might need to become students of other fields to understand their own in a new light. The fact is that, as the world becomes more complex, and as religious language is found to be mythic rather than historical, churchmen and women need to seek the advice of literary scholars and other specialists who understand metaphor and myth. In searching through the literature on demythologization, I was gratified to find this rebuke of Bultmann from the philosopher Karl Jaspers:

> Demythologization contains a half-truth: thinkers of all ages, and Bultmann too, are right in denying assertions which give myth the tangible reality of things in the world. But the demand for demythologization is justified only if at the same time it insists on restoring the reality of mythical language.[19]

The "half-truth" is that we are forced to admit that myths have gone cold in today's world. But to assume that our only response is to abandon myth is inappropriate. Jaspers makes this important point:

> Only he has the right to demythologise who retains the reality contained in the symbolic language of myth.[20]

What myth contains is vital and we have to "retain the reality" held in its symbols. Myth may appear synonymous with a defunct worldview, but its content needs to be made new in every epoch. Admittedly it is hard to resurrect this modality, given centuries of logocentric thinking. But myth is not "a thing of the past"; it is the language of revelation that has to be restored to its original dignity.

What I detect in Bultmann is a kind of vocational exhaustion. He is jaundiced by centuries of misreading of myth and wants to do away with it, to discover something more primary. But literary scholar Northrop Frye could have informed him that there is nothing more primary than myth. Bultmann's theological frustration is foolhardy, because myth is the legacy we have been bequeathed. Bultmann keeps imagining that there is a "proclamation"—which he calls *kerygma*—which is more basic than myth, and in every work he hacks away at myth with implements of destruction to reach this illustrious core. His frustration is palpable:

> What is at issue is the truth of this proclamation, and the faith that affirms its truth is not to be bound to the New Testament's world of [mythic] representations.[21]

Bultmann wants to get to the truth and is impatient. There is something more basic than the stories, but it is not to be found by dismantling them, but by moving deeply into them. There is a hidden meaning in every story, and we have to go beyond the denotation (outward appearance) to the connotation (the meaning to which it points), and we can only achieve this by understanding the metaphorical mode. In a sense, the medium is the message, or the message is revealed as we deepen the medium using imagination and insight. As Bultmann tries to discover a "New Testament proclamation that is independent of the mythical world picture,"[22] Frye points out that

> What one needs is a criticism that, instead of trying to cut away the myth as an accretion... would tell us something about why the books of the Bible exist as they now do in their present form.[23]

The Bible is written in the genre of myth, and we can't pretend otherwise. Although Frye, like Bultmann, is an ordained minister, his love of literature and his feeling for the poetry of Blake makes him able to respect mythic language.

Throwing Out the Baby

Bultmann wanted to tear down the structures of religion and start again, using concepts borrowed from existential philosophy, in particular

Heidegger. The irony of his project is that while an "existentialist reinterpretation" of the Bible may have been stimulating in his day, in our time existentialism has faded. The high-water mark of existentialism has passed, and today's intelligentsia might want a postmodern or post-structuralist interpretation that would suit its tastes. But even if we had that, it would still be avoiding the encounter with myth, and the fact that the Bible is built on myth. If we set about to "modernize" religion, we have to beware of getting caught in trends that disappear with the tides of fashion.

If we pull everything down, we end up with nothing rather than something. We cannot replace myth with concepts, because only myth and metaphor are capable of "carrying us over" (*metaphorein*) to the transcendent, compelling faith and "rebinding" us to the sacred.[24] Bultmann carries to its logical conclusion a dynamic that has been the bane of Western religion for centuries: the notion that religion can be reduced to reason, and mysticism and sacrament can be tossed away to make way for something more efficient. The truth is that an efficient revelation of the divine does not exist, and progressives are on a wild-goose chase. The mind won't, can't, carry us over the abyss between our consciousness and transcendental reality. Only the nonrational can manage that, which is why the Catholic tradition, for all its many faults, retains the possibility of carrying us over to the sacred, whereas Reformists often appear to stand resourceless before God, as literal believers or enlightened doubters. Eventually I see Protestants and Catholics coming together again in a united cause to experience the mystery of God.

The fact is that we need to *participate* in the sacred, in ritual, sacrament, and enactment. There is no point in observing it through the intellect alone, or through our day-world consciousness. Jung referred to the Reformation as a "spiritual catastrophe" from which we are still, today, recovering.[25] Jung's natal religion was Protestant, and he felt his spiritual development suffered because of it. The fact is that we need resources beyond the mind and morality to shift consciousness and direct us toward the sacred. Good works, serving others, social justice and thrift are "good" in themselves, but not enough to allow us to see the kingdom of heaven, which can only be glimpsed in an altered state. By which I mean, a state altered by prayer, reflection, *lectio divina*, liturgy, ritual or mystical experience.

Bultmann inspired the "progressive religious thought" movement, which tries to understand religion by rational means.[26] I am wary of anything that calls itself "progressive" because progress has delivered many evils of our time. Where "progress" is advocated without restriction, it is responsible for injustices and wrongdoings, whether these are of the secular kind, as in getting rid of religion, the urban-industrial kind, as in getting rid of trees and open spaces, or the religious kind, as in getting rid of myths. Progress is an idea dictated by the intellect, at the expense of the soul. It is sacrilegious when it starts to dismantle the temples of religion, replacing its time-honored constructs with new concepts borrowed from the modern world.

One aspect of the progressive religious movement is exemplified in Lloyd Geering's essay "The Legacy of Christianity":

> In the attempt to reform the Christian stream people often speak of the danger of throwing out the baby with the bathwater. That is misleading, for in actual fact there is no baby. It is all bathwater.[27]

Geering was tried for heresy in New Zealand, and progressives believe this was unfair. But his disrespect for tradition is astounding. If religion is said to be "all bathwater," with no baby, we have betrayed the tradition. The arrogance of the modern, and the aridity of the progressive mind, is a pitfall into which we can land, and disaster looms if we don't find respect for the sacramental dimension.

The predilection for throwing out reminds me of the Walt Disney cartoon in which Donald Duck is trying to start his car. He opens the hood and proceeds to extract various mechanical parts that his muddle-headed brain does not understand: the carburetor, the fuel pump, the starter motor. All are tossed out, and, pleased with his intervention, Uncle Donald closes the hood, jumps in the car, winks to Huey, Dewey, and Louie in the back seat, and turns the key. Nothing happens. He is puzzled because he thought he threw out what was extraneous. I see this as a symbol of the progressive religious spirit that has become riotous: it gets rid of too much, and eventually nothing works. It throws out myths and symbols it does not understand, and thinks it has made all the right adjustments. It is destined to fail, just as Bultmann's demythologization failed.

Jung put it best when he said this about the "rationalizing intellectuals" and their dismissal of religious myth:

> The really dangerous people are not the great heretics and unbelievers, but the swarm of petty thinkers, the rationalizing intellectuals, who suddenly discover how irrational all religious dogmas are. Anything not understood is given short shrift, and the highest values of

symbolic truth are irretrievably lost. What can a rationalist do with the dogma of the Virgin Birth or with Christ's sacrificial death, or the Trinity?[28]

The old myths have to be explained to a modern world, and this is what the Jews called midrash, making sacred truths meaningful in a new era. We have to unpack them, and put them back together in their original form. In my own practice, I do not unpack myths to cast them aside, as debris from the past. My view is that only myth is large enough, generous enough, and deeply embedded enough in our souls to enable any revitalization of the religious life.

Progressives in the Rationalistic Mode

Progressive religious thought attracts minds from numerous countries, walks of life, and academic disciplines. The movement offers a typically liberal critique of traditional theology and its metaphysical assertions. Inspired by such figures as Don Cupitt, John Spong, Lloyd Geering, Gretta Vosper,[29] and Robert Funk and his "Jesus Seminar," it accepts the modern position that miraculous events in the Bible are to be viewed as metaphors. But it is apparent that when such people refer to metaphors, they do not have in mind what I mean by the term. They tend to mean something more reductive, as is evident in the language used: "only metaphors," "just metaphors." They mean metaphors in a decorative sense, as if talking about metaphors in a novel. For them, biblical metaphors are dead, devoid of anything marvelous, and thus all the more able to be cut away as unnecessary accretions. In this sense, the progressive movement is caught in a similar blind alley to the "mythicists" whom I discussed earlier. The mythicists are secular atheists, but the progressive religious are moving in the same direction.

It was a shock for me to discover that metaphors are so heavily discounted by progressives. They are viewing metaphors through the lens of a disenchanted consciousness.[30] Progressives tend to inhabit a world in which spiritual realities are things of the past, in which sacred forces are literary conceits. They live in a buffered world, not permeable to the sacred. Bultmann's sense of reality is closed off to the sacred:

> Modern man acknowledges as reality only such phenomena or events as are comprehensible within the framework of the rational order of the universe.[31]

His thinking assumes a worldview in which the universe is a closed system of causality that excludes the possibility of extramundane influences. If God is conceived as "supernatural," God is dead in our age. But let us think this: an understanding of God that is not supernatural but profoundly natural. If God is not a supernatural being, but Being itself, as Tillich says, then God can and does influence the human order. The problem with progressive thinking is that it has not reconstructed God, but still thinks of God in premodern terms. There is a new understanding of God to be discovered, and until it is all we can expect is the rejection of the God-concept as unbelievable. For thinkers like Bultmann the world is two-dimensional, with no openings to the divine.

One of the ironies of progressive religious thinkers is that they reject the historical positivism of the churches, and embark on a new historical positivism of their own. They have been championing the search for the "historical Jesus" for some time, trying to find the Jesus beneath myth and legend, the Jesus of actual history. Dominic Crossan has spent a lot of time and effort trying to find forensic evidence for a historical Jesus, but it has not yielded much insight or information.[32] He discovers "the life of a Mediterranean Jewish peasant," but everything remarkable and significant about this figure has disappeared.[33] Admittedly, this search for the historical Jesus began long before the birth of the progressive movement, and came to modern attention with scholars such as Albert Schweitzer (1875–1965) and others who sought to find traces of the man behind the myth.[34] But we can't locate a historical Jesus because everything we know about Jesus, even from the beginning, is saturated with myth, and the notion that we can peel away the mythic layers to reveal the person is naïve and self-defeating.

The "progressive" search is vain, and shows that this movement is still wedded to literalist thinking, but now carried out at the natural instead of the supernatural level. It has not recognized the power of myth to reveal truth. It is still operating in a rationalistic mode, much like the old religious thinking it is reacting against. The literalism has merely shifted from heaven to earth. We are never going to find a secure historical platform for faith. Faith is precisely that which requires no historical evidence. The point of faith is that it is a leap into the uncertainty of mystery—which is not going to satisfy any modernist program. Bultmann's attempt to translate religion into existential philosophy failed because the content of religion is not rational. Nor is it irrational. The territory of religion is nonrational. The most enlightening commentator on this is Rudolf Otto, whose *The Idea of the Holy* attempts to lay out the true ground of religion.[35] That ground is based on the experience of the numinous, and has nothing to do with reason or dogmatics.

The Sea of Faith at Ebb Tide

Donald Cupitt is a progressive with a high profile today, since he gave birth to the Sea of Faith movement. Cupitt was based at Immanuel College, Cambridge for many years, and his early works on the philosophy of religion were typically academic and impossible for most people to understand. But later he found a popular voice and an international following. I appreciated his early work, some of which was produced with the assistance of the BBC in London.[36] But the demon of progress got into him, and he lost his way. He moved from liberal theology to negative theology,[37] which in the hands of some is interesting. Negative theology, or the *via negativa*, insists that we cannot know God because God is ineffable. But from this stage he moved into near-atheism[38] and then full-blown atheism.[39] He decided that since all we can know of God is metaphorical, God most likely does not exist. He concluded that "God was nothing more than a human construction."[40]

This is the pit into which a lot of progressive minds fall. Why do they make this mistake, over and over again? Since we cannot know God directly, they assume that the quest for God has been deluded, and we had better give it up and accept, at best, a humanist vision of the world. If a "real" God cannot be located in space, and if the literal statements of religion cannot be affirmed, they lapse into atheism. After writing *After God*, Cupitt then wrote *Life, Life*, claiming that all we can know is what we can see and touch. When the "magical" elements of religion fall away, many cannot imagine anything apart from physical matter. Such people have no imaginations and underestimate the power of metaphor to convey truth. As my colleague Matthew Del Nevo once said, religious metaphors are not empty, they are metaphors *of* something.[41] They point to something real, although not participating in that reality themselves. But when the literal approach falls down, the power of metaphor often does not rise up to replace it.

I once shared the podium with Don Cupitt at a progressive conference in New Zealand, organized by Lloyd Geering, the man who said all is bathwater. I accepted the invitation to see what kind of thinking was involved in progressive thought. Cupitt was an affable, highly cultured man with a quick wit and bright mind. But when I expressed my religious faith before the assembled audience in Palmerston North, Cupitt was horrified. Cupitt said I must be the only person in the conference who still believed in God. Some chuckled in the crowd, but I did not find it funny. Cupitt announced with smug finality that there was no God up there, out there, or in here, and my thinking was out of date. It took me weeks to recover from this event, which I experienced as a form of spiritual abuse. It is unfortunate that those who live disenchanted lives try to force their views on others.

Cupitt recognizes the metaphorical nature of religion and concludes that it points to nothing, only ourselves. I could not shift his prejudices, no matter how hard I tried. It made me think that too much education is not good for the soul. He had a smart answer to every question, and all of them moved toward nihilism. Strangely, he remained cheerful despite the emptiness of his thought. But Cupitt succumbs to the perils that await the purely intellectual approach to religion: rationalism, reductionism, relativism, atheism. We need more than an intellectual life to connect us to the sacred. The intellect works on a hermeneutics of suspicion, but faith requires a hermeneutics of affirmation. To connect with the sacred we need to affirm what we cannot see, and the intellect is unable to do this.

From Passive Belief to Active Faith

Bultmann, Cupitt, Geering, and others are signs that religion is in a state of disintegration. They are the conscience of a dying tradition, screaming its protest from rooftops. They are necessary voices at this time, but I find them depressing. One must forego the naïve enchantment of belief, not to enter a state of desolation, but to move toward an enchantment in which the metaphors are allowed to live again as carriers of meaning. How can this rebirth of meaning be effected? Clearly not by rational thinking, but by giving over intellectual suspicion to a hermeneutics of affirmation, to use the terms of Paul Ricoeur.[42] Perhaps we should stop *thinking* about metaphors, and attempt to "feel" them. Certainly the new approach to religion demands much more from us than the passive acceptance of a cluster of beliefs. Faith in the true sense is an active engagement in the symbols that point to the sacred.

Paul Tillich is helpful in leading us out of the quagmire of modernist thinking. In his *Theology of Culture*, Tillich asks: "Why do we need symbols at all?"[43] He answers: "The main function of the symbol is the opening up of levels of reality which otherwise are hidden and cannot be grasped in any other way." He continues:

> Every symbol opens up a level of reality for which non-symbolic speaking is inadequate. All religious symbols are designed to open

up a level of reality which otherwise is not opened at all, which is hidden. We can call this the depth dimension of reality itself. Religious symbols open up the experience of depth in the human soul.[44]

Then he says something that is interesting, even exciting. In order to respond to symbols adequately, "something needs to be opened up in our soul, in our interior reality." Our interior lives "must correspond to the levels of exterior reality which are opened up by a symbol." Tillich explains:

> So every symbol is two-edged. It opens up reality and it opens up the soul. There are, of course, people who are not opened up by music or who are not opened up by poetry, or more of them (especially in Protestant America) who are not opened up at all by visual arts. The "opening up" is a two-sided function—namely, reality in deeper levels and the human soul in special levels.[45]

This is a vital directive at this time. We ought not expect religion to do all the work for us. Perhaps it once did, when we existed in the era of belief, and all we had to do was believe in the miracles that were told to us by churches. But since this world has collapsed, we have to do more work ourselves. In the past, we were handed a supernatural world and asked to believe it. Now we have to produce some of the magic ourselves, and not rely on ministers or priests to do it all for us, to generate the magic of spiritual transformation.

Tillich suggests we have to use our imaginations to make the symbols come alive, to make them meaningful. He writes:

> One simply has to ask, "What is the relationship to the ultimate which is symbolized in these symbols?" and then they cease to be meaningless. They become, on the contrary, the most revealing creations of the human mind, the most genuine ones, the most powerful ones, those that control human consciousness, and perhaps even more the unconscious.[46]

He grasps something that Bultmann and his imitators fail to grasp. We cannot get rid of this ancient symbolism, because it is grounded in the soul, in what Tillich calls the "ground of being." Tillich saw that the project of demythologization was doomed. If we get rid of the myths and symbols, we get rid of religion, and end up with humanism or social realism, or what Tillich called "naturalism." We lose the sense that religion is pointing to another dimension of the world, and in this regard, Tillich had some sympathy for the antimodern brigade, those who emphasized that God, heaven, and spirit were otherworldly and supernatural. Tillich said, with a nod of approval to conservatives: liberal, demythologized theology paid the price of adjustment to the scientific era. Liberals reduced religion to humanism, and threw the baby out with everything else. He went on:

> Liberal theology paid the price of adjustment by losing the message of the new reality which was preserved by its supernaturalistic defenders.[47]

However he then criticized liberals and conservatives, and said both had missed the point. The point is not that God, heaven, spirit represent the incursion of another world. They are deeper dimensions of this world, but dimensions that rational thought cannot open for us, cannot communicate. There is another world, but it is in this one. This doorway to depth can only be opened for us by sacrament, imagination, vision, poetry, music, and iconography. The arts and imagination are what convey the sacred in today's disbelieving world. It is through the symbolic that the spirit takes flight and is released into life.

Stages of Faith

Perhaps we might think in terms of three stages of faith. At first we approach religion in literal terms. Then we say goodbye to naïve faith and mourn its loss for a time. Then we approach our experience through critical thinking, and learn to see the world through new eyes. But we can't stop there. We need to move to a third stage. Each person would have to define this third stage in his or her way, because there can be no formula that gets us from learned doubt to renewed faith. Jesus shows the way to this new state, when he says:

> Unless you change and become like little children you will never enter the kingdom of heaven.[48]

Jesus did not ask us to *remain* as children, stuck in a childish belief system. He asks us to *become* like little children, which is a new stage, after childhood and beyond adult rationality. In my case, I experienced literal belief as a child, and intellectual questioning as a young adult. But I saw that intellectual ascendancy was a kind of game we play in today's society, and it is a dangerous game at that. It is a poor consolation to give up childhood belief, only to win intellectual atheism. The second stage was anticipated by Jesus when he said:

> For what is a man profited, if he shall gain the whole world and lose his soul?[49]

Intellectual ascendancy is like winning the world. Society and its institutions, its pathways of reward and acknowledgement, its prizes and scholarships, its professions and promotions to positions of prestige, open up to a person who thinks critically about everything, especially religion. Disbelief and disenchantment is synonymous with career success. There is so much worldly reward in remaining at stage two, but Jesus continues:

> What shall a man give in exchange for his soul?

We must move on from intellectual enlightenment, addiction to materialism and the hermeneutics of suspicion. The worldliness of the world resists this shift from stage two to three, because it entails loss, surrender, and humility before a mystery we cannot understand.

Remaining as a little child means continuing to read Bible stories as children read them. Remaining as an adult means dismissing the stories as fairy tales. It means ditching the stories because they belong to an ancient worldview that can no longer be supported. Becoming a little child means returning to the stories again, but seeing them through new eyes. They are no longer literally true, no longer supernatural tales, but narratives that speak to us in a symbolic code. They only divulge their meaning if one is able to crack the code and see beyond the external features to the connotations. Finding this mystery is like discovering buried treasure in the field, which was one of Jesus' parables of the kingdom of God. It is like finding the pearl of great price, the jewel in the lode. The myths speak to us in a new way, rather like dreams once we learn their symbolic language. And like dreams, the untrained mind discards them as junk, but the trained mind discerns in them a meaning that is supportive and life changing.

The three stages are: enchantment, disenchantment, re-enchantment.[50] They aren't necessarily sequential or age related. We can experience these stages at any point in our lives. I have met young adults who know exactly what mature faith means. In the third stage, we return to where we began and "know the place for the first time," as T. S. Eliot said.[51] In the world of scholarship, there is already a small library on these three stages, and I have myself written a book on how the shift to the third stage might be conducted.[52]

Recreating the Fables

Many get stuck at the second stage, which views religion through rationality. The progressive movement gets stuck there, and does not appear to graduate to the innocence that Jesus commended. In his reply to Bultmann, Jaspers moves toward a definition of the third stage. It understands myth as myth, not as history. It does not treat myth with disdain, nor try to replace mythic structures with concepts. It recognizes that something mysterious is expressing itself in myth, and mythic thinking is here to stay:

> The myth, says Bultmann, is to be divested of its mythological garb, and translated into a truth valid today. I deny this. Mythical thinking is not a thing of the past, but characterizes man in any epoch.[53]

Myth cannot be destroyed in the interests of modernity, because myth is the vehicle of truth. We cannot put truth in any "better" way. Jaspers goes on to offer one of his most eloquent defenses for the code of myth:

> Myth is not a cloak or disguise put over a general idea, which can be better and more directly grasped intellectually. The myth is a carrier of meanings which can be expressed only in the language of myth. The mythical figures are symbols which, by their very nature, are untranslatable into other language. They are accessible only in the mythical element, they are irreplaceable, unique. They cannot be interpreted rationally; they are interpreted only by new myths, by being transformed.[54]

Jung argued that the symbol is "a living thing, it is an expression for something that cannot be characterized in any other or better way."[55] He put it memorably:

> Even the best attempts at explanation are only more or less successful translations into another metaphorical language. Indeed, language itself is only an image. The most we can do is to *dream the myth onwards* and give it a modern dress.[56]

We can "demythologize" to reach a new understanding, but ultimately we have to "retain the reality" contained in the symbolic forms. Jaspers, Jung, and Frye agree that although we may try to adapt myths to our sensibility we have to remain within the metaphorical domain. The task of interpretation is to update the mysteries by relating them to contemporary life, thus maintaining the link between eternity and time, present and past. But of crucial importance is that the return to myth cannot be a return to supernaturalism. It can only involve a rediscovery of the spiritual as an unseen dimension of the natural.[57]

We ought not destroy myths, but dream them onward, opening them to new possibilities of thought and imagination. As Frye says, this task is best left to the creative arts: "Mythology is recreated by the poets in each generation." The poet A. D. Hope said something similar in verse:

> Yet the myths will not fit us ready made.
> It is the meaning of the poet's trade
> To re-create the fables and revive
> In men the energies by which they live.[58]

Ancient myth will never fit us ready made, and that is why we have to reinterpret it using creativity and the arts. What are artists for? They enable us to "recreate the fables and revive in men the energies by which they live." Such creativity does not replace the myths, but builds on them, so they might speak to new generations. Reworking the myths, "dreaming them onward," and attuning our imaginations to their symbolic mode is the way to deepen faith and reawaken spirit.

Notes

1. Antonio Gramsci, in Q. Hoare and G. Nowell Smith, trans. and ed., *Selections from the Prison Notebooks* (New York: International, 1971), p. 276.
2. Christopher Hitchens, *God is Not Great: How Religion Poisons Everything* (New York: Twelve Books, 2007), p. 120.
3. This work by Bauer was published in two volumes in German as *Kritik der evangelischen Geschichte der Synoptiker* (Leipzig, 1841), and to my knowledge has not been translated into English.
4. I present a longer study of this in "The Storm Gods and the German Psychosis," chapter 8 of *Gods and Diseases: Making Sense of our Physical and Mental Wellbeing* (Sydney: HarperCollins, 2011; London and New York: Routledge, 2013).
5. Arthur Drews, *Die Christusmythe* (Berlin: Eugen Diederichs, 1910); translated into English as *The Christ Myth* (Chicago: Open Court Publishing, 1910).
6. James Thrower, *Marxist-Leninist "Scientific Atheism" and the Study of Religion and Atheism in the USSR* (Berlin: Walter de Gruyter, 1983).
7. See *Lamentabili Sane Exitu*, Pius X July 3, 1907, at: www.papalencyclicals.net/Pius10/p10lamen.html.

8. See *Pascendi Dominici Gregis, Encyclical of Pope Pius X on the Doctrines of the Modernists* : www.vatican.va/holyfather/pius_x_enc_1970908_pascendi-dominici-gregis_en.html.
9. Arthur Schopenhauer, "The Christian System" in Thomas Bailey Saunders, trans. *Religion: A Dialogue, and Other Essays* (1899; Westport, Connecticut: Greenwood Press, 1973) trans. Thomas Bailey Saunders, p. 106.
10. Arnold, in Robert H. Super ed., *The Complete Prose Works of Matthew Arnold* (Ann Arbor: The University of Michigan Press, 1960–1977), Vol. VI, p. 143.
11. Kevin Treston, *Emergence for Life, Not Fall from Grace* (Melbourne: Mosaic Pres, 2013), p. 19.
12. Eugen Drewermann, *Discovering the God Child Within: A Spiritual Psychology of the Infancy of Jesus* (New York: Crossroad, 1994), p. 32.
13. Drewermann, *Discovering the God Child Within*, p. 31.
14. Rudolf Bultmann, "New Testament and Mythology: The Problem of Demythologizing the New Testament Proclamation" (1941), in Schubert M. Ogden, ed., *New Testament and Mythology and Other Basic Writings* (Philadelphia: Fortress Press, 1984), p. 11.
15. Ibid.
16. Bultmann, "New Testament and Mythology," p. 3.
17. Rudolf Bultmann, *Jesus Christ and Mythology* (New York: Charles Scribner's Sons, 1958), pp. 35–36.
18. G. B. Caird, *The Language and Imagery of the Bible* (London: Duckworth, 1980), p. 193.
19. Karl Jaspers, "Myth and Religion" (1953), in Joseph Hoffmann, ed. and Norbert Guterman, trans., Karl Jaspers and Rudolf Bultmann, *Myth and Christianity: An Inquiry into the Possibility of Religion Without Myth* (1954, New York: Prometheus Books, 2005), p 32.
20. Ibid.
21. Bultmann, "New Testament and Mythology," p. 10.
22. Bultmann, "New Testament and Mythology," pp. 2–3.
23. Northrop Frye, "History and Myth in the Bible" (1975), in Alvin A. Lee and Jean O'Grady, eds., *Northrop Frye on Religion* , Collected Works of Northrop Frye , Vol. 4 (Toronto: University of Toronto Press, 2000), p. 18.
24. It may be useful to repeat here that "metaphor" comes from the Greek, *metaphorein*, meaning to "pass over" from one state or understanding to another.
25. C. G. Jung, "Basic Postulates of Analytical Psychology" (1931), *CW* 8, § 649.
26. Robert W. Funk and James M. Robinson, eds., *The Bultmann School of Biblical Interpretation* (Tubingen: J.C.B. Mohr, 1965).
27. Lloyd Geering, "The Legacy of Christianity," in Robert W. Funk, ed. *The Once and Future Jesus: The Jesus Seminar* (Santa Rosa, California: Polebridge Press, 2000), p.133.
28. Jung, *Symbols of Transformation* (1912/1952), *CW* 5, § 339.
29. Gretta Vosper, *With or Without God: Why The Way We Live is More Important than What We Believe* (Toronto: Harper Collins, 2008).
30. The notion of a disenchanted modernity comes from Max Weber, *The Protestant Ethic and the Spirit of Capitalism*, trans. Talcott Parsons (1905; London: Unwin Hyman, 1989).

31. Bultmann, *Jesus Christ and Mythology*, p. 37.
32. John Dominic Crossan and Jonathan L. Reed, *Excavating Jesus: Beneath the Stones, Behind the Texts* (San Francisco: Harper San Francisco, 2001).
33. John Dominic Crossan, *The Historical Jesus: The Life of a Mediterranean Jewish Peasant* (San Francisco: Harper San Francisco, 1991).
34. Albert Schweitzer, *The Quest of the Historical Jesus: A Critical Study of its Progress from Reimarus to Wrede* (New York: Macmillan, 1910).
35. Rudolf Otto, *The Idea of the Holy*, trans. John W. Harvey (1923; London: Oxford University Press, 1958).
36. Don Cupitt, *The Sea of Faith* (London: British Broadcasting Corporation, 1984).
37. Don Cupitt, *Christ and the Hiddenness of God* (London: Lutterworth Press, 1971).
38. Don Cupitt, *Taking Leave of God* (London: SCM Press, 1980).
39. Don Cupitt, *After God: The Future of Religion* (London: Weidenfeld and Nicolson, 1997).
40. Don Cupitt, in Nigel Leaves, *Odyssey on the Sea of Faith* (Santa Rosa, CA: Polebridge Press, 2004), p. 4.
41. Matthew Del Nevo, in a private communication, August 2013.
42. Paul Ricoeur, *The Conflict of Interpretations: Essays in Hermeneutics*, trans. Willis Domingo (1969; Evanston: Northwestern University Press, 1974).
43. Paul Tillich, "The Nature of Religious Language" (1955) in Robert C. Kimball, ed., *Theology of Culture* (London: Oxford University Press, 1959), p. 56.
44. Tillich, p. 59.
45. Tillich, p. 57.
46. Tillich, p. 60.
47. Tillich, p. 45.
48. *The Jerusalem Bible*, Matthew 18:3.
49. Matthew 16:26.
50. These three stages of thought and feeling are outlined, in reverse, in Patrick Sherry, "Disenchantment, Re-Enchantment, and Enchantment," in *Modern Theology* (Oxford: Blackwell), 25:3 July 2009, pp. 369–386.
51. T. S. Eliot, "Little Gidding" (1942), in *Collected Poems 1909–1962* (London: Faber, 1965), p. 222.
52. David Tacey, *Re-Enchantment* (Sydney: HarperCollins, 2000). Some other works in this genre include: Gordon Graham, *The Re-Enchantment of the World* (Oxford: Oxford University Press, 2007); and Christopher Partridge, *The Re-enchantment of the West*, Vols. 1 & 2 (London: T & T Clark, 2004).
53. Jaspers, "Myth and Religion," pp. 30–31.
54. Jaspers, "Myth and Religion," p. 31.
55. Jung, "Definition of Symbol," in *Psychological Types* (1921), *CW*, 6, § 816.
56. Jung, "The Psychology of the Child Archetype" (1940), *CW* 9,1, § 271.
57. David Ray Griffin, *Reenchantment without Supernaturalism* (Ithaca, NY: Cornell University Press, 2001).
58. A. D. Hope, "An Epistle from Holofernes" (1960), in *Selected Poems* (Sydney: Angus & Robertson, 1992), p. 56.

Conclusion

Unveiling the Soul

Heaven is cheap because it is on sale to everyone at the price they can afford.
— *Meister Eckhart*[1]

Rebirth of the Sacred

The soul is being born out of the collapse of literalism. Indeed, it seems to me that, historically speaking, the whole point of religious literalism was that it would eventually collapse, thus revealing the wealth of the human soul that it had systematically disguised. I refer to this as the "unveiling of the soul," and this surely is the real apocalypse of our time.[2] Like all forms of apocalypse, it is greeted with foreboding. There is an attitude of dread in religious traditions, a sense that the spirit of religion is passing away and has to be shored up by a strengthening of resolve and toughening of commitment. Religious authorities feel compelled to "tough out" the battle with science and modernity, but the appropriate response, in my view, is to let the ossified persona of religious literalism slide into the sea, so we can experience religion in a new way. One religious dispensation will collapse, but another will replace it.

We are talking about the collapse of a falsely historicized tradition that has used factual claims to bolster its truth status. What will replace it will be a more mystical tradition that understands that religious reality is found within the soul and is not something that is frozen in history or revealed in one holy revelation. We are talking about an ongoing incarnation of the divine and the collapse of the notion that one revelation had a monopoly on the incarnation. In the past, we were expected to become "religious" by deferring to, and worshipping, the time-specific Christ event. What traditionalists did not understand was that the Christ was greater than Jesus, who represented one manifestation of Christ. Every person who reaches for God and attempts to live his or her life in accordance with divine imperatives becomes a son or daughter of God. The earlier obsession with history prevented us from experiencing the mystical reality of God in the present, and in the world around and within us.

As institutions mourn the collapse of the old, the spirit delights in the confusion of the present, because perhaps for the first time spirit has the opportunity to reveal its reality. Historical positivism has obscured the living soul, and while many will lose their morale as it is undermined, a great many more will come to life in new and unexpected ways. The religious opportunity of our time is almost unparalleled in history. There is much to discover, and much to be born that has not yet been born. The soul of humanity has not fully emerged; it is a slow and gradual birth, and painful too, like any birth.

In this book I have tried to show that depth psychology can help with the birthing of the soul. It could be argued that the whole point of depth psychology is not to enhance the methods of clinical psychology, which has rejected it anyway, but to enhance our understanding of religion and symbolic life. Depth psychology, one of the most recent sciences, can come to the aid of religion as it struggles with what it sees as the death throes of tradition. Depth psychology can help us discover "another world in this one." All is not lost, religion has a future, but it is not "more of the same," or "business as usual." The world of religion and its metaphysical vistas can be rediscovered as hidden aspects of this world. This is the exciting opportunity of the present, which few seem to know about. We are still too caught up in mourning the collapse of the old—or, in the case of atheists and rebels, celebrating the collapse of the old. They see the collapse as a sign of our coming of age and maturity. But from the religious side, it is a time of darkness and despair. The religious project seems poised at the edge of an abyss, with science and philosophy keen to provide that extra shove, so it goes hurtling into the abyss.

All of this is about to be consigned to the void: a supernatural, interventionist God able to perform miracles and wonders that run counter to the laws of science; a three-tiered metaphysical reality composed of earth, heaven, and hell; a pantheon of metaphysical figures who are "seated" at the right and left hand of the Pantocrator.[3] This is not to mention the creeds, dogmas, and teachings that are based on this archaic view of the world, and the structures of authority, hierarchies, and institutional lines of command that see themselves grounded on this model. All of this is in the process of being sacrificed on the altar of history, lost to the past, and consigned to meaninglessness. Jung understands the predicament facing those who have believed in the reified metaphors:

> Anyone who has lost the historical symbols and cannot be satisfied with substitutes is certainly in a very difficult position today: before him there yawns the void, and he turns away from it in horror.[4]

But the God-shaped hole that opens before us is not as terrifying as some imagine. Out of this vacuum will arise something new: "I am convinced that the growing impoverishment of symbols has a meaning. It is a development that has an inner consistency."[5]

From the God-Shaped Hole

From the depths of the God-shaped hole a new image of God will emerge. This image will be shorn of its literalistic and dogmatic trappings. In fact, the new God will emerge from below, not above. It's location will be reversed, as is the tendency of the divine, once it former expression has been lost. It finds a new abode, and Jung uses the story of the resurrection to explain the transformations that take place in the reappearance of the sacred:

> I only know—and here I am expressing what countless other people know—that the present is a time of God's death and disappearance. The myth says he was not to be found where his body was laid. "Body" means the outward, visible form, the erstwhile but ephemeral setting for the highest value. The myth further says that the value rose again in a miraculous manner, transformed. It looks like a miracle, for, when a value disappears, it always seems to be lost irretrievably. So it is quite unexpected that it should come back.... The fact that only a few people see the Risen One means that no small difficulties stand in the way of finding and recognizing the transformed value.[6]

One of the challenges of our time is to identify the new locations of the sacred. False prophets abound in our era, each claiming that the sacred is to be found here or there—in locations of their making. But we can be sure of this: the sacred will emerge where we least expect it.

Now, what is the least valued thing from the point of view of religion? It would have to be the human soul, since our souls are, from a traditional perspective, tarnished with original sin and incapable of beholding the divine. As one old priest said to me: "Anyone who adopts himself as a spiritual director is adopting a fool." The entrenched view is that the self is incapable of providing spiritual guidance. It can only lead us to increased selfishness and narcissistic absorption. The old order has taken a very literal-minded approach to Genesis and the Fall. If this is the case, and the psyche is the most undervalued thing in Western religion, that would be the obvious place to witness the rebirth of God. If in earlier times it was felt that nothing good could come out of Nazareth, and behold, an image of God emerges in that place, the same could be said today of the psyche. In the gospel of John, Nathanael says to Philip:

> "Can anything good come out of Nazareth?" Philip said to him, "Come and see."[7]

We are having similar conversations today: "Can anything good come out of the psyche?" The answer should be: "Come and see." The old order despises interiority and tries to hide from it, but the new order has to approach interiority with the expectation that something good can emerge from it. We need to have faith that our interiority can deliver what has been lost to traditional religion.

My grandfather used to tell me about the future of religion. He was an Irish mystic, and some in our family thought he was mad, mainly because he dared to contradict the teachings of the church on a number of issues. He once said to me: "the Old Testament was about the reign of the Father, and the New Testament about the reign of the Son. We are moving to a new world in which the Holy Spirit will be revealed to all." I told my parents about this, and they expressed disapproval, saying, "You can't believe everything Grandpa says." Grandpa had trained as a priest as a young man, but gave it up when he came into conflict with church teachings. He used to warn me about differentiating between "Churchianity" and "Christianity." Although these could be dismissed as the ravings of a lunatic, I found seeds of truth in what he told me, and those seeds have grown in my heart over time.

At the time, I had no idea that he was expressing the mystical views of esoteric Christianity, in particular the ideas of Joachim de Fiore, a Calabrian monk of the twelfth century.[8] Joachim arrived at the theory of the three ages. He believed humanity was at the edge of the third age of the Holy Spirit, and this would be different from the former two. While the age of the Spirit would proceed from the gospel of Jesus, it would transcend the letter of the gospel and move beyond its focus on the Jesus of history to an experience of universal Spirit and the mystical Christ. According to Joachim, only in this third age would it be possible to understand the words of God in their deepest meanings. Joachim believed that as God speaks through the soul of human beings, the old order would collapse, and its hierarchical structures become unnecessary. Naturally the pope of the day, Alexander IV, condemned his theories and charged him with heresy. That might be an indication that he was on the right track. His theories can be considered millenarian, and as we progress into a third millennium, his ideas of a third age have particular relevance.

Heretical or not, we are moving into a new understanding of religion. I agree with Joachim that to understand the meaning of the gospels, we have to place less emphasis on the letter of the law. We can no longer afford to take the gospels literally, as this freezes their meaning in time and prevents us from seeing the coming of the kingdom as a personal event. The gospels speak to us about our present condition, and not merely to the ancient past. The metaphorical approach ensures that the personal dimension is not siphoned off into historical positivism. Theologian Karl Rahner said, "The future Christian will be a mystic or he [or she] will not exist at all."[9] The best way to ensure that people become mystics is to learn the language of metaphor and symbol, because they will then see that the symbols point to themselves, to the interiority of their lives. So long as the scriptures are framed as history the interiority of our lives is bypassed in favor of an external reading. As soon as sacred texts point to ourselves, we are in the spotlight and have to take the psyche seriously.

Paradoxically, to realize what Jesus was saying we have to place less emphasis on his divine status, and more emphasis on what he was pointing to. The construction of Jesus as God has done enormous damage to Jesus, and to ourselves insofar as Christianity became Jesusolatry by turning him into an idol. Idols are obstacles to spiritual growth, as by fixating on the idol we forget to take spiritual responsibility for our lives. We fail to take Jesus as a living metaphor for the Christ element in us. Thus as the dogmatic idea that Jesus is God disintegrates we are more likely to move toward the realization that God is found everywhere, and not in one incarnational event. What was invested in the particular is now shared as a universal experience. The true eucharistic event is realizing that the body and blood are found everywhere, and this is not the exclusive experience of believing Christians. The triumph of Christianity is found by dissolving Christianity into the universal life of humanity. Joachim was moving in this direction, as was his near-contemporary, Meister Eckhart.

The birth of God in the soul had long been foreshadowed by Eckhart:

> People think that God became human only in the Incarnation, but this is not the case, for God has become human just as surely here and now as he did then, and has become human in order that he might give birth to you as his only begotten Son, and no less.[10]
>
> The Father gives birth to the Son in the soul, and the soul is spoken to.[11]

This brought Eckhart into collision with tradition, but all great thinkers have trouble with tradition. Tradition is forever trying to foreclose the sacred and limit it to a particular historical revelation. But the sacred cannot be contained in these man-made structures, and will always break out of whatever dogma in which it is encased. Creative thinkers understand this, and it is their responsibility to be heretical, antinomian, and suggest possibilities that move contrary to convention. If this did not happen, we would kill God with familiarity. As infinite being, God has to keep surprising us with new possibilities. As soon as we are sure what God is like, we can be just as sure that we have killed off the thing we are enshrining.

As Eckhart put it, the soul is "spoken to" by the divine. This is certainly the case today; as traditional dogmas fall into irrelevance, the soul is commanded to take itself seriously. It is asked to recognize the element of divinity residing in the human breast. Blake had something similar in mind when he wrote:

> Thus men forgot that all deities reside in the human breast.[12]

Blake did not mean that deities are manufactured by humans. He was talking about the appearance of deities, which are given their shape by human imagination. The deities are not reducible to appearances, which are at best metaphorical forms that ought not to be worshipped as such—as in the second commandment.[13] Deities are powers found throughout the cosmos, as well as in the human breast. It is important to emphasize that the psyche "constructs" gods, but the gods are prior to our constructions. Atheists note the anthropomorphic appearances and say the gods are frauds. This is to misunderstand religion. We give a human likeness to what is more than human. We give this likeness so we can relate to that which is absolutely other. If we did not create images of the divine we might not be able to relate to it at all, hence images are necessary but limited in their usefulness. They are not descriptions of reality, but approximations of what is beyond representation.

Blake is affirming a divine life in the soul, and this life is necessarily "shaped" by human agency, even though it cannot be reduced to such agency. There is something more-than-human in the soul, and that presence has been long understood in the East, where it was called the Atman, the God dwelling in the human being. In the West, the divine potentials of the soul were suppressed by our obsessive concern with sin. Thus if God reappears in the soul, we are in danger of not even noticing this incarnation because we have failed to award the soul the religious importance it deserves.

But it seems to me that Eckhart's idea of God coming to birth in the human soul is indeed in accord with the teachings of Jesus. Jesus saw the incarnation as a radically democratic event, to be shared by all. He did not want himself to be idolized as the "only begotten Son," as dogma states, but to invite everyone into the experience of sonship. This sonship is found throughout the gospels, as I have argued.[14] In the first letter of John we read:

> See what love the Father has given us, that we should be called the children of God; and so we are. The reason why the world does not know us is that it did not know him. Beloved, we are God's children now.[15]

This dimension of the faith, its fiery spiritual core, got lost in the process of dogmatization, and in the tradition called "Christology," which seems to be a history of blinkered thinking about Jesus. But with the collapse of this baggage, the living core of faith is able to be revealed and experienced.

The birth of the soul is like a consolation awarded to modernity after the collapse of old religion. The vast empyrean above us has fallen, but we begin to sense a new world opening within. It is a mammoth shift in perspective, a "changing of the gods." Jung put it this way:

> Since the stars have fallen from heaven and our highest symbols have paled, a secret life holds sway in the unconscious. That is why we have a psychology today, and why we speak of the unconscious. All this would be quite superfluous in an age or culture that possessed symbols. Symbols are spirit from above, and under those conditions the spirit is above too. . . . Our unconscious, on the other hand, hides living water, spirit that has become nature, and that is why it is disturbed. . . . The "heart glows," and a secret unrest gnaws at the roots of our being.[16]

One world collapses, another opens—in the most unexpected place. The depths of the self, as I've said, is the last place religious leaders would look for the rebirth of the sacred. Their focus is outward facing: the sacred comes from elsewhere, from other worlds. But today we seem to have nowhere to turn but inwardly. If we have the courage to turn within, we see a vast "other" world beckoning with a sense of mystery. As literalism collapses, we discover buried treasure in the field. We attribute the collapse of traditional religion to the rise of materialism and science, but there may have been, all along, a spiritual meaning behind this collapse.

Depth Psychology as Midwife

My aim is not to reduce religion to psychology, but to build a bridge to religion using the methods and ideas of psychology. "The bridge from dogma to the inner experience of the individual has broken down," Jung wrote. "Dogma no longer formulates anything, no longer expresses anything; it has become a tenet to be accepted in and for itself, with no basis in any experience that would demonstrate its truth."[17] We might build a bridge by finding resonances between the contents of the psyche and the symbols of religion:

> It is high time we realized that it is pointless to praise the light and preach it if nobody can see it. It is much more needful to teach people the art of seeing. For it is obvious that far too many people are incapable of establishing a connection between the sacred images of religion and their own psyche: they cannot see that there are equivalent images lying dormant in their own souls. In order to facilitate this inner vision we must first clear the way for the faculty of seeing. How this is to be done without psychology, that is, without making contact with the psyche, is, frankly, beyond my comprehension.[18]

Psychology is the threshold where science and religion meet. It is ironic that science, which played a role in bringing about the collapse of religion, might play another role in bringing religion to a new stage of realization. We have to take the plunge into interiority, becoming psychologically literate, and able to take up a dialogue with the inner life. A depth psychology based on the exploration of the unconscious becomes the locus for the recovery of wisdom in a post-secular age.

Jung alerts us to the fact that his method of reading "the statements of Holy Scriptures [as] utterances of the soul" will be "suspected of psychologism."[19] This prediction has been fulfilled, as we see critics claiming that Jung is reducing the mystery of God to the "known" field of science. In recent times, the Vatican has made an assault on Jung for purportedly reducing metaphysics to metapsychology. But this is a misreading, with the express purpose of throwing a cloak of invisibility over the soul so we do not look there for the presence of God. The Vatican misreads the psyche as ego, thus reducing depth psychology to narcissism. It sees no soul behind the ego, no inner self behind the persona, and thus appears adamant that there is no Atman-equivalent in Western religion. The Vatican is unable to give birth to the third age of the Spirit, which is why it is futile to look there for guidance. The psyche is a small infinity, not bound by limits and not reducible to processes in the brain. It is a threshold between worlds, which we are only in the process of discovering.

If we can bring religion home to our psychological experience, we might save it from being redundant, from pointing to supernatural worlds that science claims do not exist. If religious images become metaphors pointing to the soul, we have made a start in the revival of religion. The discovery of the unconscious has made us aware that activity takes place in the psyche that is not known to consciousness. Religion can be interpreted as a symbolic code that discloses the inner wealth of human interiority. Psychology does not have the capacity to found a new religion, but it can take ailing religions and revitalize them. Jung uses alchemical imagery to explain his approach to religious systems:

> To gain an understanding of religious matters, probably all that is left us today is the psychological approach. That is why I take these thought-forms that have become historically fixed, try to melt them down again and pour them into moulds of immediate experience.[20]

The way to renew religion is to deconstruct old forms, "melt down" dogmas, and pour them into the molds of experience. This seems like a destructive activity to religious conservatives. But this method serves to preserve what is most precious about tradition, saving it from extinction and releasing it into new forms of thought. Jung sees his method as redemptive and salvational; he is not merely interpreting religious statements, but saving them from irrelevance. He writes:

> Once metaphysical ideas have lost their capacity to recall and evoke the original experience they have not only become useless but prove to be actual impediments on the road to wider development. Thus in the course of time the meaningful turns into the meaningless. This is unfortunately the fate of metaphysical ideas.[21]

Here he sounds like the radical theologian Bultmann, but the argument is not moving in the direction of destroying the myths. Jung is working in the spirit of what Judaism calls *midrash*, that is, a "making new" of ancient truths that are in danger of being lost for want of being understood. These truths are too significant to lose, and thus the use of psychological ideas is

> important because it is possible, through them, to relate so-called *metaphysical* concepts, which have lost their root connection with natural experience, to living, universal psychic processes, so that they can recover their true and original meaning.[22]

Like Drewermann, Frye, Campbell, Armstrong, and others used in this book, Jung believed that the psycho-spiritual dimension of religion is its actual and true domain. We are not "distorting" religion to fit the mold of psychology, we are redeeming the original message of religion.

According to Thomas Merton, a Cistercian monk and mystic, the "melting down" of old religious forms needs to take place, if we are to move beyond clichés and achieve a new connection with the sacred. The seeker who burns with the love of God has to "burn away" a lot of hackneyed and worn-out understandings:

> What a holocaust takes place in this steady burning to ashes of old worn-out words, clichés, slogans, rationalizations! The worst of it is that even apparently *holy* conceptions are consumed along with all the rest. It is a terrible breaking and burning of idols, a purification of the sanctuary, so that no graven thing may occupy the place that God has commanded to be left empty: the center, the existential altar which simply is.[23]

Merton and Jung are preoccupied with the same desire, to clear away dogmas and ready oneself for the incursion of a living experience of the divine. This "burn off" seems almost antireligious, but springs from the deepest religious desire, which is to keep the spirit relevant and connected to experience.

The project of linking religious statements to psychological ideas can only be effective if the psychology we use is based on soul and spirit. If it is academic psychology, based on the study of behavior or laboratory experiments, it can only be detrimental. Only a psychology based on the unconscious is able to "dream the myth onward" and relate the experience of God to contemporary understanding. Jung wrote:

Conclusion

> Were it not a fact of experience that supreme values reside in the soul, psychology would not interest me in the least, for the soul would then be nothing but a miserable vapour. I know, however, from hundredfold experience that it is nothing of the sort, but on the contrary contains the equivalents of everything that has been formulated in dogma and a good deal more, which is just what enables it to be an eye destined to behold the light. This requires limitless range and unfathomable depth of vision.[24]

Perhaps we might ask where this "limitless range and depth of vision" are to come from. I cannot see such range or vision on the current religious horizon, but it is unfolding in contemporary science, philosophy and psychology. The idea that the interior self is an *eye destined to behold the light* has been kept from us, withheld from knowledge. We have to win this back, claim it as our own, and if our guides are not available in the religious institutions, we have to search for them in new areas, including the mystical traditions of East and West.

Psyche as an Opening to Infinity

The sense of an inward transcendence has a long history. The philosopher Heraclitus said:

> You could not discover the limits of the psyche, even if you travelled every road to do so; such is the depth of its meaning.[25]

The understanding that the soul might be limitless and represent a "small infinity" is ancient and long-standing. The idea can be found in pre-Socratic philosophy, and in Plato, the Neoplatonic tradition, the hermetic sciences, alchemy, and gnosticism. Plotinus, the founder of Neoplatonism, based his teaching on the connection between psyche and the sacred: "Strive to lead back the god within you to the divine in the universe."[26]

Later in the philosophical tradition, Nietzsche saw that the collapse of religion would result in the unexpected outcome of the development of the soul. The secular expectation was that the collapse of formal religion would see the end of the sacred. The sacred can never be extinguished, because it is the basis of humanity. Nietzsche saw this in the nineteenth century and argued that the soul is *born* as and when the traditional religious view collapses:

> All instincts that do not discharge themselves outwardly turn inward—this is what I call the *internalisation* of man: thus it was

that man first developed what was later called his "soul." The entire inner world, originally as thin as if it were stretched between two membranes, expanded and extended itself, acquired depth, breadth, and height, in the same measure as outward discharge was inhibited.[27]

As the "outward discharge" of the religious instinct is inhibited by enlightenment, the soul "expands" and acquires "depth, breadth, and height." As if to compensate for the lack of religious expression, we find the soul expanding beyond its normal bounds. Psychic energy invested in religions does not go away, but falls back into the unconscious, activating its spiritual potential. There is no getting rid of the religious urge, because humanity is *homo religiosus* and destined to remain such. Nietzsche calls it the "internalization of man," and it is ironic that this philosopher, known for his atheistic repudiation of religion, can see with such clarity that the future of religion must be psychological, because that is the new area of richness that is opening before us.

The soul is a cosmos, vast and wide as the universe. It seems to intersect with the physical, to run as it were alongside it, and forms the basis of all that exists. As I have argued, this insight is foundational in the East and poorly developed in the West. Jung became interested in Eastern philosophies because he saw in them an acknowledgement of the cosmic nature of mind. The difference between East and West is that the West sees mind originating in the human, and the East sees it as an expression of the cosmos. We tend to link consciousness with ego, but "the Eastern mind has no difficulty in conceiving of a consciousness without an ego. Consciousness is deemed capable of transcending its ego condition; indeed, in its "higher" forms, the ego disappears."[28] The West says there is no evidence for the existence of mind outside the human; as such we ought to be alarmed at what a shrunken thing the mind has become. We have cut psyche from cosmos, and this is one reason why we cannot locate religious forces in our interiority. "It is just possible that our mind is nothing but a perceptible manifestation of a Universal Mind."[29]

We have to win back this lost heritage of humanity, for in that heritage lies our potential for recovering the spiritual dimension. We need to revise our worldview to include the reality of the universal soul. In his last work, Jung wrote:

> Man's greatest instrument, his psyche, is little thought of, if not actually mistrusted and despised. "It's only psychological" too often means: it is nothing. Where, exactly, does this immense prejudice come from?[30]

Conclusion

Mystics who attempt to ground religion in the experience of the ordinary were regarded as heretics because they brought religion too close to the everyday. For theology, God is thinkable as a vast, superhuman presence, but unthinkable as a presence in the psyche. Clearly we have to revise our concept of the real.

It seems to me that what we have called "reality" is nothing more than an optical illusion, or an intellectual prejudice. Blake is illuminating on this point:

> If the doors of perception were cleansed every thing would appear to man as it is, infinite. For man has closed himself up, till he sees all things through narrow chinks of his cavern.[31]

It is because we have shrunk reality to the size of our rationality that we have had to invent "other" worlds, and supernatural deities, angels, and demons. The reality we have fashioned for ourselves is a prison that precludes any spiritual dimension, and this is why our culture has been plagued by fantasies of other worlds. In the past these other realities were theological and supernatural; today they tend to be fashioned by science fiction and fantasy. We will look everywhere for spirit and soul except under our noses. Reality is not what the rational ego can see and touch, but what intuition senses below the surface, and increasingly, what post-Newtonian physics is able to discern. The ego reduces reality to its proportions, and if we take the ego's version of the real as true, we are forced to add layers of "super-reality" to accommodate spirit and soul. From this came the error that God is a being outside creation who "intervenes" in history, rather than a creative force at work in and through creation, on the inside of reality and not external to it.

Our present reality is enchanted, already possessed of cosmic powers and full of spiritual potential. We don't need to invent heaven, hell, and purgatory as literal places, because these are metaphors that point to states of mind that exist in our experience. "Our arbitrarily delimited reality is continually menaced by the "supersensual," the "supernatural," the "superhuman," and a whole lot more besides. Eastern reality includes all this as a matter of course."[32] The Western concept of reality is inherently defective, and its theology has been forced to build new layers upon this defective base. It built castles in the air, which have collapsed in our time. The idea of a multi-layered universe is the result of the machinations of the semi-blind ego, which does not grasp the

245

complexity of the real. The future of Western thought is to study the East, see how it has understood reality, and find mystical resources for building a similarly complex view of reality. Contemporary science and emergence theory seem set to accomplish this based on our own traditions. When we realize how complex reality is we won't be "menaced" by the supernatural, but we will see the miraculous in the everyday and the mysterious in the ordinary.

Notes

1. Meister Eckhart, Sermon 6, in Oliver Davies, ed., *Meister Eckhart: Selected Writings* (London: Penguin, 1994), p. 131.
2. One of Jung's major essays was entitled "Die Entschleierung der Seele," which in English is "The Unveiling of the Soul." Unfortunately, this evocative title never made it to English, as the essay was translated with the pedestrian title "Basic Postulates in Analytical Psychology" (1931), *CW* 8, § 649–688.
3. "Pantocrator" is used by Paul to refer to the character of God, translated into English as "Almighty"; see 2 Corinthians 6: 18.
4. Jung, "Archetypes of the Collective Unconscious" (1934/1954), *CW* 9, part 1, § 28.
5. Jung, ibid., § 28.
6. Jung, "Psychology and Religion" (1938/1940), *CW* 11, § 149.
7. John 1: 46.
8. For further on Joachim, see Marjorie Reeves, *Joachim of Fiore and the Prophetic Future: A Medieval Study in Historical Thinking* (London: Sutton Publishing, 1999).
9. Karl Rahner, "The Spirituality of the Church of the Future," in tr. Cornelius Ernst, *Theological Investigations*, Vol. 20 (Baltimore: Helicon Press, 1981), p. 149.
10. Eckhart, ibid., Sermon 4, p. 124.
11. Meister Eckhart, Sermon 5, in Oliver Davies, ed., *Meister Eckhart: Selected Writings* (London: Penguin, 1994), p. 130.
12. William Blake, "The Marriage of Heaven and Hell" (1793), in ed., Geoffrey Keynes, *Blake: Complete Writings* (London: Oxford University Press, 1976), p. 153.
13. Exodus 20:4: "You shall not make for yourself a graven image, or any likeness of anything that is in heaven or that is in the earth beneath, or that is in the water under the earth; you shall not bow down to them or serve them."
14. See chapter 4.
15. 1 John 3:1–2.
16. Jung, "Archetypes of the Collective Unconscious," § 50.
17. Jung, "The Psychology of Christian Alchemical Symbolism" (1951), *CW* 9, 2, § 276.
18. Jung, *Psychology and Alchemy* (1944), *CW* 12, § 14.
19. Jung, "Answer to Job" (1952), *CW* 11, § 557.
20. Jung, "Psychology and Religion" (1938/1940), *CW* 11, § 148.
21. Jung, "The Self," in *Aion* (1952), *CW* 9, 2, § 65.
22. Ibid.

23. Thomas Merton, *New Seeds of Contemplation* (1961, New York: New Directions, 1972), p. 13.
24. Jung, *Psychology and Alchemy*, § 14.
25. Heraclitus, Fragment 42, in Philip Wheelwright, *Heraclitus* (Princeton, N.J.: Princeton University Press, 1959).
26. Plotinus, quoted in John Gregory, ed., *The Neoplatonists* (London: Kyle Cathie, 1991), p. 6.
27. Friedrich Nietzsche, *The Genealogy of Morals*, Walter Kaufmann trans. (1887, New York: Random House, 1989), pp. 84–85.
28. Jung, "Psychological Commentary on *The Tibetan Book of the Great Liberation*" (1939/1954), *CW* 11, § 774.
29. Jung, ibid, § 760.
30. Jung, "Symbols and the Interpretation of Dreams" (1961), *CW* 18, § 605.
31. Blake, "The Marriage of Heaven and Hell", p. 154.
32. Jung, "The Real and the Surreal" (1933), *CW* 8, § 743.

Index

Aboriginal cultures, 46
　ceremonies, 124
Abraham, 65, 66
Adler, Alfred, 62
Adorno, Theodor, 62
After God (Cupitt), 223
Aion (Jung), 120, 173
Allegro, John, 16
Alpha (original self), 139
Ancient psychology, myth as, 39–42
Anima mundi, 107
Annunciation sequence, Luke's gospel, 95, 96, 98
Answer to Job (Jung), 196, 200
Anti-Semitism, John's gospel, 152
Apocalypse, 131–149. *See also* Ego
　etymology, 132
　new world order, establishment of, 146–148
　as psychology, 131–132
　rapture, 145–146
Apostles, 21
Aquinas, Thomas, 31–32, 98
Archetypal contents of psyche, personifying, 63–65
Archetype of Apocalypse (Edinger), 132–133
Arianism, 75
Aristophanes, 128
Arius of Alexandria (250–336 CE), 75
Armstrong, Karen, 20, 37–39
　on logos, 42
　on psychological dimension of myth, 40–42
Arnold, Matthew, 15, 16–17, 26–27, 212
Art, mythos in, 47–48
Aryanism, 210

Assumption of Mary, 200–203, 204
Atheism, 5, 223
　crisis of, 5
　faith and, 5
　in Russia, 210
Atheists
　celebrity, 4–5
　on fundamentalism, 37
Atman, 239
　in Hinduism, 73–74
　Jung and, 74
Augustine, St., 31–32, 168
Augustus (Roman Emperor), 94
Awakening. *See* Ego; Kingdom of heaven; New self

The Bacchae (Euripides), 184
Baptism of Jesus, 75
Basileia (Greek), 108
The Battle for God (Armstrong), 38
Bauer, Bruno, 20, 22, 209
Belief
　faith *vs.*, 12
　faith without, 212–213
　and miracles, 6
Ben-Chorin, Schalom, 97
　on Annunciation in Luke, 98
Bible
　Allegro on, 17
　being historical, 2–3, 5
　Caird on, 3
　code language of, 17
　credibility of, 22
　Frye on, 2–3
　as holy history, 19
　literary construction in, 21
　as mythopoesis, 19

reading, 19
symbols and myths in, 17–18, 19
Biblical language
  Bultmann on, 217
  Caird on, 217
  code and symbols, 17–18
  conventional readings of, 4
Biblical writers, 1, 11
  Arnold on, 16
  Caird on, 16
  Frye on, 17
Birth. *See also* Rebirth
  of the divine child, 99
  of Jesus, 23. *See also* Virgin birth
Bishop, Paul, 189
Bishop of Paderborn, 88
Blake, William, 9, 19, 164, 214, 238–239, 245
  "antinomian" thinking of, 162
  on churches, 60
  on eternity, 145
  on evil, 162
  "Jesus the Imagination," 24, 59
  on natural man, 59–60
  on New Jerusalem, 147
  on religious literalism, 60–61
  on sacred metaphors, 59
  on secret life, 63
Book of Revelation, 131–132
Borg, Marcus, 67
Brown, Norman, 25
Buddhist monks, 73
Bultmann, Rudolf, 9, 10
  on biblical language, 217
  on church, 215–216
  existential philosophy and, 218–220
  progressive thinking of, 215–216
  on resurrection, 167

Caird, George, 3–4
  on biblical language, 217
  on biblical writers, 16
Campbell, Joseph, 75
  Moyers and, 172
  on resurrection, 170–173, 174
  on virgin birth, 96
The Case for God: What Religion Really Means (Armstrong), 37
Cassirer, Ernst, 17, 43, 48
Cathars, 75
Catholic Church, 210
Celebrity atheists, 4–5

Christ
  appearance before disciples, 184
  and Christianity, 161
  Harpur on, 70–71
  historical Jesus *vs.*, 21–22
  John of Patmos on, 139
  myth of, 2
  religious authorities on, 62
  secret life, 62–63
Christianity
  in Germany, 210
  history of, 4
  Jung on, 190–192
  materialistic attitude, 173
  mythical nature, 210
  psycho-spiritual death and, 124
  rebirth and, 124–125
  revilement of, 68
Christians
  early, as primitive thinkers, 174
  interfaith dialogue, 68
  myth and, 61–62
  prayer, 47
Christmas story, 98–99
"Christ myth theory," 22, 209
  Lenin and, 210
Christology, 67. *See also* Theology
Churches
  intelligent minds, 32
  literalism and, 20–21
  on resurrected spirit of Jesus, 170
  scriptures and, 2
Churinga, 124
Civilisation and Its Discontents (Freud), 120
Civilizations of ancient world, 38
Cleopas, 180
Commandment, of Jesus, 119–120
Common sense, 155–156
Communists, 210
Consciousness, 192
  Eastern *vs.* Western philosophy of, 244
  ego and, 244
  emotionalism and, 81
  myths and, 18, 55
Constantine, 78, 79, 81
Consumerist societies, 98–99
Corbin, Henry, 89–90
Costello, Tim, 102
Council of Lyons, 169
Council of Nicea (325 CE), 75
Cox, Harvey, 4, 79

Index

A Critique of the Evangelical History of the Synoptics (Bauer), 209
Crossan, Dominic, 16, 222
   on resurrection and Road to Emmaus, 178–183
Cupitt, Donald, 9, 10, 223–224

Dark Ages, 83
December 25, 98, 99
Demythologization, 215
   Jaspers on, 217
Depth psychology, 42, 234
   ego and new self, 134
   mythology and, 63
   sexual addictions in, 155
   Socrates and, 128
Derrida, Jacques, 109, 128, 133
Desire, spirituality and, 161–162
Devil, 154
   approach to rebirth, 155
   Jesus encounter with, temptation narrative, 157–164
   as personification of literalism, 157–160
   in psychological terms, 159
Die Christusmythe (Drews), 210
Dionysus, 184, 189
Directed *vs.* nondirected thinking, 49–50
Discovering the God Child Within: A Spiritual Psychology of the Infancy of Jesus (Drewermann), 101
Disenchantment, 227
Divine insemination, 96–98, 99
Doppelgänger, 159
"Double vision," 24
Doubting Thomas, 167–168
"Dover Beach" (Arnold), 27
Dreams, 54, 63–64
Drewermann, Eugen, 4, 20, 87–89, 213–214
   on infancy narrative, 96, 97
Drews, Arthur, 209–210
Dualism, and literal thinking, 164
Dupois, Charles, 22

East
   inward divinity, 73–74
   literalism and idolatry in, 73
   reality, 245–246
   West *vs.,* 73–74, 245–246
Eckhart, Meister, 100–101, 237, 238
Edict of Thesalonica, 81
Edinger, Edward, 132–133, 145–146

Ego, 113
   consciousness and, 244
   destruction and punishment, 141–143
   individuating, 117
   judgment, 140–141
   loss of, 116–117
   as master, 116
   original self, 138, 139
   psychopathology and, 139–140
   reality and, 245
   response to new self, 118–119
   second self, 138–139
   self-overcoming, 134
   soul and, 112–113
   transformation of, 134
   values and attitudes, 115–116
Einstein, Albert, 31
Eliade, Mircea, 52, 123, 124
Eliot, T. S., 2, 227–228
Emmaus parable. *See* Road to Emmaus
Enchantment, 227
Entertainment, mythos in, 47–48
Epiousios, 158
Eternity, myths and, 47
Eucharist, 183
Euripides, 183
Evangelical fundamentalism, 20
Evangelism, 82
Evil, 37, 162
Existential philosophy, 218–220

Facts, truths *vs.,* 18–19
Faith
   atheism and, 5
   proof and, 12
   stages of, 226–228
   without belief, 212–213
Fear of myth, 61–62
Feedings, miraculous stories, 6–7
"Feeding the Lord's Flock," 210
Feminine self-sufficiency, 93
Filius philosophorum, 139
Fiore, Joachim de, 236–237
Fraud, religion as. *See* Pious fraud, religion as
Frazer, James, 19, 22
   on virgin births, 94, 95, 96
Freud, Sigmund, 15
   on incest taboo, 156
   Jung and, 189
   on perfection/perfectionism, 120
   on religion as metaphor, 15

Frye, Northrop
  on Bible, 2–3
  on myth and psychology, 40
  on virgin birth, 102–103
Fundamentalism, atheists on, 37

Gabriel, 97
Geering, Lloyd, 9, 220, 223
Genesis, 176
Germany
  Christianity in, 210
  nationalism in, 210
  National Socialism, 210
Giegerich, Wolfgang, 159, 160, 161, 163
Gimbutas, Marija, 92
Glorified body (Paul), 168, 176, 179
Gnosticism, 74–75
God
  being poet, 32
  as cartoon figure, 25
  continuing incarnation of, 100–101
  emergence as new image, 235–240
  as fairy-tale character, 25
  human order and, 222
  as interruption, 143–145
  motif in disguise, 183–185
  mystical reality of, 234
  ongoing incarnation, 67–70
  reign of, 108
  relationship with, 16
  spirit of, 25
  supernatural being, 222
  unknowable nature of, Jung on, 199–200
"God and Philosophy" (Levinas), 143
"God Must Not Die!" (Giegerich), 159
God parents, 99
God-shaped hole, 235–240
Gogh, Van, 23
The Golden Bough (Frazer), 95, 96
Gospel of Thomas, 124
Gospels, 2
  biblical criticism, 21
  chronology of being written, 21
  interpretations of events, 22
  miraculous feeding stories, 6–7
  reading, Treston on, 18
  representation of Jesus in, 21–22
The Great Gatsby (Fitzgerald), 140
Griffiths, Bede, 73

Haggadah, 7. *See also* Midrash
Harpur, Tom, 70–71, 90
Harvey, Andrew, 77
Head-in-the-sand approach, 216
The Heart of Christianity (Borg), 67
Heaven
  condition of consciousness, 108
  as metaphor, 23. *See also* Kingdom of heaven
Heraclitus, 243
Hidden Treasure, 178
Higgins, Godfrey, 28–29
Hillman, James, 39
Historical events, 2–3
History
  Bible and, 2–3
  of Christianity, 4
  Eliot on, 2
  facts *vs.* truths, 18–19
  mythos and, 1–5
Hitchens, Christopher, 22, 209
Holloway, Richard, 32
Holy Trinity, 214
Holy war. *See* Jihad
Homo religiosus, 244
Hope, A. D., 229
Horkheimer, Max, 81
Hubris, 71
Human, and divine persons of Jesus, 75
Huskinson, Lucy, 236
Hypostatization, 200

The Idea of the Holy (Otto), 222–223
Ideology, 9
Idol
  Jesus as, 237
  obstacles to spiritual growth, 237
Idolatry, 125, 126
  in East, 73
  literal thinking as, 24–26
Idolization of Jesus, 83–84
Imagination
  miracles as, 1–13
  purpose of, 24
  and reality, 59–61
  as vehicle of revelation, 24
Incarnation, 67–70
Incest, 154–157. *See also* Sexual abuse
Incest and Human Love (Stein), 155
The Incredible Shrinking Son of Man (Price), 67

252

Index

Insemination, by divine, 96–98
Intellectual Enlightenment, 20, 89
Interfaith dialogue, 68
"Internal oracle," 125
The Interpretation of Dreams (Freud), 51
Islamic faith, 25

Jaspers, Karl, 1, 126, 217, 228
The Jerusalem Bible, 175, 179
Jesus
    baptism of, 75
    becoming God, 77–81
    Christ of theology *vs.*, 21–22
    commandment, 119–120
    devil and, temptation narrative, 157–164
    healing powers, 7–8
    as historical figure, 21–22
    idolization of, 83–84
    as idol *vs.* icon, 72
    Jews and, 65–66
    kingdom, 107–110
    message, 70–72
    as metaphor, 59–84
    miracles of, 5–8
    and Nicodemus, rebirth narrative, 151–157
    ongoing incarnation, 67–70
    in Pilate's court, 160, 163
    representation in gospels, 21–22
    resurrection, 167–186
    Road to Emmaus, 178–183
    secret life, 62–63
    and Socrates, and soul awakening, 125–128
    spirit personified in, 65–67
    spiritual master, 107
    spiritual nourishment by, 6
    virgin birth of, 23, 87–105
Jesus Christ and Mythology (Bultmann), 216
"Jesus the Imagination," 24
Jews, 65–66
Jihad, 143
John of Patmos, 132
John's gospel
    anti-Semitism, 152
    incest fantasies, 154–157
    metaphorical thinking, 151–154
    rebirth narrative in, 151–157
    sexual abuse, 154–157
    time of writing, 21
    virgin birth in, 95
Johnston, William, 73
Joseph (earthly father of Jesus), 23
    Spong on, 95
Judaism
    John's gospel and, 152
Jung, Carl, 15, 42, 88, 187–205
    on Aboriginal cultures, 46
    on Assumption of Mary, 200–203
    Bishop on, 189
    on Christianity, 190–192
    on consciousness, 45
    criticism, 190
    on demythologizing, 188
    directed *vs.* nondirected thinking, 49–50
    on encounter with the devil, 162–163
    Freud and, 189
    on God's unknowable nature, 199–200
    on human proximity to spirit, 71
    on incest fantasies, 156, 157
    as midrashic scholar, 188
    on miracles, 197–198
    on myth, 191–192
    on mythic thinking, 52–53
    on Protestantism, 201–202
    on psychic truth, myth as, 194–196
    on rationalizing intellectuals, 220–221
    on religious truth, 197
    on resurrection, 173–174
    sacrosanct unintelligibility, 187, 203
    on scriptures, 196–197
    spirituality and, 190
    on symbols, 228
    on *teleios* translation, 120
    on therapeutic function of myth, 192–194
    "the two million-year-old man," 55

Kalachakra mandalas, 73
Kant, I., 200
Keats, John, 27–28, 153, 179
Kershner, Frederick D., 82
Kerygma, 218
Kingdom of heaven, 23, 107–110. *See also* Ego; Jesus; New self
    concept, 107
    location, 108
    ministry, 108–109, 123
    spiritual transformation, 123–124

King James Version, 175
Kuhn, Alvin, 15, 29–30, 40, 78–79

"A Lamentable Departure Indeed," 210
The Language and Imagery of the Bible (Caird), 3
"Late Thoughts," 190
Lazarus story, 8
Leda and the Swan (Greek myth), 97
"Leda and the Swan" (Yeats), 97
"The Legacy of Christianity" (Geering), 220
Legend, 1
Lenin, Vladimir, 210
Levinas, Emmanuel, 143–145
Liberal theology, 226
Life, Life (Cupitt), 223
Literalism, 20
  churches and, 20–21
  devil and, 157–164
  in East, 73
  evangelical fundamentalism and, 20
  idolatry, 24–26
  mystery without, 196–199
  religious advocacy and, 4
  spiritual death and, 25, 26
Literal readings, 1
The Little Prince (Saint-Exupéry), 22
Logos, 24, 214
  intellect and, 43
The Lost Light (Kuhn), 30
Lost Sheep, 178
Love's Body (Brown), 25
Luke's gospel
  Annunciation sequence, 95, 96, 98
  Gabriel, 97
  Road to Emmaus, 178–183
  time of writing, 21
  virgin birth in, 95

Macchioro, Vittorio, 23, 191–192
Machado, Antonio, 107
Macnab, Francis, 9
Mark's gospel
  miraculous feeding story, 6
  postmortem sightings, 174
  resurrection in, 174
  time of writing, 21
  virgin birth in, 95
Martyr, Irenaeus, 177
Martyr, Justin, 177

Mary, 23
  virginity, 92–93
Matthew's gospel
  miraculous feeding story, 6
  temptation narrative, 157–164
  time of writing, 21
  virgin birth in, 95
Mead, G. R. S., 22
Mental health, mythos and, 40–41
Merton, Thomas, 73, 242
Metanoia, 123, 124, 161
Meta-phorein, 26
Metaphorical thinking, 151–154
  for spiritual and sexual health, 156
Metaphors
  being allegories, 9
  etymology, 24
  hazards of, 8–10
  miracles as, 5–8
  progressive Christian thinkers and, 9–10
Midrash, 6–7, 188, 242
  Haggadic, 7
Miller, David, 121, 122
Miracles
  belief and, 6
  Bible and, 3
  feeding stories of gospels, 6–7
  as imagination, 1–13
  of Jesus, 5–8, 113
  Jung on, 197–198
  as metaphors, 5–8
  significance of, 9
  Spong on, 10–11
Miraculous feeding stories, 6–7
Modernity, 211
Modern society, 124
Moses, 7
Müller, Max, 19
Murdock, Dorothy, 32
Mustard seed parable, 117–118
Mystery, without literalism, 196–199
Myth(s)
  "allegories" of external experiences, 45
  as ancient psychology, 39–42
  archetypal configurations, 63
  Cassirer on, 17–18
  cosmos and, 46
  eternity and, 47
  fear of, 61–62
  Frazer on, 19

254

Index

history and, 2, 38–39
in popular language, 18
as psychic truth, 194–196
recreating, 228–229
in religious stories, 18
saving, 216–218
soul and, 46, 63
spiritual function of, 30
supernatural "beings," 1
terminological inferences, 2
therapeutic function, 192–194
universal patterns, 45–46
of virgin birth, 87–105
Mythic figures, 1
Mythicist tradition, 209
Mythic thinking, 53
Mythologem, 96, 191
Mythology, 15
Kuhn on, 40
Müller on, 19
as science of spiritual life, 40
theology and, 191–192
Mythopoesis, 19
Mythos. *See also* Myth(s)
in art and entertainment, 47–48
Greek terminology and meaning, 2
history and, 1–5
as language of psyche, 43–45
logos *vs.*, 42–43
mental health and, 41–42

National Socialism, in Germany, 210
Naturalism, 225
Natural man/person, 59–60
abolition of, 123
Negative theology, 223
Neoplatonists, on spirit, 107
Nestorians, 75
Nestorius, 75
Neville, Bernie, 63
Nevo, Matthew Del, 223
The New International Study Bible, 179
New Jerusalem, 147
Newman, Cardinal, 31–32
New self
archetypal reality, 114
directed to goal/*telos*, 115–116
as dormant, 114
ego and. *See* Ego
entrance into, 118–119
kingdom and, 110–123

liminal reality, 114
mustard seed parable, 117–118
mystery of, 113
as original self, 138–140
of Paul, 112
New Testament, 3, 21, 138, 178, 236
telos, 119
virgin birth, 23
New world order, 146–148
New York Times, 55
Nicodemus, and rebirth narrative, 151–157. *See also* John's gospel
incest fantasies, 154–157
sexual abuse, 154–157
Nietzsche, Friedrich, 19, 202, 210, 243–244
Nihilism, 214
Nondirected *vs.* directed thinking, 49–50

Old Testament, 137, 143, 236
Olympian gods, 126
Omega (second self), 139
Ongoing incarnation, 67–70
Ontogeny, 53
Origin (185-254), 20–21
Otto, Rudolf, 222–223

Palestine, 171, 172
Pantocrator, 234
Papal Bull, 202
"The Parents of Jesus: Fictionalized Composites" (Spong), 95
Paul, St., 167
letter to the Ephesians, 111
pneumatikos, 120
on resurrection, 168, 169, 170, 175–178
Personifying archetypal contents, 63–65
Philosophy of Symbolic Forms (Cassirer), 48
Phylogeny, 53
Physical resurrection
Paul on, 175
vs. spiritual resurrection, 167–170
Pilate, Pontius, 160, 163
Pious fraud, religion as, 27–30
Pius X, Pope, 210
Plato, 126
"Pleasure principle," 161
Plotinus, 243
Pneuma, 182

Pneumatikos, 120, 176
"Poetics of mind," 39
Poetry, religion as, 26–27
The Power of Parable: How Fiction by Jesus Became Fiction about Jesus (Crossan), 23–24, 178
Prayer, 47
Price, Robert, 67
Primitive thinkers, 174
Prodigal Son, 178
Progressive Christian thinkers, 9–10
Progressives
   Bultmann, 215–216
   in rationalistic mode, 221–223
Psyche
   antique thinking and, 53
   as opening to infinity, 243–246
   personifying, 55
   personifying archetypal contents, 63–65
   sacred and, 243
   symbol and, 187–207
   as transcendental factor, 198–199
Psychic truth, 194–196
Psychoanalysis, 29, 39
   archetypal images, 64–65
   Jung on, 189
   "projection," 64–65
Psychology, apocalypse as, 131–132
Psycho-spiritual death, 124

Rabbis, 69, 152, 154
Rahner, Karl, 237
Rapture, 145–146
Rationalism, 210
Rationality, and reality, 245
Reality
   Eastern *vs.* Western concept of, 245–246
   ego and, 245
   as intellectual prejudice, 245
   as optical illusion, 245
   rationality and, 245
   of universal soul, 244
Rebirth
   Christianity and, 124–125
   incest fantasies and, 154–157
   narrative, and Nicodemus in John's gospel, 151–157
   of sacred, 233–235
   sexual abuse and, 154–157
Re-enchantment, 227

Religion
   Armstrong on, 37–38
   crisis of, 30–33
   demise of supernatural, 27
   Einstein on, 31
   Keats on, 27–28
   misrepresentations of, 37
   as pious fraud, 27–30
   science *vs.*, 31
   theology and, 27
   as unconscious poetry, 26–27
Religious authorities, 233
Religious stories, 1–2
Remythologizing, 188
Repentance, 123
Resurrection, 167–186
   Campbell on, 170–173
   Crossan on, 178–183
   Jung on, 173–175
   Moyers on, 172
   Paul on, 175–178
   Road to Emmaus, 178–183
   Schneiders on, 169–170
Revised Standard Version, 156
Road to Emmaus, 178–183
Ruether, Rosemary Radford, 92
Russia, 210

Sacred, rebirth of, 233–235
Sacrosanct unintelligibility, 187, 203
Sanford, John, 122–123
Satan. *See* Devil
Schmidt, Roger, 47
Schneiders, Sandra, 169–170
Schopenhauer, Arthur, 31, 211
Schweitzer, Albert, 222
Science *vs.* religion, 31
Scriptures
   being sacred, 3–4
   children and, 13
   churches and, 2
   criticism of, 27–30
   Higgins on, 28–29
   historical event narratives, 3
   historical reporting, 15–16
   Jung on, 196–197
   literal reading, 12–13
   literary mode of, 15–21
   misread as doctrine, 17
   poetic intentions of, 27–28
   teachers of, 32

Index

Scripture writers, 1, 11. *See also* Biblical writers
Sea of Faith movement, 223
Secret life, 62–63
Self
  concept of, 74
  Eastern *vs.* Western philosophy, 73–74
  as ego, 74
  Jung on, 74, 110, 144–145
  new. *See* New self
Sermon on the Mount, 115, 119
Sexual abuse, 154–157. *See also* Incest
Sexual addictions, in depth psychology, 155
The Shadow of the Third Century (Kuhn), 78
"Sick Rose" (Blake), 9
Smith, Huston, 116
Socrates, 109, 125–128
  as an atheist, 125
  depth psychology and, 128
  as divine emissary, 125
  as enemy of state, 125
  gods as external beings, 125
  immortality of the soul, 128
  sentenced to death, 126–127
  teachings, 126, 127–128
  trial of, 125
Socratic method, 127
  first strategy, 127
  second strategy, 127–128
Soma, 176
Soul, 190
  antique thinking and, 53
  as cosmos, 244
  Greek philosophy, 178
  historical positivism and, 234
  myth and, 46, 63
  Nietzsche on, 243–244
  secret life, 62–63
  symbolic code of, 37–56
  unveiling, 233–246
Soviet Union, 210
Spirit, 107
  archetypal configurations of, 63
  common sense to, 155–156
  Neoplatonists on, 107
  personified in Jesus, 65–67
Spirituality, and desire, 161–162
Spiritual rebirth, 98–101
Spong, John Shelby, 10–11
  on Joseph (earthly father of Jesus), 95
  on Mary, 95
  on virgin birth, 95–96
Stages, of faith, 226–228
Stein, Robert, 155
Stevens, Anthony, 134
Strauss, David, 20, 22
"The Study of Poetry" (Arnold), 26
Supernatural "beings," 1
Supernatural happenings, 1
Supersubstantialis, 158
"Syllabus Condemning the Errors of the Modernists," 210
Symbolic code, of soul, 37–56
Symbolic language, 2
Symbols, 15, 213–214
  being idol, 81
  psyche and, 187–207
  spiritual aliveness of, 214
  third eye to, 214
  Tillich on, 224–225
Symbols of Transformation (Jung), 49, 156

Teaching story. *See* Nicodemus, and rebirth narrative
Teleios, 119–123
Tertullian, 171
Theology
  mythology and, 191–192
  and religion, 27
Theology of Culture (Tillich), 224
Theo-poesis, 90
Theotokos, 93
Therapeutic function, of myth, 192–194
Thinking
  directed *vs.* nondirected, 49–50
  literal, 157–163
  metaphorical, 151–154
  nonliteral, 15
Tibetan monks, 73
Tillich, Paul, 224–226
Todd, Peter, 12–13
"Transcendent function," 163
Treston, Kevin, 18, 213
Truths, 22–23
  facts *vs.*, 18–19, 22
  historical events and, 2

Unconsciousness, depth psychology of, 39
Unconscious poetry, religion as, 26–27
Unimaginative readings, 2

Unmerciful Servant, 178
"Unveiling of the soul," 233

Valuable Pearl, 178
Van Gogh, Vincent, 23, 30, 180
Vatican, 241
Violation, of ego's boundaries, 136–138
Virgin birth, 87–105
    background, 93–96
    believe in, 102–103
    divine insemination, 96–98
    feminine self-sufficiency, 93
    institutional literalism, 101–102
    New Testament on, 23
    sexual politics over, 91–93
    spiritual rebirth, 98–101
    women and, 91–92
Vocatus atque non vocatus deus aderit, 184
Volney, Constantin, 22
Voltaire, 82
Vosper, Gretta, 9

Warner, Marina, 92
Wells, G. A., 22
West
    Eastern moment in, 73–74, 245–246
    idolatry and, 25–26
    images and, 25–26
    reality, 245–246
    self in, 73–74
Western prejudice, 173
When Jesus Became God (Rubenstein), 78
Williams, Rowan, 102
Word of God, 199
Writers. *See* Biblical writers

Yeats, W. B., 97

Zen Buddhism, 73
Zeus (Greek god), 97